Punishment for Sale

Issues in Crime & Justice

Series Editor
Gregg Barak, Eastern Michigan University

As we embark upon the twentieth-first century, the meanings of crime continue to evolve and our approaches to justice are in flux. The contributions to this series focus their attention on crime and justice as well as on crime control and prevention in the context of a dynamically changing legal order. Across the series, there are books that consider the full range of crime and criminality and that engage a diverse set of topics related to the formal and informal workings of the administration of criminal justice. In an age of globalization, crime and criminality are no longer confined, if they ever were, to the boundaries of single nation-states. As a consequence, while many books in the series will address crime and justice in the United States, the scope of these books will accommodate a global perspective and they will consider such eminently global issues such as slavery, terrorism, or punishment. Books in the series are written to be used as supplements in standard undergraduate and graduate courses in criminology and criminal justice and related courses in sociology. Some of the standard courses in these areas include: introduction to criminal justice, introduction to law enforcement, introduction to corrections, juvenile justice, crime and delinquency, criminal law, white collar, corporate, and organized crime.

TITLES IN SERIES:

Effigy, by Allison Cotton

Perverts and Predators, by Laura J. Zilney and Lisa Anne Zilney

The Prisoners' World, by William Tregea and Marjorie Larmour

Racial Profiling, by Karen S. Glover

Punishment for Sale: Private Prisons, Big Business, and the Incarceration Binge by Donna Selman and Paul Leighton

Punishment for Sale

Private Prisons, Big Business, and the Incarceration Binge

Donna Selman and Paul Leighton

ROWMAN & LITTLEFIELD PUBLISHERS, INC.
Lanham • Boulder • New York • Toronto • Plymouth, UK

8-23-11
LN
$24.95

Published by Rowman & Littlefield Publishers, Inc.
A wholly owned subsidiary of The Rowman & Littlefield Publishing Group, Inc.
4501 Forbes Boulevard, Suite 200, Lanham, Maryland 20706
http://www.rowmanlittlefield.com

Estover Road, Plymouth PL6 7PY, United Kingdom

British Library Cataloguing in Publication Information Available

Library of Congress Cataloging-in-Publication Data

Selman, Donna, 1967–
  Punishment for sale : private prisons, big business, and the incarceration binge /
Donna Selman and Paul Leighton.
      p. cm. — (Issues in crime & justice)
  Includes bibliographical references and index.
  ISBN 978-1-4422-0172-9 (cloth : alk. paper) — ISBN 978-1-4422-0173-6 (pbk. :
alk. paper) — ISBN 978-1-4422-0174-3 (electronic)
  1. Corrections—Contracting out—United States. 2. Prisons—United States.
  3. Privatization—United States. I. Leighton, Paul, 1964– II. Title.
  HV9469.S45 2010
  365'.973—dc22   2009030713

♾ ™ The paper used in this publication meets the minimum requirements of
American National Standard for Information Sciences—Permanence of Paper for
Printed Library Materials, ANSI/NISO Z39.48-1992.

Printed in the United States of America

For

Mom, Dad, and Kaitlyn

And

For my family

Contents

List of Tables, Figures, and Boxes

Preface

Private prisons are for-profit businesses that build and/or manage prisons for local, state, and federal governments. They emerged in the 1980s in response to two powerful forces. First, President Ronald Reagan declared in his first inaugural address that "government was the problem" and set out on a course to outsource and privatize as many government functions as possible. Second, the United States has been waging a relentless "get-tough-on-crime" campaign that focuses excessively on harsher punishments for crime after it occurs rather than considering crime prevention. The result is a multinational incarceration business whose Securities and Exchange Commission (SEC) filings discuss sentencing reform as a risk factor. This book examines how we ended up in this situation and provides a portrait of the companies in America's public-private "partnership" that maintains the highest incarceration rate in the world.

We have been curious about private prisons since the early days of this free market experiment in punishment. We have watched as Wall Street praised these companies as "theme stocks" of the 1990s, as the Corrections Corporation of America flirted with bankruptcy and their stock price fell well under $1 a share, and as they "rehabilitated" themselves and produced strong profits by housing immigrant detainees after September 11. With this book we intend, first, to provide the social, political, and economic context for the two main drivers of modern-day private prisons: the war on crime and government outsourcing. Second, we intend to provide a more detailed look at private prisons as businesses. While we note some of the management problems they have had (e.g., riots, escapes), our emphasis is on reviewing their congressional testimony, their SEC filings, and the contracts they have made with governments. While we are

Preface

both criminologists interested in prisons, researching this book has forced us into new and unfamiliar areas as we have tried to "follow the money" to understand the emergence and future of companies traded on the stock exchange that have entrenched themselves in core areas of our criminal justice system.

In many places, we draw on the words of representatives of the private prison companies to explain events and their business environment. However, the framework of this book is best described as a critical analysis of the private prison industry and the trends that gave rise to it. The massive increases in America's prison population have been costly and provided minimal reductions in crime while devastating minority communities. Private prisons are born of this unjust trend, and the profitability of the industry requires that it continue. Further, the belief in the greater efficiency of the private over the public sector fuels beliefs in great cost savings that research has failed to substantiate. Our examination of the overhead costs suggests a few reasons: multi-million-dollar executive pay, fees for securities lawyers to do SEC filings, fees for Wall Street investment banks, merger-and-acquisition costs, expenses associated with "business development" and "customer acquisition," requirements for headquarters in several countries, and so forth. Many of these items mean that shifting incarceration from a state-run enterprise to a private business, which saves money by paying guards less, directly contributes to inequality in income and wealth.

While our opinions and conclusions are our own, we wish to acknowledge the support and encouragement we have received along the way. Thanks to our editor, colleague, and friend Gregg Barak. Along with setting the example of an admirable career marked by academic rigor and pushing the boundaries of criminology, Gregg has provided prompt and constructive suggestions regarding this manuscript. Both of us also wish to acknowledge Eastern Michigan University's (EMU) Faculty Merlanti Ethics Award for recognizing the importance of this work on private prisons in the context of corporate social responsibility. The award also provided support during the final stages of manuscript preparation.

Donna Selman would like to thank the Josephine Nevins Keal Fellowship and the EMU Women's Commission for their support, which covered the costs of obtaining the contracts analyzed in chapter 4. Paul Leighton wishes to thank EMU for a sabbatical leave that enabled him to complete some of the research based on SEC filings for this book.

Both of us wish to thank Dana Radatz for her help with the references. Dana also contributed to the research on chapter 5, which was originally a coauthored presentation with Paul Leighton for the 2008 American Society of Criminology Conference. We also wish to thank Donna's graduate assistant, Chadd Powell, who was instrumental in securing many of the contracts discussed in chapter 4.

Introduction

The news from early February 2009 stated that the Reeves County Detention Center in Texas had started burning because of an inmate uprising. Again. The latest series of problems started on December 12, 2008, when an inmate died and fellow inmates started rioting and demanding better health care. Inmates rioted again on January 31, 2009, setting fire to various buildings and causing heavy damage (Barry 2009). Several days later, the GEO Group, a private prison business that manages the detention center, released a statement claiming they reached a "positive outcome" in meetings with the inmates. But several days later, "plumes of smoke were once again rising from the prison," followed by more reassuring statements from county officials. "Even as the county judge's office was handing out its latest statement, fire trucks and county deputies were speeding out to the prison, sirens blaring and lights flashing" (Barry 2009).

Prison riots are not new, although this one was a little ironic, given that it occurred at a private prison whose existence is based on the argument that the private sector can handle the task of incarceration better and cheaper than the government—and has generally failed to live up to that promise. Private prison companies use private funds to build prisons that they lease to government, and they also manage prisons owned by government. Although most people would agree that having private companies conduct executions would be inappropriate, even if they could do so more cheaply and somehow "better," the United States has embarked on a process whereby the lowest bidder is managing the deprivation of liberty of more than one hundred thousand inmates.

Two companies—the Corrections Corporation of America (CCA) and the GEO Group—both of which are traded on the stock exchange and must regularly report financial information to shareholders, hold most of these inmates. These for-profit corporations need to work constantly on expanding their business and returning a profit after paying off overhead like multi-million-dollar executive pay, fees for lawyers to prepare Securities and Exchange Commission (SEC) filings, fees for Wall Street investment banks to provide credit lines, and fees for lobbyists. Indeed, the GEO Group was formerly Wackenhut Corrections Corporation. It acquired its current name after it spun off and reacquired a real estate investment trust (REIT) and a larger multinational security company acquired its parent company, the Wackenhut Corporation. A great deal of money from these transactions went into fees for Wall Street bankers and lawyers, and the executives of Wackenhut/GEO Group received handsome payouts because of a "change-in-control event" that did not really change that much about the company or their jobs.

The corporate history of GEO Group mattered much less to Reeves County than the jobs provided by the thirty-seven hundred bed "law enforcement center," which "county officials have dreams of expanding to 7,000 prison beds" (Barry 2009). That part of Texas used to be known for produce like cantaloupe, but "the farm and ranch boom ended in the early 1960s when the water wells ran dry." There was some economic development tied to oil, which was good during the booms of the 1970s and 1980s but devastating during the bust parts of the cycle when prices fell dramatically. So,

> the town fathers envisioned another economic boom for Pecos. This one wouldn't depend on nonrenewable resources like before—water, oil, the soil of the arid plains—but on a resource that seemed to be abundant in modern America. They dreamed of making Pecos a destination for prisoners. They could offer a remote location, a county willing to issue nearly $100 million in revenue bonds for prison construction, and a downtrodden, desperate, despairing workforce left behind by previous booms. All this would make Pecos "competitive," as county officials say, in a national market that seemed bustproof. (Barry 2009)

Across America, many other communities had similar dreams of replacing lost jobs with prisons. Processes of globalization threaten manufacturing and some service jobs, but prison construction and guard jobs cannot easily be moved overseas. So, areas with high unemployment and unstable job bases offered tax breaks and other subsidies to have a prison built, be it public or private. While the logic of this idea may work for an individual community, the aggregate national effect is irrational: the country overbuilt prisons to house minor offenders for long periods while cutting funds for crime prevention, education, and community development. This process has been called "mopping water off the floor while we let the tub overflow" (Currie 1985, 226). (Private prisons work to sell allegedly better and cheaper mops as the solution.)

Early dreams of the prison-based, recession-proof economy were not tied to private prisons, which during the mid-1980s were just starting to come into existence. The United States forged ahead with private management of prisons after President Ronald Reagan declared in the opening lines of his first inaugural address that "government was the problem." Part of the "Reagan revolution" involved privatizing as many government activities as possible, based on an economic theory about free markets that contained assumptions that frequently did not match reality. The election of Reagan and the veneration of an extreme version of free market theory was the first of two important factors necessary for the idea of private prisons to gain traction.

Normally, prisons would not be considered seriously for privatizing, but the second factor, relentless prison overcrowding, created the appearance of a problem that privatization could solve. From the early 1900s through to the 1970s, the incarceration rate (the number of people in prison for every one hundred thousand citizens) had been relatively stable, and few new prisons were needed. Nixon's "law-and-order" campaign responded to social protest and black empowerment and ushered in decades of "get-tough-on-crime" proposals. Enacting numerous laws to increase prison sentences and incarcerate more people had the obvious effect of increasing the number of people in prison, but little prison construction had been done to prepare for the larger prison populations. The easily foreseeable increase in incarceration led to a crisis as prisons became overcrowded, inmates filed suits, and courts started declaring entire prison systems in violation of Eighth Amendment prohibitions against cruel and unusual punishment.

The ideology that business is more efficient than government led to easy and widespread acceptance of the claim that government mismanagement was generating inmate lawsuits rather than to an investigation into the effectiveness of harsher sentencing policies. The alternative was to ask difficult questions about race (what does "tough on crime" mean when most people associate criminals with African American men?) and the desirability of using an incarceration binge to rebuild the economy (turning the United States, the land of the free, into the country with the highest rate of imprisonment). Needless to say, the country continued to endorse tough-on-crime slogans, which funneled trillions of dollars into prison construction, payroll, and supplies.

The increasing amounts of money going into corrections and the dynamics supporting continuation of the trend caught the eye of many business people. Businesses look out for growth opportunities, and in this sense private prisons were just one among many business interests looking to cash in. The CCA spent its first year trying to land a contract to manage a prison and lost money for the next two years, but it still had a successful public stock offering to raise money. Other companies followed, especially after stock analysts started promoting private prisons and labeling them "theme stocks" for the 1990s. While theoretically any member of the public can purchase shares, the reality is that the wealthiest 50 percent of the population owned 99.4 percent of all directly held stocks and 99.1 percent of all bonds in 2004 (Kennickell 2006). In other words, private prisons took money from the wealthy to build prisons to lock up poor and disproportionately minority citizens, giving the rich an opportunity to get richer from the poor getting prison.

So far, this introduction has mentioned corporations, corporate takeovers, stock exchanges, lobbyists, and economic development in the context of prisons. These relationships are outside of the usual take on prisons based on crime rates, retribution, deterrence, and the occasional nod toward rehabilitation. We believe that understanding contemporary criminal justice policy requires "following the money." Private prisons have billions of dollars in outstanding stock and billions more in debt to Wall Street banks, and they spend millions on lobbyists. Studying developments in criminal justice or corrections without attention to these private interests will produce an incomplete picture. Worse still, traditional approaches to criminal justice policy produce a blindness to how business profit affects public safety and the deprivation of liberty.

To be sure, private prisons are not the only profit-minded actors influencing policy. Further, the criminal justice system and prisons have contracted with private businesses to provide guns, handcuffs, bars, alarms, and many other goods. Prisons have frequently contracted out food service, health care, laundry, education, and drug treatment. We thus see private prisons as an important actor within the context of a prison-industrial complex that itself is situated within a criminal justice–industrial complex. These complexes are literal and figurative successors to the military-industrial complex President Dwight Eisenhower warned of in his Farewell Address. At that point, he was concerned about the establishment of a permanent military industry and the "potential for the disastrous rise of misplaced power [that] exists and will persist" (Eisenhower 1961). He worried about its effect on "our liberties or democratic processes" and concluded that "only an alert and knowledgeable citizenry can compel the proper meshing of the huge industrial and military machinery of defense with our peaceful methods and goals, so that security and liberty may prosper together" (Eisenhower 1961).

Between the 1970s and 1990s, the modest number of smaller businesses serving the criminal justice system morphed into a criminal justice–industrial complex. Unlike the concerns giving rise to the military-industrial complex, there is not a single event or year that ushers in a criminal justice–industrial complex. The growth in the number of businesses involved with criminal justice and the dollar volume of that commerce—not to mention politicians and communities dreaming of a prison economy—produce powerful vested interests that affect people's liberties and make crime policy something other than a tool for public safety and justice. At their worst, some of these interests threaten to make crime policy a tool for private gain and profit rather than the public good; criminal justice comes to be about "bodies destined for profitable punishment" (Davis 1999, 2). Having businesses that are traded on the stock exchange owning and running prisons is qualitatively different from past privatization, especially when their SEC filings list sentencing reform as a "risk factor." In this environment, only a knowledgeable public, one attuned to business models of prison profitability, can compel the proper meshing of multi-billion-dollar business beholden to shareholders with public safety, public accountability, and social justice.

We wrote this book to help inform the public about private prisons. While we set these businesses in the larger context of a criminal justice–industrial complex, this volume does not give a broad overview of all the vested interests in criminal justice (Christie 1993; Shichor 1995); rather, it provides a focused look at private prisons. We have read through congressional testimony, SEC filings, and numerous contracts between government agencies and private prison operators. Overall we aim to provide readers with a more thorough examination of the business model upon which private prisons operate, as well as the financial and economic context within which they exist. This book is not just a recounting of escapes, riots, and the numerous blunders of private prisons (Mattera, Khan, and Nathan 2004), although we do use these as examples of larger problems. Instead, we follow the money to understand the mind-set and objectives of the "partner" that has entrenched itself in the world of corrections.

Because our data come from congressional testimony, SEC filings, and contracts obtained (with difficulty) under the Freedom of Information Act, this book largely describes the U.S. experience with private prisons. Both CCA and GEO Group are multinational corporations operating in a half dozen other countries and seeking inroads elsewhere. We believe that much of what we have written here will help those in other countries understand the nature and character of a private prison corporation operating in their jurisdiction, as well as the problems that might be expected over time. In the future, we hope we can add insights from the experiences of other countries and/or incorporate the insights of those who have followed similar research strategies.

Through the data, we try to let the companies speak for themselves; however, we provide a critical context through which to interpret their actions.

As we demonstrate later in this book, we believe that the incarceration binge has imposed a large financial cost on all taxpayers, yet it is responsible for only a small part of the drop in crime rates that started in the early 1990s. The disproportionate confinement of minorities has caused racial tension and injustice. And the high incarceration rates have made certain neighborhoods more crime prone by eroding informal social controls like families and neighborhood ties.

Private prisons were not responsible for the incarceration binge, although they have helped it along by promoting tough-on-crime legislation. The larger critique is that they were born of a fundamentally unjust incarceration binge, and they require the continuation of those dynamics in order to grow in their current form. They can expand into other areas of corrections—and they are—but this is deeply problematic since they try to lock up information behind the veil of "trade secrets" and reject both greater transparency for political contributions and attempts to tie executive pay to social responsibility (e.g., human rights, fair labor). Private prisons also pay their executives millions of dollars and make up for it by paying their staff less than those with similar government jobs, directly contributing to economic inequality.

In making sense of a prison- or criminal justice–industrial complex, it is helpful to understand the political economy of punishment. This is a structural analysis of how politics, law, and economics influence each other. As such, the political economy of prison looks not to crime rates to explain patterns of punishment but to factors such as social stratification and the surplus population—those who are unemployed or unemployable and are thus considered the "dangerous class." Conditions that cause increases in the surplus population or require work will be of interest, as will technology and the prevailing ideologies. For example, historically, the rise of the prison as factory coincides with the Industrial Revolution. But history confirms that mixing punishment via the criminal justice system with profit for a private interest creates conflicts in which the public good suffers so a small group of private interests may gain.

In the United States, early-nineteenth-century prisons relied on the "silent system," which required that inmates not talk to each other for the entire duration of their sentence—it was a sort of moral quarantine from criminality while programs aimed at rehabilitation could take effect. One form of the silent system, the Pennsylvania system, relied on the isolation of single-person cells to enforce silence. The production of crafts was lauded as a means to occupy otherwise idle, troublesome prisoners when they were not reading the Bible. Labor had to be simple enough that one person could perform it within the confines of his cell. Shoe and hat making and coopering were easily broken down into component parts that required little training and fit these requirements nicely. The work was done under a contract with private parties (Gildemeister 1987). The state provided suitable workshops, food, clothing, religious instruction, and security. Contractors, in turn, provided raw materials, tools, and instruction. In theory, the prison would pay for itself. However, even at this early date the power differential favored the contractors. Prison personnel from guards to wardens were political appointees, and the contractors had their own political power through friends and business associates, plus their own positions as former, prospective, and even current officeholders (Shichor and Gilbert 2001). (As later chapters in this book will demonstrate, not much has changed.)

Auburn, New York, employed another form of the silent system during this period. It featured congregate, factory-type work in total silence during the day and the isolation of single-person cells at night. The Pennsylvania and Auburn systems competed for a time, but the Auburn system of congregate labor emerged as the model of choice. The prisons using this system were cheaper to build because the Pennsylvania system required larger cells for inmates to live and work in for their entire sentence. Monitoring prisoners working in assembly-line type groups rather than individually was cheaper, and groups of men working together under harsh discipline were more productive than the Pennsylvania system's solitary workers. The production of materials at low labor cost increased the attractiveness of utilizing prison labor to private contractors. As modes of production changed to include more machinery, the Auburn system could adapt.

While the history of American prisons rightly highlights bold experiments in rehabilitation, the emergence of the Auburn model was not based on outcomes for individual inmates as much as on its greater cost-effectiveness and fit with the emerging Industrial Revolution. The prison made a conscious effort to instill discipline through an institutional routine—a set work pattern, a rationalization of movement, a precise organization of time, and an overall uniformity. The model of regularity and discipline was thought to reawaken the prisoners to these virtues and thus contribute to social improvement by promoting a new respect for order and authority, but the main focus was to turn criminals into obedient (and therefore more productive) workers. As Robert Johnson explains, the congregate penitentiary "forges a crude urban creature, a tame proletarian worker, oppressed and angry but hungry and compliant: a man for the times forged by a prison for the times" (1987, 31).

Under this system, prison labor was in the hands of private citizens and lined the pockets of private capital (Shichor and Gilbert 2001). On a day-to-day basis, many prisons left discipline within the shops to the private contractors (Colvin 1997, 97–98), who used extensive punishment to exact productivity. The practice of noncommunication with the outside served to shelter the public from the brutal conditions within the penitentiary, and the profits of the system satisfied the legislatures. Moreover, the contract labor system proved highly lucrative to prison administrators, whose control over the highly sought contracts gave them political and financial power. This contract labor flourished for nearly twenty years, until both businesses and emerging unions saw contract labor and its products as unfair, state-subsidized competition. Businesses did not want to compete with contract prison industries for raw materials or markets, and unions were unhappy that the use of prison labor undercut their demands for shorter workdays and -weeks and for higher wages. By 1890, six northern, largely industrial states had abolished contract labor, but the South continued this practice well into the 1930s (Shichor 2001, 17).

The South did not have the same interest in factory prisons, but in the aftermath of the Civil War, convict leasing became a popular for-profit activity. Slavery, rather than prison, had been the dominant form of social control. When the Thirteenth Amendment (ratified in 1865) freed the slaves, it lifted that type of control and created serious anxiety among the white population. Slaves went from property to economic competition; black men were freed at a time when many Southern white women were widowed or single because of the large number of young white men killed during the war. Southern whites wanted another system for social control, but building prisons at that time was impossible. The war had been fought primarily in the South, and that was where most of the destruction had occurred. The repairs required labor, which was in short supply, again, because of the large number of young white men killed in the war. Additionally, the labor needed to take place outside the prison walls. The labor-intensive crops grown on plantations also required attention.

The answer was to round up blacks, convict them, and lease them out for labor to serve their sentence. The Black Codes facilitated this process by penalizing a number of behaviors by blacks that whites found rude, disrespectful, or threatening. Plantation owners could now lease inmates rather than own slaves. Reformers of the time argued that this new convict leasing was merely a replication of, or an economic replacement for, slavery without a capital investment in workers (Mancini 1996). The cheap lease rates attracted a variety of private contractors, who put the prisoners to work in the most dangerous conditions doing the most arduous work. The system was brutal for blacks, who rarely lived to see the end of their sentence and whose condition is captured by the title of David Oshinsky's book *Worse Than Slavery* (1996). But responsibility for housing, feeding, and disciplining convicts was turned over to contractors, relieving the states of a financial burden. And the criminal justice system took a cut from the lease money, so everyone with power wanted the system expanded.

The inmates, who were raw materials for profit making, were expendable: "One dies, get another" (Mancini 1996). State-appointed commissioners or inspectors were to ensure care and safety at these privately owned sites. In reality, inhumane conditions, deadly epidemics, and excessive brutality ruled because of nepotism, neglect of duty by prison commissioners, and conflicts of interest involving state employees (Myers 1998, 20). At best, the commissioners issued critical reports that fell on deaf ears; at worst they were men who profited monetarily and politically from leasing. (Unfortunately, as chapter 4 demonstrates, the use of contract monitors and private prison commissions to reduce problems in today's private prisons is as ineffective as it was in the past.)

In most states, challenges from labor unions or economic conditions accompanied the end of the leasing system. Economic conditions rather than humanitarian concerns brought about the end of convict leasing in Tennessee. There, mining dominated the lease program, and the economic depression of the 1890s hit the mining industry hard. Free miners who saw convict labor as a drain on their wages stormed the camps, set fire to the stockades, and shipped prisoners out. As the conflict escalated, both the mining companies and the state wanted out of the contract relationship; convict labor was no longer financially viable in the state of Tennessee (Shichor and Gilbert 2001). Alabama finally abolished the use of convict labor in the coal mines in 1928. Although incidents of mine explosions, resulting in the deaths of hundreds of mostly black convicts, were common, fiscal concerns spurred the ultimate end of convict leasing (Mancini 1996). When the coal mines were running dry in Georgia, the national good-roads movement was getting under way, so the convict labor was put to use on chain gangs to build and maintain roads. Journalistic outcries and corruption scandals were not enough to bring down the leasing program. Again, leasing only ended when it became economically necessary: the bottom dropped out of the labor market and low-paid, free workers who could be fired rather than maintained at company expense became more desirable than leased convicts. In Texas, convict leasing ended only when the economic troubles hit the labor-intensive sugar cane industry (Walker 1988).

With this background, it is easier to see how the racialized wars on crime and drugs, popular for several decades, fueled an incarceration binge. The loss of jobs in the United States due to processes of globalization added to the need for prisons to stimulate economic development while at the same time providing an increasing number of unemployed who could be swept into the system. The harsh laws and demand for prison economies produced a demand for prison beds that outstripped government's ability to supply them. The stage was set for private prisons, and the opening curtain lifted with President Reagan's extreme free market ideology and desire to outsource government functions wherever possible (wherever business could make a profit).

In the modern incarnation of for-profit punishment, proponents argued that the lease system and other misadventures were not relevant. But Michael Hallett (2007) ties the long-standing role of private entrepreneurs in shaping punishment policy with the history of slavery, race and class relations, and deals that funnel public monies to capitalists. By drawing parallels between the historical convict lease system and the contemporary war on drugs, he demonstrates that both culminated in the disproportionate imprisonment of African Americans while serving the interests of the capitalist system. Hallett's careful analysis demonstrates how political and industrial leaders often amassed capital, be it financial or political, on the backs of convicts through specific policy decisions; at the same time he shows how the for-profit imprisonment movement can only be understood in the context of both historical and contemporary racism.

Punishment for Sale uses the ideas of political economy and the criminal justice–industrial complex as a departure point for a detailed study of private prisons. Private contractors finance and build facilities, provide food service, medical care, and commissary supplies, and use inmate labor, but we focus on the private ownership, operation, and management of prisons. This operational privatization plays a significant role in the daily lives of inmates, and these multi-billion-dollar companies are at the forefront of shaping criminal justice policy. To facilitate understanding of this issue, *Punishment for Sale* is divided into two parts and has some supplementary materials. Part I contains two chapters that examine the origins of private prisons. Part II contains three chapters that drill into understanding them as businesses. An appendix presents a brief overview of how to use the SEC website to research the private prisons traded on the stock exchange. This allows readers to use the main source of public information about private prisons to keep up to date on developments and concerns presented here. Finally, Paul Leighton has posted some supplemental material and links, including a version of the appendix, on his website (http://paulsjustice page.com > Punishment for Sale).

More specifically, chapter 1, "America's Incarceration Binge: The Expansion of Prisons, Budgets, and Injustice," sets the stage. It describes how the United States came to build more prisons in two short decades than at any other time in its history. We review the nature and extent of the increased use of incarceration and critique this phenomenon to establish the case that private prisons and the larger criminal justice–industrial complex are providing little social good and contributing to societal harm. Specifically this critique demonstrates that increases in the prison population have little effect on crime rates, there has been a tremendous opportunity cost in building prisons and expanding the criminal justice system, and the incarceration binge has caused social harm by undermining public safety, disrupting communities, disenfranchising millions, and contributing to racial and economic inequality. To better understand how America, the land of the free and home of the brave, came to have the highest incarceration rate in the world, we examine the ideology and "ideas" justifying the incarceration binge. The chapter explains how the sociohistorical context—including the rise of "law and order," the Republican ascendancy to power in the 1980s, and media images—has driven the popularity of "tough on crime" that in turn created an overcrowding crisis and massive expansion of budgets for criminal justice.

Chapter 2 examines the second requirement for interest in privatizing prisons: the antigovernment/pro-business ideology of the 1980s. We begin by contextualizing President Reagan's statement in his first inaugural address that "government is the problem." In the chapter's first section, we review critiques of New Deal policies and programs and how blame for the economic crises of the late 1970s and early 1980s came to be placed on "big government," "generous" social welfare programs, excessive government spending and bureaucracy, lack of incentives for investors, and weak foreign policy—a combination dubbed the "welfare state." This is followed by a brief overview of the justifications for the privatization of a variety of government functions in general and how these rationales overcame the earliest concerns about privatizing prisons, including questions regarding the legitimacy, moral implications, and legality of privatizing punishment. The chapter's second section explores the origins and development of the first private prison business, the Corrections Corporation of America, which received backing from the same group that built Kentucky Fried Chicken. Specifically, we critically examine the strategies and techniques of private prison proponents: claims of superior service and cost savings. The chapter's final section examines the 1988 President's Commission on Privatization, which further paved the way for privatization.

Chapter 3 starts the portion of the book on business operations by exploring some of the financial aspects of CCA. Specifically, we examine in depth the strategy of "going public"—offering shares of stock on the New York Stock Exchange—to provide some understanding of the general process as well as the numerous offerings of private prison–related businesses. We study closely the SEC filings of several industry leaders to understand from the companies themselves how their business models work, how they depend on the government for inmates, and how they manage their business risks. Being accountable to shareholders and creditors means working to mitigate risks and expand business, a process that involves lobbying and making political donations (and arguing against a shareholder proposal for greater transparency about donations), as well as participation in professional policy-advocacy groups.

Chapter 4 begins by examining some of the most serious problems encountered by the industry and how, in light of the multitude of human rights violations and lawsuits, industry leaders are able to continue growing profit. When bad situations arise, private prison companies blame inmates, government, the contracts they signed with government, or a combination of the three. We then examine a number of contracts obtained after a frustrating experience with filing Freedom of Information Act requests, one of the few avenues other than the SEC to gain access to information. Using this intelligence, we explain the legal costs of crafting the government's requests for proposals (RFPs) and negotiating contracts and provide an understanding of provisions on compensation calculations, facility maintenance fees, and staffing requirements. Ultimately, the base rate paid by government, which is typically used in research on cost savings, does not reflect the total cost of the contract to government. Finally, we discuss the bailout of CCA, which was deeply troubled financially, and how fear, racism, and political connections in the aftermath of September 11 are critical components of growth in the industry.

Chapter 5 looks beyond the ideology of "business is more efficient than government red tape" to the overhead costs of private prisons. We focus attention on expenses that private prisons incur that governments do not. Of particular interest are executive pay and the compensation consultants that work with the compensation committee to set salary, target levels for stock awards and stock options, deferred compensation, and other benefits. To the extent that executive pay is higher than compensation for comparable government positions, private prisons have overhead costs that need to be recouped if the business is really going to provide the service more cheaply and turn a profit. We try to quantify this amount, not just by citing that the CEO of GEO Group's 2007 compensation was $3.8 million but by focusing on cash salary and comparing that with the highest salaries at state departments of correction of a similar size. (Governments also do not give $2.2 million change-in-control payments.) To further raise questions about the efficiency of private prison firms traded on the stock exchange, we review some of the costs associated with CCA's unfortunate experiment with spinning off, then reacquiring, an REIT. Less than a year after splitting, the companies had to spend $26 million to merge, deal with shareholder lawsuits, shell out millions in advisory fees to Wall Street companies and millions more to restructure credit lines and pay change-in-control compensation to executives, and so forth. Along the way, SEC filings report efficient maneuvers, such as "Old CCA granted to New CCA the right to use the name 'Corrections Corporation of America.'"

The book's conclusion, "Back to the Future," points to areas in which private prisons have tried to diversify their revenue base and move to higher-profit-margin services. While it is important to provide mental health services in prison, we note that the root of the "crisis" of incarcerated mentally ill people relates to the lack of community mental health treatment, which causes much of the incarceration in the first place. But the private prison industry wants to profit from the mentally ill in prison rather than fixing the bigger problem. Just as private prisons have no interest in crime prevention, the "service" and "innovation" here are very narrowly defined. We noted above that focusing on incarceration to control crime is like mopping the floor while the tub is overflowing. Once again, private interests claim to be serving the public with better and cheaper mops than government can provide while obscuring the root problems. Similar problems apply to other initiatives to house the families of suspected illegal aliens and to community corrections. We detail problems due to conflicts of interest arising from public officials' "consulting" for private prisons as well as to private probation schemes that act as collection agencies that can threaten imprisonment. The industry's move toward using Global Positioning Systems to track parolees and probationers—Big Brother, Inc., and Satellite Tracking of People, LLC—generates some disconcerting thoughts about the future of privatized criminal justice.

I

THE CRIME "PROBLEM" AND
THE FREE MARKET "SOLUTION"

1

America's Incarceration Binge

The Expansion of Prisons, Budgets, and Injustice

Joel Dyer comments, without exaggeration or hyperbole, that the increase in the number of inmates in the United States "reflects the largest prison expansion the world has ever known" (2000, 2). This "incarceration binge" (Irwin and Austin 2001) entails building, stocking, and staffing an increasing number of prisons and jails, which in turn requires dramatic increases in corrections budgets. This pot of money increased dramatically from the early 1970s until the 2008 financial crisis, and it has been an important factor in the creation and growth of both private prisons and the larger criminal justice–industrial complex. Indeed, in *The Perpetual Prisoner Machine*, Dyer follows the money and reports that "today's prison industry has its own trade shows, mail-order catalogs, newsletters and conventions, and literally thousands of corporations are now eating at the justice-system trough" (2000, 11). The recipients of taxpayer money became vested interests who lobbied government to maintain or expand their piece of the pie, which created stronger vested interests lobbying for more money, and so on, ultimately creating a seemingly perpetual incarceration binge.

Understanding the origins of modern private prisons is thus more than a perfunctory historical exercise because the same factors that gave rise to prison privatization are still present and continue to drive the growth of what is now a multi-billion-dollar, multinational incarceration business. The dynamics that created private prisons—an increasing prison population and government outsourcing—not only continue to shape it today but also provide insights into future directions and problems. The introduction to this book noted the historical problems associated with efforts to privatize or introduce profit motives into state-sanctioned punishment, yet private prison companies gained a foothold during the 1980s. They generated venture capital from the backers of Kentucky Fried Chicken, and a number of private prison companies later raised money through initial public offerings (IPOs) to become public companies traded on the stock exchange (see chapter 3). While this phenomenon generated resistance along the way, Wall Street analysts labeled private prisons as hot stock picks in the 1990s, and the degree of comfort with the idea of prisons having publicly traded stocks was so high that one prison had a sign out front advertising the closing stock price of its parent company (Dyer 2000).

Such changes in sentiment, while drastic, do not occur overnight; governments and business tend to be conservative and incremental. So, this chapter outlines the first of two main factors that created prison privatization starting in the 1980s and helped give it the legitimacy necessary to expand. The first important trend, covered in this chapter, is the explosive growth in the numbers of prisoners in the United States. This unprecedented expansion in the prison population required rapidly increasing criminal justice expenditures for the "war on crime" and provided the basis for politicians to seek unconventional solutions to the problem caused by decades of "getting tough" on street crime. The second important trend, covered in chapter 2, is elected leaders' professing an antigovernment ideology that justified smaller government and the outsourcing of many services to for-profit businesses. During the Great Depression, people and politicians saw government as the answer to widespread problems, and in the late 1960s President Lyndon Johnson premised his Great Society on an assumption that combating social problems requires government involvement. But in the 1980s, President Ronald Reagan and Republican leaders maintained that big government was the problem, not the solution. Government was inefficient, so they argued for a smaller government that would benefit by outsourcing services to business, which would allow free market competition to reduce cost and improve service.

Thus, the immediate task is to examine why, from 1980 to 2000, the United States built more prisons than it had in the entire rest of its history (Vieraitis, Kovandzic, and Marvell 2007, 590). During the 1800s, prisons were among the largest structures in the United States, and our experiments with rehabilitation attracted the curiosity of Europeans. One of many who braved the journey here to study our prison system was Alexis de Tocqueville, who somewhat ironically ended up writing the classic *Democracy in America* (1904). Less than two hundred years later, our experiments with rehabilitation have long since ended, and of all the countries in the world, the United States has incarcerated the largest percentage of its population. The irony now is that the country founded on a revolutionary notion of democracy and the inalienable right to liberty has become *Lockdown America* (Parenti 1999).

In order to explain the incarceration binge, this chapter starts by describing the nature and extent of the increased use of imprisonment. It also provides a critique of this phenomenon to make clear that private prisons and the larger criminal justice–industrial complex are providing little social good and contributing to societal harm. The second section examines the ideology and "ideas" justifying the incarceration binge, starting with the rise of "law and order." The Republican ascendancy to power in the 1980s and media images further drove the popularity of "tough on crime" that has created an overcrowding crisis and massive expansion of budgets for criminal justice.

AMERICA'S INCARCERATION BINGE

One major method for understanding changes in the use of prisons involves the incarceration rate, which expresses the number of prisoners for every one hundred thousand people in the population. This standardized rate allows comparisons in one country over time as the population grows or across countries of different sizes. Figure 1.1 illustrates the incarceration rate from 1925 to 2005 in the United States, which had a relatively stable level from 1925 until the early 1970s when President Richard Nixon ran the first "law-and-order" campaign. "Law and order" became a "war on crime" as the rhetoric about "getting tough" continued over decades and resulted in policies that pushed the incarceration rate from about 100 state and federal prisoners per 100,000 of the population in the mid-1970s to almost 509 by midyear 2008 (Bureau of Justice Statistics 2009, 2).

Notably, figure 1.1 only includes state and federal prisoners and not inmates in local jails because similar historical data are not available. According to the Bureau of Justice Statistics, by midyear 2008 the incarceration rate for jails plus federal and state prisons stood at 762 per 100,000 (2009, 2), or 1 in every 100 residents (Pew Center on the States 2008). Even before it reached this level, the United States had the highest incarceration rate in the world. In the last year for which there was comparable international data, the United States had an incarceration rate of 760, ahead of the Russian Federation at 628. Other North American countries had substantially lower rates, with Canada at 116 and Mexico at 207; America's industrial democratic peers were also much further down the list, with England and Wales at 151, Germany at 88, Italy at 97, and Japan at 63 (International Centre for Prison Studies 2009).

Another way to look at the growth in incarceration is to consider the change in the actual number of inmates in the United States. By this measure, the state and federal prison population increased fourfold—quadrupled—between 1980 and 2008, going from about 320,000 inmates in

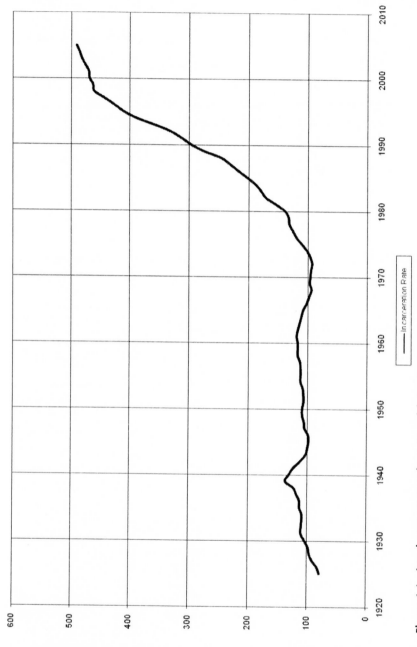

Figure 1.1   Imprisonment rates in state and federal prisons.
Source: Sourcebook of Criminal Justice Statistics online, Table 6.29, 2005.

state and federal prisons to more than 1.5 million. In addition, those incarcerated in local jails increased from 182,000 in 1980 to almost 750,000 in 2005. Taken together, the United States went from having roughly a half million inmates in 1980 to more than 2.3 million by midyear 2008 (Sourcebook Online, table 6.1.2005; Bureau of Justice Statistics 2009, 16). (By 2007, an additional 5.1 million Americans were on parole or probation [Bureau of Justice Statistics 2008a, 1], another large area of expansion for corrections and a major new growth area for privatized services, which we explore in this book's conclusion.) Locking up that many Americans requires not just large budgets for corrections but also increasing numbers of police to make arrests and courts to process offenders. Indeed, according to the Bureau of Justice Statistics, "If increases in total justice expenditure were limited to the rate of inflation (184%) after 1982, expenditures in 2003 would have been approximately $65.7 billion ($35.7B × 184%), as opposed to the actual $185.5 billion" (2006, 3).

Many people believe that spending such large amounts is regrettable but necessary, or even that the increased expenditures successfully caused the declines in crime rates during the early 1990s. However, criminologists have called the incarceration binge a natural experiment in crime reduction that failed, and many see it as causing social harm by diverting money from other important priorities and adding to social injustice by fueling inequality, racial tension, and community breakdown. We believe these critiques have merit, meaning that private prisons and the criminal justice–industrial complex were born from a social movement that has fostered injustice and that these entities, pursuing their own economic interests rather than the public good, perpetuate policies that cause further injustice because they profit from them. Indeed, with privatization, we use quotation marks around the word "solution" to indicate our belief that it has created more problems than it has solved. Therefore, it is important to explain briefly the failure of the incarceration binge to reduce crime and its contribution to social harms.

The first point in the critique of the incarceration binge is that increases in the prison population have little effect on crime rates, which makes them an inefficient way to reduce crime. The incarceration rate increased every year since the early 1970s, but crime rates did not start to fall until the early 1990s. Using the all-time highest crime rate to start a comparison of violent crime rates and the incarceration rate in the early 1990s produces a flawed chart, like that in figure 1.2a, which shows a misleadingly clear picture of the relationship between incarceration and crime. Politicians and businesses wanting to justify the enormous budget increases for criminal justice and prisons frequently make this type of comparison. Figure 1.2b, which takes into account a longer time frame, indicates a more complex relationship: while the incarceration rate

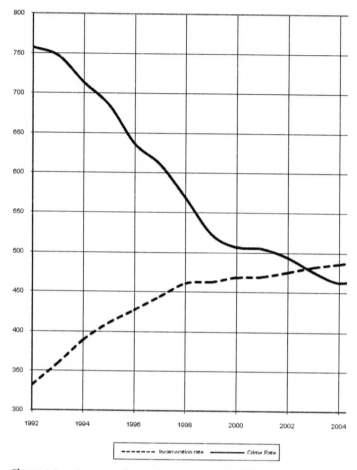

Figure 1.2a Incarceration and crime rates for different time periods, 1992–2004.
Source: Sourcebook of Criminal Justice Statistics online, Table 6.29, 2005.

increases, the crime rate fluctuates and has cycles. Thus, surveying the last thirty-five years, the argument that prisons reduce crime requires a problematic "heads I win, tails you loose" reasoning: increases in the crime rate necessitate getting tougher, while declines in the crime rate prove tougher sentences are working (Reiman and Leighton 2010).

However, criminologists point to a number of facts that question the efficacy of the incarceration binge. For example, states that enacted the strictest laws did not necessarily experience the sharpest declines in crime. Indeed, Canada and other countries did not follow the U.S. lead in getting tough but still saw crime rates fall (Currie 1998; Zimring 2007). Of course it would be hard to increase the incarceration rate by 600 percent without

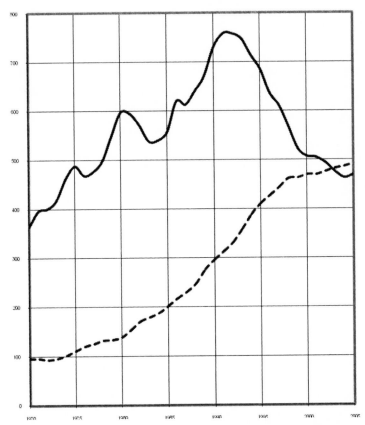

Figure 1.2b   Incarceration and crime rates for different time periods, 1970–2005.
Source: **Sourcebook of Criminal Justice Statistics online, Table 3.106, 2005.**

having some effect on crime, but the Texas comptroller of public accounts discovered what many criminologists already know: the state criminal justice system cannot solve the crime problem. He performed an audit of expenditures on criminal justice and writes in *Texas Crime, Texas Justice: A Report from the Texas Performance Review* that "the only point on which virtually all students of Texas crime agree is that the ultimate answer to the state's rising crime must come from outside the sphere of criminal justice. Economic hardship, the growing 'underclass,' drug addiction, the decline in moral and educational standards, psychological problems and other root causes will never be cured by punitive measures" (Sharpe 1992, ix).

Little accountability or oversight at the local, state, or federal level has accompanied these vast sums of money to ensure that taxpayers are getting good value for their hard-earned money. The Texas comptroller's audit is unique but noteworthy because this political and fiscal conservative's striking conclusion is that

> despite the need for real solutions, public debate over crime in Texas revolves around hollow calls for the state to become "tougher." In fact, this is a call for the status quo—for more of the same, only more so. It is a call for a continuing cycle of cynical quick fixes and stop-gap measures, for costly prison construction that cannot keep pace with the demand for new prison space—*for a constant drain on state and local treasuries that makes Texas taxpayers poorer, not safer.* (Sharpe 1992, emphasis in the original)

In the first book to examine systematically the drop in crime rates, *The Crime Drop in America*, two mainstream criminologists used different quantitative techniques to arrive independently at the conclusion that the enormous increase in incarceration contributed, at best, 25 percent to the crime reduction that started in the mid-1990s (Blumstein and Wallman 2000). Alfred Blumstein and his colleagues credit "multiple factors that together contributed to the crime drop, including the waning of crack markets, the strong economy, efforts to control guns, intensified policing (particularly in efforts to control guns in the community), and increased incarceration" (Blumstein 2001, 2). In another book not based on original research, *Why Crime Rates Fell*, John Conklin posits that incarceration had a slightly larger impact but concedes that "the expansion of the inmate population certainly incurred exorbitant costs, both in terms of its disastrous impact on the lives of offenders and their families and in terms of the huge expenditure of tax revenue" (2003, 200). Thus, even those inclined to see incarceration as more effective in reducing crime seem to question whether it has been an overall "success." Yet another book on the crime drop by criminologist Franklin Zimring emphasizes the cyclical nature of crime rates (2007, 131) and suggests a "best guess of the impact" of incarceration on crime rates "would range from 10% of the decline at the low end to 27% of the decline at the high end" (55).

Imprisonment may prevent an inmate from committing crimes in the outside world, but research shows that a small number of career criminals commit a disproportionate number of offenses, so after they are locked up, further increases in the prison population have a declining effect on crime (Vieraitis, Kovandzic, and Marvell 2007, 597). More and more trivial, nonviolent offenders received harsh sentences as the decades progressed: "Between 1980 and 1997 the number of people incarcerated for nonviolent offenses tripled, and the number of people incarcerated for drug offenses increased by a factor of 11. Indeed, the criminal-justice researcher Alfred Blumstein has argued that none of the growth in incarceration between 1980 and 1996 can be attributed to more crime" (Loury 2007).

For example, William Rummel was convicted of a felony involving the fraudulent use of a credit card to obtain $80 worth of goods, another felony for forging a check in the amount of $28.36, and a third felony for obtaining $120.75 under false pretenses by accepting payment to fix an air conditioner that he never returned to repair. For these three nonviolent felonies that involved less than $230, Rummel received a mandatory life sentence under Texas's recidivist statute. The Supreme Court affirmed the sentence despite Justice Louis Powell's dissent, which noted, "It is difficult to imagine felonies that pose less danger to the peace and good order of a civilized society than the three crimes committed by the petitioner" (*Rummel v. Estelle* 1980, 445 U.S. 263, 295).

Unfortunately, the Supreme Court recently reaffirmed *Rummel* in a case involving a fifty-year sentence for two instances of shoplifting videos. In 1995, Leandro Andrade, a nine-year army veteran and father of three, got caught shoplifting five children's videotapes from Kmart, a heist yielding a value of around $85. Two weeks later, he was caught shoplifting four similar tapes—including *Free Willie 2* and *Cinderella*—worth about $70 from another Kmart. Under California law, Andrade's 1982 convictions for residential burglary were his first "strikes" under the Three Strikes Law, and the prosecutor decided that Andrade was a repeat offender whose current shoplifting charges should count as strikable offenses. The two current Kmart shoplifting charges thus became strikes three and four—each carrying a mandatory penalty of twenty-five years. The thirty-seven-year-old Andrade received a mandatory fifty years, meaning he will likely die of old age before being released (and incurs a cost to taxpayers of about $25,000 to $35,000 a year for the early years of his incarceration). Andrade contended that his sentence was grossly disproportionate to the crime and violated the U.S. Constitution's Eighth Amendment prohibition against cruel and unusual punishment. The Supreme Court decided the sentence was not unreasonable and found that "the gross disproportionality principle reserves a constitutional violation for only the extraordinary case" (*Lockyer v. Andrade* 2003, 538 U.S. 63, 77); Leighton and Reiman 2004).

The second point in the critique of the incarceration binge is that there has been a tremendous opportunity cost in building prisons and expanding the criminal justice system. The idea behind an opportunity cost is that because money, time, and effort are spent on one thing, other projects go unfunded, and other ideas are ignored. With the imprisonment binge, the United States spent hundreds of billions on an inefficient method of crime reduction, and the opportunity cost involves thinking about how that money could have been put to more socially beneficial uses. One legislator bluntly stated, "For every dollar you're spending on corrections, you're not spending that on primary and secondary education, you're not spending it on colleges and tourism. It's just money down a rat hole, basically" (Huling 2002, 205).

Some trade-offs are inevitable, but government decisions have usually entailed funding prison expansion by slashing budgets for education, crime prevention, community programs, drug and alcohol treatment, and a host of other programs that seek to create law-abiding citizens rather than simply punish people after they commit a criminal act. One criminologist likens this tactic to "mopping the water off the floor while we let the tub overflow. Mopping harder may make some difference in the level of the flood. It does not, however, do anything about the open faucet" (Currie 1985, 227). Worse still, programs that prevent crime can have a high return on investment because by intervening early, "you not only save the costs of incarceration, you also save the costs of crime and gain the benefits of an individual who is a taxpaying contributor to the economy" (Butterfield 1996, A24).

Once again, Andrade's case provides an example because he was stealing to support a drug habit. The presentence report noted he had been a heroin addict since 1977: "He admits his addiction controls his life and he steals to support his habit" (Lockyer 2003). The obvious question is why he didn't just go for treatment. While Andrade's personal history is unknown, another person in a similar situation tells a common story about drug addiction and prison. Charles Terry, one of the "convict criminologists" who served time in prison then earned a PhD wrote in *The Fellas*,

> Before that particular arrest, I made phone calls to various hospitals or "recovery" centers asking for help because I was hopelessly addicted. I was tired of the pain, the remorse, and the sure knowledge that sooner or later I was going back to prison. When someone on the other line answered, I'd say, "Hi. I need help. I'm a heroin addict who has already been to prison twice. I'm hooked like a dog. I'm doing felonies everyday to support my habit, and I can't stop!"
>
> In response came the inevitable question, "Do you have insurance? . . . The cost is five hundred dollars a day." (2003, 4)

Needless to say, Terry did not have that kind of money and committed more crimes that landed him back in prison. His book does not suggest that drug rehab is an easy cure-all, and his stories of "the fellas" show that drug rehabilitation among hard-core convicts is extremely difficult. But it is also true that the best time to reach people is when they want help. Not funding drug treatment on demand is one of the many opportunity costs of funding an incarceration binge. The emphasis on building prisons made fewer programs available for prisoners already incarcerated, let alone creating new drug-treatment programs. During the 1990s, prisoner participation declined in educational, vocational or job, drug and alcohol, and prerelease programs (Vieraitis, Kovandzic, and Marvell 2007, 592). All these programs help make reintegration more successful and thus contribute to public safety by decreasing the likelihood of crime.

The third point in the critique of the incarceration binge is that it has caused social harm in a variety of ways, including undermining public safety, disrupting communities, disenfranchising millions, and contributing to racial and economic inequality. The most serious concern centers on findings that excessive use of incarceration can increase crime and violence. For example, *The Crime Drop in America* notes,

> It is somewhat ironic that the growth in violence with handguns was at least partly a consequence of the drug war's incarceration of many of the older drug sellers. . . . As older sellers were taken off the street, the drug market turned to younger individuals, particularly inner-city African-Americans. . . . The reduction in age of the workers in the crack trade entailed a predictable increase in violence, as the inclination to deliberate before acting is simply less developed in the young. (Blumstein and Wallman 2000, 4–5)

In addition, excessive use of prison that results in high levels of incarceration concentrated in poor communities can cause social disorganization and weaken informal social controls like family, neighborhoods, and community groups (Clear 2002). Offenders exit prison with diminished job prospects; many have been hardened or brutalized as well, and they return to communities already stressed by dealing with social problems. This movement from the community to prison and the subsequent return to the community leads to "neighborhood instability and low informal social control [both of which] have been linked to higher crime rates" (Vieraitis, Kovandzic, and Marvell 2007, 590). The effects from high levels of incarceration in certain neighborhoods exist in addition to a general finding that prisons are criminogenic, meaning that "imprisonment causes harm to prisoners," who go on to "commit more crimes than they would have had they not gone to prison" (Vieraitis, Kovandzic, and Marvell 2007, 614).

These harmful dynamics have hit inner-city minority neighborhoods especially hard because as the prison population has grown, the proportion of incarcerated minorities has also increased. According to the Bureau of Justice Statistics, "On June 30, 2006, an estimated 4.8% of black men were in prison or jail, compared to 1.9% of Hispanic men and 0.7% of white men. More than 11% of black males age 25 to 34 were incarcerated" (2007a, 1). Table 1.1 presents the data more systematically; it also expands on the normal counts that provide a snapshot of a particular day and considers the cumulative impact of high incarceration rates across a lifetime. The table highlights the disproportionate number of minorities, especially blacks, who are in prison—explaining why many feel the war on crime is a war on minorities (Miller 1996). But the detail by gender—almost one-third of black males born in 2001 will go to prison at some point during their lives—underscores problems like weakened families and social disorganization mentioned above.

Table 1.1. People under Control of the Criminal Justice System by Gender, Race, and Ethnicity

	Jail (rate per 100,000) Midyear 2006	Prison (rate per 100,000) 2008	Percentage of Adult Population Ever Incarcerated in Prison 2001	Percentage Ever Going to Prison during Lifetime if Born in 2001
White	170	N/A	1.4	3.4
Male		727	2.6	5.9
Female		93	0.5	0.9
Black	815	N/A	8.9	18.6
Male		4,777	16.6	32.2
Female		349	1.7	5.6
Hispanic	283	N/A	4.3	10
Male		1,760	7.7	17.2
Female		147	0.7	2.2

Source: Bureau of Justice Statistics (2003, 1 and tables 5 and 9; 2007a, 6; 2009, 18). BJS does not regularly report overall incarceration rates for race and has not recently reported jail incarceration rates by race.

Because of the high number of minorities who have been to prison at some point, minority communities are disproportionately affected by felony disenfranchisement, the denial of voting rights to incarcerated felons after their release, at which point they have supposedly paid their debt to society. These laws, which became widely used in the South after the Fourteenth Amendment gave newly freed slaves the right to vote, now disenfranchise 2 percent of the U.S. population and 13 percent of African American men (King 2006, 1). The census's method of counting prisoners further erodes the electoral power of inner-city minorities because inmates are counted as residents of the rural county where the prison is located instead of having their "usual and customary residence" be the city where they formerly lived and to which they will return. The census then becomes the basis for apportioning legislators, so the number of elected representatives from (white) rural areas increases because their prison populations have inflated their overall population counts (Prisoners of the Census 2007). Census counts are also the basis for distributing various payments to cities and counties, leading to a redistribution of aid away from racially diverse and impoverished inner cities.

As part of sentencing reform, many jurisdictions are enacting "truth-in-sentencing" laws, which require offenders to serve at least 85 percent of their sentence. But criminologist Todd Clear notes that a sentence's length is a small part of the "truth" about its underlying irrationality. He imagines a judge telling the full truth, which nicely summarizes some of the critique of the imprisonment binge:

For the crime of selling drugs, I sentence you to 10 years in prison. I am doing so even though we know that this sentence will not prevent any more drugs from being sold, and that it will probably result in someone not now involved in the drug trade being recruited to take your place while you are locked up. I impose this sentence knowing that the main reason you have been caught and convicted is that we have concentrated our police presence in the community where you live, and that had you lived where I live, your drug use and sales would probably have gone undetected. I impose this sentence knowing it will cost the taxpayers over a quarter of a million dollars to carry it out, money we desperately need for the schools and health care in the area where you live, but instead it will go into the pockets of corrections officers and prison builders who live miles away from here and have no interest in the quality of life in your neighborhood. I impose this sentence knowing it will most likely make you a worse citizen, not a better one, leaving you embittered toward the law and damaged by your years spent behind bars. You think you have trouble making it now? Wait until after you have served a decade of your life wasting in a prison cell. And I impose this sentence knowing that it will make your children, your cousins, and your nephews have even less respect for the law, since they will come to see you as having been singled out for this special punishment, largely due to the color of your skin and the amount of money in your pocket. I impose this sentence knowing that its only purpose is to respond to an angry public and a few rhetorically excited politicians, even though I know this sentence will not calm either of them down in the slightest. This is the truth of my sentence. (Welch 1999, x)

This critique is fundamental to understanding private prisons because they, along with the larger criminal justice–industrial complex, were created from the same movements that gave rise to a sprawling, expensive, inefficient, and sometimes socially harmful prison system. Both also now have an interest in perpetuating this system, thus its problems, because the duty of business executives is to maximize profit, which they do by expanding business opportunities, which in turn is best accomplished through an expanding prison and criminal justice system. While the United States has a long history of the rich getting richer while the poor get prison (Reiman and Leighton 2010), the current situation—private prisons listed on the stock exchange and an expanding number of businesses profiting from the expansion of the criminal justice system—means that rich whites get richer *from* poor minorities being sent to prison.

IDEOLOGY AND "IDEAS"
JUSTIFYING THE INCARCERATION BINGE

"Following the money" is a useful exercise, especially as the criminal justice–industrial complex gets larger (see chapter 3), but we can better understand several important steps that created the foundation for the present situation by looking at political discourse and "ideas," or ideology. Indeed, the role of ideology is to justify the present, which means that current social dynamics come to seem natural, inevitable, and fair. As the previous discussion indicated, this state of affairs is deeply unfair. It is not natural and inevitable, but its unfolding does have a logic, which this section of the chapter explores. Indeed, the deeply problematic nature of the current situation and the ideological inertia to continue along this "commonsense" path make understanding how the United States came to this self-perpetuating dynamic of injustice imperative.

During the 1960s and early 1970s, crime changed from a local concern into a federal one, with conservative national politicians conflating civil rights protests, urban unrest, and crime into one problem that required "law and order" as a solution. Unfortunately, too few people thought to ask, whose law? And what social order is being upheld? Also, the flexible sentences that prospered under a system of rehabilitation gave way to more determinate ones. Because of the continued popularity of "tough on crime" and the continued election of conservatives espousing it, fixed sentences became harsher (and harsher). The process of getting tough continued to ensnare large numbers of nonviolent and trivial offenders, but media depictions of crime aided in perpetuating the belief that building more prisons was necessary for public safety. Finally, the obvious result of enacting harsher mandatory sentences was that more people were in prison, but overcrowding quickly became a crisis. The easy option of building prisons to continue "tough on crime" quickly ran into conflict with politicians' other popular line about cutting taxes.

THE RISE OF "LAW AND ORDER"

The 1960s were troubling times for Americans because of marches, riots, and acts of civil disobedience related both to the civil rights movement and protests over the Vietnam War. For those with conservative leanings, war protests and civil rights marches threatened the social order and exacerbated what they saw as the erosion of traditional values. The increasing acceptance of divorce, free love, teenage parenthood, and drug use, in addition to women's liberation, were all indicators of the unraveling social fabric. On the other side, liberals saw some traditional values as tolerating and even perpetuating racism, sexism, and inequality. They waged extensive legislative battles for civil rights and voting rights laws, only to face further battles over implementing those pieces of landmark legislation. As one of many examples, in his 1963 inauguration speech as governor of Alabama, George Wallace declared, "In the name of the greatest people that have ever trod this earth, I draw the line in the dust and toss the gauntlet before the feet of tyranny, and I say segregation now, segregation tomorrow, segregation forever." Later that year Governor Wallace himself would stand in front of a door at the University of Alabama and block the first two black students from entering, a move that required the National Guard's intervening to enforce the law.

During this same period, a dramatic shift in the national attitude transformed crime from a local into a national problem that warranted a national solution. The 1964 presidential campaign battle among Republican senator Barry Goldwater, Independent candidate George Wallace, and Democrat Lyndon B. Johnson brought crime into the national spotlight as a policy issue. Goldwater and Wallace stressed formal social control rather than social welfare as the government's primary responsibility. The "permissive society" needed to be reigned in, and they promised to repress crime with a stricter enforcement of the criminal code. In reaction to civil rights demonstrations and a rising crime rate, both Goldwater and Wallace included a strong law-and-order plank in their campaign platforms. Glenn Loury (2007) notes that this

> punitive turn represented a political response to the success of the civil-rights movement. Weaver describes a process of "frontlash" in which opponents of the civil-rights revolution sought to regain the upper hand by shifting to a new issue. Rather than reacting directly to civil-rights developments, and thus continuing to fight a battle they had lost, those opponents—consider George Wallace's campaigns for the presidency, which drew so much support in states like Michigan and Wisconsin—shifted attention to a seemingly race-neutral concern over crime.

Johnson ultimately won the election and sought to build his Great Society by spreading the benefits of America's successful economy to more citizens. Early in his administration, President Johnson stressed the need to address crime's "root causes" and argued that programs attacking social inequality were, in effect, anticrime programs: "There is something mighty wrong when a candidate for the highest office bemoans violence in the streets but votes against the war on poverty, votes against the Civil Rights Act, and votes against major educational bills that come before him" (Beckett and Sasson 2000, 52). But through the conservative Southern strategy, "anxiety over racial change and riots, civil rights and racial disorder—initially defined as a problem of minority disenfranchisement—were defined as a crime problem, which helped shift debate from social reform to punishment" (Loury 2007). By the end of the decade, even President Johnson would turn away from long-term structural solutions like "the war against poverty" toward shorter-term punitive practices like "the war against crime."

Conservatives further argued that the criminal justice system had become so concerned with civil rights that it was benefiting criminals rather than preventing the victimization of innocent citizens. Throughout the 1960s, the Supreme Court under Chief Justice Earl Warren strengthened individual rights, including the protections offered to criminal defendants. For example, the court ruled in *Mapp v. Ohio* (1961) that search warrants must be obtained before the search for or seizure of evidence, *Gideon v. Wainwright* (1963) guaranteed defendants the right to legal counsel, and *Miranda v. Arizona* (1966) required that suspects be informed of their legal rights. In the eyes of conservatives, such decisions established "criminal's rights" rather than logically extending the individual rights enshrined in the Constitution that protect all individuals, innocent and guilty, from abuses of state power. After an unsuccessful campaign to impeach the chief justice, on whom the Constitution confers a lifetime appointment in order in insulate the Court from political passions, conservatives settled in to argue the need to strengthen the state control apparatus in other ways to prevent criminals from getting the upper hand.

Of additional critical importance to the successful promotion of increased punitiveness was the growing support for the "culture-of-poverty" thesis, which attributed poverty to the immorality of the impoverished. For example, Democratic senator Daniel Patrick Moynihan's much-discussed 1965 report on the black family attributed black poverty to the "subculture of the American Negro" and described crime, violence, and disorder in urban ghettos as a deserved consequence of poor choices and a lack of morals and values. Moynihan specifically cited female-headed households as a problem (Wilson 1987). The release of the report touched off widespread discussion, much of it emphasizing poor individual choices rather than larger social conditions and disenfranchisement. Loury notes that "before 1965, public attitudes on the welfare state and on race, as measured by the annually administered General Social Survey, varied year to year independently of one another: you could not predict much about a person's attitudes on welfare politics by knowing their attitudes about race" (2007). Correlations are used to measure the strength of relationships between two items, with a value of one indicating perfect similarity or predictive ability and a value of zero indicating the absence of any similarities. The "correlation between an index measuring liberalism of racial attitudes and attitudes toward the welfare state over the interval 1950–1965 was 0.03. These same two series had a correlation of .68 over the period 1966–1996. The association in the American mind of race with welfare, and of race with crime, had been achieved at a common historical moment" (Loury 2007).

The effect of these shifts was to transform the image of the impoverished, especially poor minorities, from needing social justice to not deserving rights, financial assistance, and rehabilitation. By emphasizing street crime and framing that problem as the consequence of bad people making bad choices, conservatives made it much less likely that members of the public would empathize with, and support measures to assist, them (Beckett and Sasson 2000, 53). Historian Michael Katz points out that "when the poor seemed menacing they became the underclass" (1989, 185). Through "law-and-order" and "tough-on-crime" campaigns, society could be protected from them—unwanted, unworthy of help, and increasingly portrayed as dangerous. The end result was that race eclipsed class as the organizing principle of American politics. By 1970, when Nixon declared a "war on crime," quickly followed in 1971 by his declaration that "America's Public Enemy No. 1 is drug abuse," both were firmly associated in the public's mind with minority populations (Ray 1972, 38).

A key aspect of the transformation of these attitudes into criminal justice policy started with the overthrow of rehabilitation and the indeterminate sentences that supported it. Indeterminate sentences were flexible and open-ended commitments—say, five years to life, with the parole board deciding release based upon the offender's participation in programs and an evaluation of his or her progress toward rehabilitation. Criticism of rehabilitation would come from both the political Left and Right, although for different reasons. The bipartisan agreement on the problem of discretion in flexible sentences and concerns about rehabilitation precipitated the shift to both the era of the prison warehouse (Irwin 2005) and ever-increasing fixed sentences as Republicans gained power with their "tough-on-crime" rhetoric.

With rehabilitation, critics on the Left pointed to a variety of faulty theoretical assumptions, the harm done under the guise of therapy, and the use of the therapeutic ideal to administer justice in a discriminatory manner. For example, new therapeutic techniques, such as drugs, electroshock, sterilization, and psychosurgery, used under the guise of benevolence often left inmates with irreversible physical and psychological damage. The logic of "behavior modification" became the ultimate coercive custodial weapon used to deny inmates basic human rights; the critique of mental institutions in *One Flew over the Cuckoo's Nest* (Kesey 1963) applied equally to penal institutions. Also, critics argued that prison officials used the indeterminate sentence as a coercive tool to achieve their own custodial goals rather than treatment goals. The criterion for release became institutional conformity rather than "cure." In addition, critics pointed to the furtherance of class and race discrimination because of discretionary practices by parole boards that had almost no official accountability (especially for decisions to continue incarceration). Finally, rehabilitation, by explaining crime in highly individualistic terms as perpetrated by sick offenders rather than a symptom of a problematic society, legitimated the expansion of numerous state administrative powers used in practice to discriminate against already

disadvantaged groups whose crimes were frequently minor in comparison with the immensely destructive actions of corporations and the state
(Greenberg and Humphries 1980).

Where the Left saw discrimination, the Right generally saw leniency for
offenders. Too many programs "coddled" offenders who were undeserving
of such efforts and resources. The lower end of the range for indeterminate
sentences was increased as politicians put the "law-and-order" and "tough-
on-crime" rhetoric into practice. Pointing to soaring crime rates as evidence
that those administering our criminal justice system had tipped the scales
in crime's favor, neoclassical criminology stressed that the failure to control
crime largely resulted from the failure to punish criminals (Kramer 1984,
223). This school of thought argued that the vast majority of offenders break
the law only after they have used their rational faculties to calculate that the
benefits of committing a crime outweigh the potential costs. That the benefits
of crime outweighed its costs, it was argued, stemmed directly from leniency,
including the "soft" sentences associated with the rehabilitative efforts.

In addition, conservatives argued that it was time to "admit that we do
not know how to rehabilitate and start thinking about the criminal's victims
for a change" (cited in Cullen and Gilbert 1982, 96). The argument about
whether rehabilitation was ineffective received a substantial boost because of
an article by Robert Martinson (1974) that reviewed more than two hundred
evaluations of treatment programs. His conclusion was widely interpreted to
be that "nothing works." While other researchers studying the question had
weighed in on both sides of the debate, Martinson's article drew a great deal
of attention and even led to the author's appearance on *60 minutes* (Cavender
2004). Martinson would do a follow-up study later and write that "new evidence from our current study leads me to reject my original conclusion," but
no one paid attention, even though Francis Cullen and Paul Gendreau note
that Martinson's original "nothing works article is among the most cited of
criminological writings" (Cavender 2004). The selective nature of attention
to these studies suggests that they were "used to justify, not to form, opinions about correctional treatment" (Cavender 2004). However, Martinson's
article made the conservative critique seem grounded in reality and science.
Because liberals, rehabilitation's traditional defenders, were also critiquing it,
few voices spoke out against widespread political agreement that discretionary practices like indeterminate sentences should be abolished along with
parole boards.

REPUBLICANS AND MEDIA DRIVE "TOUGH ON CRIME"

This move to more fixed sentences was an important step, but it would not
necessarily have led to an incarceration binge without ongoing support for

the notion that "getting tough" would solve a problem the United States faced. In this sense, the second important step entails the political Right's domination of politics in general and the crime issue in particular, as well as that group's consistent emphasis on tougher criminal sentences. Indeed, even when a Democrat finally won the presidency, he did so with a largely conservative crime-control agenda: Bill Clinton favored the death penalty, advocated putting one hundred thousand more police on the streets, and expanded the drug war (he also did a great deal to increase the use of privatized prisons). While recent politics has focused more on terrorism than crime, there is no sign of a rejection of the tough-on-crime agenda (Reiman and Leighton 2010), so it is important to look beyond the early origins of this "idea" and examine its ongoing impact on politics. Indeed, it is the relentless nature of this politically popular agenda that causes overcrowding and increased criminal justice budgets. In turn, these budget increases conflict with the perennially popular and politically lucrative tax-cutting agenda—and rather than admit a basic contradiction in politically popular rhetoric, politicians will turn to privatization in order to have their cake and eat it too.

We have already noted the nationalization of crime in the 1964 election and Johnson's backtracking on fighting crime by refocusing on dealing with poverty. But the 1968 election of President Nixon signaled the first successful "law-and-order" campaign. His 1970 State of the Union address announced a resounding rejection of earlier tactics for fighting crime, which he made a high priority:

> We have heard a great deal of overblown rhetoric during the sixties in which the word "war" has perhaps too often been used—the war on poverty, the war on misery, the war on disease, the war on hunger. But if there is one area where the word "war" is appropriate it is in the fight against crime. We must declare and win the war against the criminal elements which increasingly threaten our cities, our homes, and our lives. (Nixon 1970)

As the 1970s came to an end, the American public defined crime as the number one domestic problem facing the nation, and fear of crime increased dramatically. Initially a substantial increase in the major index crimes reported by the police in the late 1960s and early 1970s aroused this anxiety. However, even as the violent crime rate declined in the early 1980s (see figure 1.2b), the public continued to believe that crime was increasing, and the level of fear remained high—a pattern that would repeat itself in the 1990s as well. Regardless of whether the crime rate was actually increasing or decreasing, national, state, and local politicians played on the media-driven fear of crime and its underlying racial anxiety to promote harsher sentences (Davey 1998).

During the 1980 presidential elections, the Democratic Party included a crime plank denouncing excessive police brutality and promising increased federal funding for jobs and education, while the Republicans emphasized swift, certain, and strong punishments, including mandatory minimum sentences for drug offenders (Woolley and Peters 2007). The Republican candidate won. In 1984 the Republican Party announced its anticrime agenda comprising largely repressive measures, including preventative detention, the reestablishment of the death penalty, and the targeting of drug dealers. The Democrats, in contrast, focused on "the elimination of poverty and unemployment that foster the criminal atmosphere" (Woolley and Peters 2007). The Republican candidate won. In 1988, the Democratic Party platform continued the education-and-prevention theme, stating that sentencing reform should include "diversion programs for first and non-violent offenders." On the issue of drugs, the platform called for "readily available counseling for those who seek to address their dependency." The 1988 Republican Party platform demanded "an end to crime" and what it called a "historic reform of toughened sentencing procedures for federal courts to make the punishment fit the crime." In addition, the party stated, "The best way to deter crime is to increase the probability of detection and to make punishment certain and swift. Republicans advocate sentencing reform and secure, adequate prison construction" (Woolley and Peters 2007). The Republican candidate won.

After almost two decades of "law and order," efforts to keep the public focused on crime and supportive of yet another round of getting tough required dramatic political stunts. Thus, in September 1989, President George Bush gave a televised speech about the drug problem in the United States that included a prop—a bag of crack cocaine that he said had been purchased right across the street from the White House. Media coverage of drug issues increased, and public concern about drugs skyrocketed. Following the speech, the Gallup Poll recorded its highest-ever response to the question about whether drug abuse is the most important problem facing the United States (Bureau of Justice Statistics 1992). Congress and state legislators responded with another round of tougher mandatory sentences. Keith Jackson, an eighteen-year-old black high school student, was indicted for drugs and became known as the kid who sold drugs to the president.

Though not well covered by the media, the story behind this "political theater" provides a good example of the symbiotic relationship politicians and the media have with the crime issue (Barak, Leighton, and Flavin 2007). Stories like this garner support for politicians and an audience for the media if told in certain ways—for instance, by highlighting a young black man's selling crack to the president. The more complex and less newsworthy story was that Jackson had no previous record and was a student in good standing; he only occasionally sold drugs for extra money because the area of Washington, D.C., in which he lived had severely limited job opportunities. His drug-sale pattern did not normally take him near the

White House, and despite his living in Washington, D.C., he did not know where it was. Drug Enforcement Administration (DEA) agents had to drive him there so he could make the sale. The DEA's special agent in charge of D.C. admitted in court, "We had to manipulate him to get him down there. It wasn't easy" (T. Thompson 1989, C1; Thompson and Isikoff 1990, D6). Worse still, a homeless woman in the park attacked a DEA agent charged with videotaping the transaction because she thought he was taping her. The jury chuckled, and the presiding judge likened the event to an episode starring the slapstick Keystone Cops.

The reality for Jackson was not so funny. He was held without bail and faced a mandatory twelve-year prison sentence. The first trial ended in a hung jury, but in the second, he was convicted of drug charges stemming from drug sales other than the one near the White House. Judge Sporkin, a former CIA general counsel appointed to the bench by President Reagan, imposed a ten-year sentence without the possibility of parole under mandatory sentencing guidelines for crack cocaine (T. Thompson 1990a, B11). The judge said he regretted having to impose a sentence of ten years (at a cost to the taxpayers of $175,000) and hoped Bush would commute the sentence (he didn't). The image on the television screen showed another black man in handcuffs for selling drugs. The media focused coverage on the rhetorically excited politicians calling for more and harsher penalties because drug dealers were selling crack near the White House. They ignored and left unsaid the other truths about sentencing mentioned by Clear (above): the lack of jobs and opportunities, the need for money to go to school rather than prison, the fact that most crack users and dealers are white, the perception that Jackson was singled out, the likelihood that he will emerge from prison a worse citizen, and the possibility that those who know him will have less respect for the law. More pointedly, Valerie Callanan sees crack dealing as part of an informal economy that flourished because of labor market crises, and she asks, "Would we have two million people incarcerated today if the links to deindustrialization and globalization had been made in the media?" (2005, 178).

Although Clinton was a Democrat, he broke from the 1980s ideas in the Democratic Party platforms mentioned above and seized the crime issue by advocating traditionally Republican positions. Governor Clinton interrupted his 1992 campaign for president to return to Arkansas for the execution of a retarded black man who wanted to save a piece of cake from his last meal for after his execution (Sherrill 2001). Clinton's proposal to put an additional one hundred thousand police on the streets won him the support of the police unions, and he later claimed they had "played a big role in the recent crime drop" despite skepticism from criminologists (Reiman and Leighton 2010, 1). While other presidents could ignore crime-rate decreases during their terms, the decline in these rates under Clinton was substantial, so he took credit for it, and he did so in a way that kept the issue alive: "Now that we've finally turned crime on the run, we have to redouble our efforts." Thus, his 1999 State of the Union address proposed more police armed with updated technologies (Reiman and Leighton 2010, 2).

State and local politicians noted the success of "law and order" and "tough on crime" at the national level. By 1974, most states had begun to build at least a few new prisons and put into place sentencing guidelines. In the mid-1970s Illinois and Arizona revised their criminal laws to increase penalties based on the argument that rehabilitation does not work and a discussion of serial killers (Cavender 2004, 342). Of particular relevance to the growth of the prison population were the state statutes relating to drug offences. For example, New York's 1973 Rockefeller drug laws set forth a mandatory sentencing scheme that requires judges to impose prison terms of no less than fifteen years to life on anyone convicted of selling two ounces or more, or possessing four ounces or more, of any illegal narcotic substance. The penalties apply without regard to the circumstances of the offense or the offender's criminal history, character, or background (Schmalleger 2003, 497). In 1978, Michigan enacted the 650 Lifer Law requiring mandatory life sentences for the possession, sale, or conspiracy to sell or possess 650 grams of cocaine or heroin. By 1983, forty states had passed such provisions (Tonry 1987). In 1984, the Sentencing Reform Act mandated the formation of the U.S. Sentencing Commission and tasked it with establishing binding sentencing guidelines to narrow judges' sentencing discretion dramatically. Increasingly, criminals were "no longer persons to be supported, but risks to be dealt with" through incarceration, so "as of 2000, 33 states had abolished limited parole (up from 17 in 1980); 24 states had introduced three-strikes laws (up from zero); and 40 states had introduced truth-in-sentencing laws (up from three). The vast majority of these changes occurred in the 1990s, as crime rates fell" (Loury 2007).

Notice that many of these laws targeted drug possession rather than violent crime, and many others increased sentences for a range of nonviolent offenses. "Get tough" started with the idea that the United States needed harsher penalties against repeat violent offenders, even though research demonstrates the United States is no more lenient with serious crimes than other Western democracies (Lynch 1993). Later rhetoric would shift to concern for leniency with repeat *and* violent offenders. Though rhetorically subtle, this shift has important implications for sentencing because a large number of repeat offenders have never done anything violent, as the stories of Rummel and Andrade discussed above illustrate. Steven Donziger calls this a "bait and switch" after the classic sales ploy of luring customers into a store with a low advertised price on one item, then shifting their focus to a more expensive one. With criminal justice, he writes, the "bait" is citizen fear of violent crime. The "switch" occurs when public officials fight crime by building more prisons *but then fill the new cells with nonviolent offenders.* This scheme profits those who wish to appear "tough" on crime but in reality are failing to make America safe. One consequence of this policy is that the criminal justice system spends tens of billions of dollars on prisons and then underfunds effective drug treatment, educational programs, and violence prevention programs by asserting that there is not enough money. (Donziger 1996, 25, emphasis in the original)

The continuing popularity of "tough on crime" and the packing of prisons with nonviolent offenders at great taxpayer expense could not have happened without increasing media coverage of crime that stoked people's fear. Just as crime had earlier changed from a local concern into a national one, 1990s television coverage of crime followed the same process: certain types of crime occurring anywhere in the country were worth reporting. The media do not directly determine people's beliefs, but they do help focus their attention on one issue (like crime) over others (like unemployment, poverty, and inequality). Further, the media provide "frames" for coverage, and crime fits into a "fear frame" that plays to sensationalize conflict, which attracts more viewers and advertising revenue—but it also sends a message about the dangerousness of contemporary society (Cavender 2004, 338), especially by implying that the violence is random in nature.

Media executives say their outlets reflect what happens in the real world, but from 1990 to 1995, a time when crime rates peaked then started to decline, the "number of crime stories on national television news broadcasts nearly quadrupled" (Callanan 2005, 8). When the increase in crime dramas, "reality" programs, and other coverage is included, it comes as no surprise that the public believed crime was continuing to increase even after crime rates had been falling for several years. Further, when compared with official crime statistics, media representations reflect a "law of opposites": "The characteristics of crime, criminals, and victims represented in the media are in most respects the polar opposite of the pattern suggested by official crime statistics or by crime and victim surveys" (Pollak and Kubrin 2007, 61). The media cover violent crimes almost to the exclusion of property crimes, even though the latter comprise the vast majority of offenses. And the more freakish the violent crime, the more coverage it gets, especially when a photogenic white female victim is involved. Further, minority men are overrepresented as offenders compared to their prevalence in arrest data and victim surveys that ask about perpetrator characteristics. Conversely, the media underrepresent minority men as victims, even though violent victimization occurs disproportionately to that portion of the population.

During the 1970s, criminologist James Q. Wilson summarized the crime problem with the words "Wicked people exist," and the increasingly corporate media repeatedly associated black men with that idea by overrepresenting them as violent offenders, underrepresenting them as victims, and downplaying social conditions as an explanation in favor of blaming individual pathology. Over decades, crime dramas, the news, and entertainment programs helped create the image of a typical criminal as overwhelmingly poor, black, male, increasingly drug crazed, and more and more dangerous. Katheryn Russell (1998) uses the term *criminalblackman* to capture the close association in the media and the public mind of black men with crime, especially the kinds of crimes white America fears most. This process, combined with the ideology about law and order discussed earlier, helped create a powerful sense that "crime was bad and getting worse, criminals were monstrous 'OTHERS' and the modern world was virtually spinning out of control" (Cavender 2004, 346).

While many Americans were coming to believe that gangs of (black) criminals were overrunning the streets randomly committing violence, the public discourse continued to focus on protecting law-abiding citizens ("us") from the dangerous population ("them") through imprisonment and executions. One important result of this crusade was the belief that there were only two choices: either build more prisons or have dangerous criminals on the streets. By showcasing extreme incidents of violent, predatory street crime, politicians and the media convinced the public to uphold the status quo policy of "lock 'em up." Anything else would be dangerous and irresponsible, even though the reality of get-tough policies involved escalating punishments for nonviolent offenders. As Grey Cavender notes, "In Governor Jim Thompson's words, we should 'send a message to the criminal.' In Dirty Harry's version, it was, 'Go ahead. Make my day.' As this response was replayed in the coverage of legislative debate across the states, and in movies and TV drama, it eventually became THE solution; and, it became common sense" (2004, 346).

THE OVERCROWDING CRISIS AND MASSIVE BUDGET EXPANSION

Set in this sociohistorical context, the upsurge in prison populations is not surprising (Ziedenberg and Schiraldi 2000). The attack on rehabilitation from political figures at the state and national levels, supported by the utilitarian calculus of neoclassical criminological thinking and coupled with the ever-increasing media focus on crime and criminals, elevated the level of fear of crime and the *criminalblackman*. However, prior to the mid-1980s, few new prisons had been built in the United States since the Great Depression, and the flood of new prisoners that began in the late 1960s overwhelmed these aging facilities (see box 2.1). Although the first private prison was still years away, the 1970s and early 1980s furnished the foundation for it by causing overcrowding that guards, prison administrators, politicians, and courts found unacceptable. Guards perceived overcrowding as a threat to their physical and mental health, while administrators viewed it as career threatening and an impediment to accomplishing the goal of providing a secure facility. Politicians saw overcrowding as having the potential to call into question their crime policies, and courts saw the totality of prison conditions as violating the Constitution.

As prison populations began to grow in the early 1970s, prisoners sought relief from the conditions produced by overcrowding. Inmates in Florida (*Costello v. Wainwright* 1975, 1980) and Alabama (*Pugh v. Locke* 1976) challenged the conditions of confinement, noting how overcrowding exacerbated sanitation and security problems, while also further limiting access to classes and what remained of rehabilitative programming. Inmates in Texas also filed a historic suit in 1972 (*Ruiz v. Estelle* 1980) because the state prison system was so overcrowded that some units were operating at 200 percent of capacity with as many as five inmates to a two-person cell and others sleeping on the hallway floors and outside in tents. In 1980, a federal judge finally decided the case: citing brutality by guards, overcrowding, understaffing, and uncontrolled physical abuse among inmates, he ruled that conditions were so dismal that the state prison system in Texas violated the Eighth Amendment's protection against cruel and unusual punishment. The state of Texas was ordered to reduce overcrowding, and the entire Texas system was placed under court supervision (R. Vogel 2004).

Given that the Alabama court found prison conditions there "wholly unfit for human habitation" (*Pugh v. Locke* 1976, 406 F. Supp 318 at 323), it is not difficult to see the connection between severely overcrowded prison conditions and riots. Overcrowding was linked to major prison riots at Attica (1971), Santa Fe (1980), and Southern Michigan Prison at Jackson (1981), the world's largest walled prison at the time. Thus, at the international meeting of the American Federation of State, County, and Municipal Employees (AFSCME) in 1982, the corrections personnel union addressed the overcrowding issue once again. In addition to the mental stress and physical danger guards faced, AFSCME added its concern over antiquated facilities because "forty-three percent of prisoners nationwide are in facilities built before 1925" (Resolution No. 69 1982). In the final analysis, AFSCME called for $6.5 billion in federal aid to build new prisons.

As inmates won lawsuits, administrators came to view the problem as a serious threat to their jobs and the autonomy of the profession. Inmate victories like *Ruiz* and *Pugh* resulted in the appointment of a "special master" to oversee policy changes and implementation (Martin and Ekland-Olson 1987). Prison litigation on this scale results in a consent decree where the two sides agree to standards and procedures for running a prison (or an entire state prison system) along with timetables for remedying conditions.

The special master is someone who typically has experience in prison administration and can potentially oversee the case for a decade or more, looking over the warden's shoulder and reporting on his decisions.

By 1985, prisons in two-thirds of the nation's states were under court order to correct conditions that violated the Constitution's Eighth Amendment prohibition against cruel and unusual punishment. Corrections officials and local politicians who failed to comply with court-established deadlines faced contempt charges. For example, the corrections commissioner of the state of Tennessee was fined and nearly jailed for contempt of court (Humphrey 1985). The state of Texas was also threatened with an $800,000-a-day fine until prison overcrowding was alleviated (T. Vogel 1987). Across the country, corrections officials and politicians alike announced that they would begin the mass release of prisoners because of caps on the prison population to prevent overcrowding. In Michigan, state corrections authorities released seven hundred inmates. In Texas, corrections officials announced the impending release of thousands of convicts unless a new prison was built (LaFranchi 1986). In 1984, a Tennessee court threatened to order the immediate release of three hundred inmates from the state prison system. In 1985, more than eighteen thousand prisoners were released on an emergency basis to alleviate overcrowding (McDonald 1990, 6).

Overcrowding in state prisons also affected county and city jails. State corrections officials began refusing to transfer state prisoners from local and county jails, essentially warehousing state inmates at no cost to state departments of corrections' budgets while draining those of local communities. In New York, jails in counties across the state filed claims against the state totaling more than $2.2 million for expenses related to operating at 50 percent above capacity. A Nassau County executive summed up the situation: "We're under a federal court order to keep the population below 900. If the sheriff had accepted the 901st prisoner he would have been in contempt of Federal Court, if he hadn't accepted number 901 he would have been in contempt of state court. We are in a bind" (*New York Times* 1984, 46).

As crowding grew, due largely to stricter sentencing guidelines and drug laws, politicians searched for a way to maintain "tough-on-crime-and-criminals" stances while at the same time protecting state- and locally run facilities from federal court interventions and appeasing corrections unions. State and local officials found themselves in a conundrum: political livelihoods and reelections were won on get-tough campaign promises, but there was no space to house criminal offenders. The easy answer at the time was to increase funding for prison building and facility renovation. Thus, the first important result of this crusade to manage the overcrowding problem was the development of widespread state-prison-expansion plans. Corrections expenditures quadrupled from approximately $6.8 billion in 1980 to $26.1 billion in 1990, and by 1995 expenditures had reached $40 billion (Bureau of Justice Statistics 2001a). In ten years during the peak of prison construction, approximately six hundred new prisons were built in the United States (Donziger 1996). But state after state built countless new prisons only to find they were quickly filled with prisoners affected by get-tough policies that increased the likelihood of incarceration following a conviction *and* increased the length of the sentence *and* ensured offenders served at least 85 percent of their time.

While prison construction was the only solution to the way the "crime problem" had been constructed, the financial burden of more prisons was proving to be a fiscal nightmare for states (see comments from the Texas Performance Review above). Any discussion of alternatives to incarceration was the political kiss of death, and even talking favorably about more prisons but appearing less tough than an opponent could harm a politician's standing in the polls. At the same time, continuing to expand the criminal justice system became a problem because politicians also liked to promise tax cuts and smaller government. They seemed unaware of the contradiction—at least in public speeches—between building a bigger criminal justice system with many expensive prisons and imposing fiscal restraint to help hold down taxes and government growth. Worse still, the public went along with it.

As economic difficulties arose in the 1980s, citizens repeatedly voted down bond issues that funded state prison expansion while at the same time demanding that more criminals be imprisoned to make their communities safer. For example, three years after the legislature enacted the 650 Lifer Law, Michigan voters turned down a proposed tax increase for prisons. Even as the Rockefeller drug laws expanded the prison population, New Yorkers organized a statewide coalition to combat a proposed $475 million bond issue for expanding and improving state and local prisons (Kihss 1981). In 1982, Texas governor Bill Clements vetoed $30 million in state-appropriated funds for a new prison under pressure from voters (LaFranchi 1986). In addition, President Reagan, following up on President Jimmy Carter's revenue restrictions, made several deep cuts to the federal government's revenue-sharing program, expenditure controls, and federal tax laws. This effectively left many states and localities without any direct federal assistance for the first time (Herbers 1987). When politicians succeeded in delivering on their promise to cut taxes, state and local governments had to scramble to cut budgets or incur deficits. Ironically, this was happening at the same time that demand for local social assistance was increasing because so many people were losing jobs. The higher levels of spending for corrections were met by funneling money from other types of services and raising local taxes.

The extended economic prosperity of the 1990s alleviated this conflict to some extent, even while it provided fertile ground for the formation of

Table 1.2. Criminal Justice Expenditures, Payroll, and Employees, 2006

	Total Expenditures (billions)	Employee Payroll (billions)	Total Employees
Criminal justice system total	$214.5	$10.2	2,427,452
Police	$98.8	$5	1,154,193
Judicial and legal	$46.8	$2.3	507,793
Corrections	$68.7	$2.8	765,466

Source: Bureau of Justice Statistics 2008a, tables 1 and 2. Detail may not add to total because of rounding.

private prisons. So, by 2006 (the latest year for which data are available) the criminal justice system consumed $214.5 billion and employed 2.4 million workers, as broken down by function in table 1.2. A Pew Center study has found that "federal and state governments are projected to need as much as $27 billion—$15 billion in additional operational funds and $12 billion in additional capital funds" for prison construction from 2007 to 2011 to accommodate projected prison expansion and operation (Pew Public Safety Performance 2007, 18). That $27 billion would be in addition to any increases necessary for the police and court systems.

CONCLUSION

An incarceration binge does not inevitably lead to private prisons with stock offerings. Still, some especially important points emerge from this discussion and interact with the growing interest in privatization discussed in chapter 2. First, from a business perspective, the data shown in figure 1.1 and the incarceration binge make corrections look like "growth area," a good place to start a profitable company or to expand the profitability of an existing one. For example, in a prospectus filed with the Securities and Exchange Commission for the sale of five million shares in 1998, the Corrections Corporation of America (CCA) noted,

OUR REVENUE AND PROFIT GROWTH DEPEND ON EXPANSION
Our growth depends on our ability to obtain contracts to manage new correctional and detention facilities and to keep existing management contracts. The rate of construction of new facilities and our potential for growth will depend on several factors, including crime rates and sentencing patterns in the United States and other countries in which we operate. (1998a)

With 2.2 million prisoners, large numbers of whom are nonviolent offenders appropriate for the minimum- and medium-security institutions private prisons favor, private prisons are seen as having plenty of potential to expand. The continual increase in that number of offenders overall means even more business opportunity. Investors would not have risked the sub-stantial amount of capital required to build the first private prisons without this promise of growth and a continuation of the overcrowding that gener-ates demand for immediate prison space.

While private prisons did not advertise themselves as antidemocratic, they took advantage of voters' defeat of prison bond initiatives. Private prison companies proclaimed to politicians that they could build a prison despite public bond defeats and even without a public vote of any kind. Money came not from tax dollars, but from venture capital, credit lines with Wall Street investment banks, and purchases of stock offerings.

Private prisons also benefited from the process of deindustrialization, which left many regions actively lobbying for a prison as an economic stimulus package. Regions that had previously relied on manufacturing or natural resource extraction had high unemployment and a weak tax base, so building a prison held out the allure of construction work followed by seemingly more permanent jobs for guards and other prison workers. In its 1994 annual report, the Corrections Corporation of America (CCA) quotes a resident of Venus, Texas, who had been part of a senior citizen's group that wrote a letter to protest locating the prison there. CCA "explained it from the ground up," she is said. "We felt like it would help Venus because we were just about as broke as you could get financially. It would help us tax-wise, and Venus would grow again like it used to be. So then we got out and worked for the prison and when they voted, it passed 100 percent."

The phenomenon of the rural prison economy is not unique to private prisons; many of these areas simply wanted a prison, public or private, although neither public nor private prisons had nearly as much positive im-pact on the local rural economies as expected or promised (Huling 2002). Politicians from economically depressed areas would lobby state represen-tatives to locate prisons in their counties, increasing pressure on states to build prisons regardless of whether doing so was wasteful in terms of public safety. As localities went into competition and engaged in "bidding wars" for prisons, private prisons cashed in and secured tax breaks, infrastructure subsidies, and other benefits paid for out of taxpayers' pockets (Mattera and Khan 2001). Indeed, one study found that "78% of CCA's and 69% of Wackenhut's prisons were subsidized" (Mattera and Khan 2001, 28), suggesting that they had aggressively turned economic desperation to their corporate advantage, shifting large sums of taxpayer money into private profit. The subsidies for so many prisons added to the incarceration binge, contributing directly to the imbalance in legislative representation, the redirection of aid, and the other harms described earlier. All of those facili-ties also represent a huge opportunity cost as those dollars and resources could have gone into other projects to rebuild local economies in socially beneficial ways rather than contributing to injustice.

But private prisons could not have taken advantage of these dynamics— and might never have been part of the story of incarceration in America—were it not for another important factor: an antigovernment ideology that led to a large-scale outsourcing and privatization of government services. Without this ideological shift, the government may never have made the leap from outsourcing prison food service to outsourcing prison design, construction, and management. Without an intense ideological shift, entrepreneurs could not have sold the idea that turning over inmates to the lowest bidder would increase quality, reduce cost, and maintain the legitimacy of punishment. So, chapter 2 provides an overview of the antigovernment ideology that gave rise to privatization, which in turn, together with the incarceration binge, gave birth to the first modern for-profit prison corporations.

2

The Big Government "Problem" and the Kentucky Fried Prison "Solution"

Americans have always had a love-hate relationship with government. The United States was founded though a revolution against King George III, and the Declaration of Independence justifies the action by citing a "long train of abuses and usurpations" that have led to "absolute Despotism" and "absolute Tyranny over these States." The U.S. Constitution could not have been approved without the addition of the first ten amendments—the Bill of Rights—which enshrine individual rights to protect against government actions like censorship, arbitrary searches, and criminal proceedings without due process, notification of charges, the ability to defend oneself, and a trial by a jury of one's peers. The Ninth and Tenth Amendments explicitly state that the people and the states retain all rights not specifically mentioned, a clear move to prevent the federal government from amassing too much power in the future. While these sentiments flow through much of American history, there are also times, like the Great Depression, when Americans not only appreciate but even count on the federal government to play an important role.

Americans also have a love-hate relationship with business, which is important for the economy and livelihoods but whose corporate charter creates an entity that "has civil rights but no civil responsibilities" and "is legally obligated to be selfish" (Hightower 1998, 34). While many individual employees make good neighbors, corporations sometimes incite outrage because their "legally defined mandate is to pursue, relentlessly and without exception, [their] own self-interest, regardless of the often harmful consequences it might cause to others" (Bakan 2004, 2). Indeed, Joel Bakan asked noted psychopath expert Robert Hare to apply his diagnostic checklist to corporations, and he found a close match: they can

47

irresponsibly put others at risk; manipulate everything, including public opinion; lack empathy for others and the ability to feel remorse; refuse to accept responsibility; and relate to others superficially (2004, 56–57). Just as psychopaths are known for their superficial charm, corporations may "act in ways to promote the public good when it is to their advantage to do so, but they will just as quickly sacrifice it—it is their legal obligation to do so—when necessary to serve their own ends" (Bakan 2004, 118). The result is a long history of outrage over businesses that injure and kill workers out of disregard for occupational safety, poison communities through pollution, and harm consumers through unsafe products or food (Reiman and Leighton 2010; Simon 2005).

Privatization thus requires both a strong antigovernment sentiment and a simultaneous pro-business bias. In the case of private prisons, this combination must be strong enough to overcome concerns about contracting out what many consider to be a core government function. For example, cities and states would not privatize their police forces, though they may also employ a large number of private security personnel, and jurisdictions would not consider privatizing courts or allowing judges to be employed by for-profit companies. Some argued that the legitimacy of state punishment would be at stake if inmates looked out from their cells at guards wearing badges that read, "Acme Correctional Corporation." The debate included both serious and sarcastic questions about the limits of privatizing punishment, like whether a state could privatize executions if a company offered to do them more cheaply.

Despite these concerns about contracting out punishment to the lowest bidder, private prisons made inroads in the 1980s, and in 1986 the Corrections Corporation of America (CCA) would be listed on the stock exchange. So this chapter examines the growth of interest in privatizing prisons, which was part of a large movement to outsource numerous government functions. (Chapter 3 discusses the public offering of stock.) The first section of this chapter contextualizes President Ronald Reagan's statement in his first inaugural address that "government is the problem" and reviews the general justifications for, as well as the concerns about, privatizing prisons. The second section explores the origins and development of prison privatization, focusing on CCA, which has become the largest private prison business in the modern era. CCA's founders believed the era of "big government" was over and that they could sell prison privatization "like you would sell hamburgers"; indeed, they received support from the venture capital that had backed Kentucky Fried Chicken (KFC). They used problems with the prison system in their home state to make a proposal to run the entire state of Tennessee's prison system for the next twenty years, even though their company had been running prisons for less than two years. But the bid attracted attention and caused them to be invited to testify before Congress, which helped them gain legitimacy and catapulted private prisons toward the mainstream (and the stock exchange). A final section of this chapter examines the 1988 President's Commission on Privatization, which further paved the way for privatization.

THE NEW DEAL BECOMES THE "BIG GOVERNMENT" PROBLEM

The excesses of the war on crime would not necessarily have led to the creation of private prisons were it not for a simultaneous push against big government in favor of "free market" forces. The "big government" under attack grew out of an accumulation of concerns starting in the late 1800s with the Sherman Antitrust Act, which set the stage for the trust busting of Presidents Theodore Roosevelt and William Howard Taft. At that time, journalists called muckrakers believed that "big business was 'bad business' insofar as it was more concerned with profit than human life" (Frank and Lynch 1992, 13). Lawyers such as Louis Brandeis, who would later become a U.S. Supreme Court justice, wrote about the "curse of bigness" and the problems with companies' becoming large in the interest of developing a monopoly, which usually violated the public trust rather than worked for the public good. "No country," he wrote, "can afford to have its prosperity originated by a small controlling class" (in Douglas 1954, 187). Supreme Court Justice Douglas explained, "Brandeis did not want America to become a nation of clerks, all working for some overlord" (1954, 187).

The working classes aggressively resisted exploitation through on-the-job actions and wide social movements. To combat challenges to the increasing concentrations of corporate power, the wealthy and ruling classes employed violence, for instance, by hiring the first private security companies, like Pinkerton's, to infiltrate and break up worker organizations (Barak, Leighton, and Flavin 2007). They also used the law as a tool to prevent unionization, the regulation of working conditions, and the establishment of a minimum wage. But with the Great Depression, people turned to government for a "New Deal," one that both provided immediate relief from effects like unemployment and developed regulations to prevent another stock market crash. The New Deal resulted in the creation of more than two dozen "alphabet agencies," from the Agricultural Adjustment Administration (AAA) to the Works Progress Administration (WPA), including today's Federal Aviation Administration (FAA), Federal Deposit Insurance Corporation (FDIC), Federal Housing Administration (FHA), National Labor Relations Board (NLRB), and the Securities and Exchange Commission (SEC). During the 1930s, Congress also finally passed a number of acts that, among other things, established a minimum wage, outlawed child labor, and regulated working conditions. However, the Supreme Court kept striking down laws passed to promote economic recovery and regulate business as violations of the "freedom of contract"; unionization was a criminal conspiracy. Many laws were finally upheld only after retirements on the Court led to changes in its philosophy.

Although America was initially isolationist when World War II broke out, entry into the conflict required mobilization and a transformation of industrial production under strong government leadership. Following the end of the war, government initiatives like the GI Bill provided benefits for former soldiers, enabling them to acquire education and housing; major initiatives, like building the interstate highway system, facilitated mobility and what many believed to be the personal freedom that came with it. Further, chapter 1 discussed some of President Lyndon Johnson's Great Society initiatives, which he premised on the need for government to intervene in social problems. Even though support for these initiatives crumbled, President Richard Nixon (a Republican) expanded government further by creating the Environmental Protection Agency (EPA).

In the late 1970s and early 1980s, however, the United States experienced both high inflation rates and a depression, an economic condition known as stagflation. Unemployment rates rose to their highest since the Great Depression (11 percent), interest rates hovered at 20 percent, energy prices reached record levels, and the American public's confidence in its government hit record lows. According to economists and conservative politicians who rose to power during this time, the culprit was "big government" and its "generous" social welfare programs, excessive spending and bureaucracy, lack of incentives for investors, and weak foreign policy—a combination dubbed the "welfare state."

As early as 1976, politicians and the mass media began to promote the images and language that shifted debate away from the policies of the New Deal to what would eventually become the 1994 Republican Contract with America. The narratives and images associated with each of the purported causes of the economic crises of the late 1970s and early 1980s profoundly shaped the remedies pursued and supported by the American public. An anecdote told repeatedly by then presidential candidate Ronald Reagan perhaps best captures the attack on "generous" social programs and their recipients, specifically welfare. He spoke of an alcohol-swilling, Cadillac-driving, inner-city black woman who had ripped the government off to the tune of $150,000, using eighty aliases, thirty addresses, a dozen social security cards, and four fictional dead husbands. The picture of the "welfare queen" driving her "welfare Cadillac" infuriated the public and became forever associated with the typical undeserving welfare recipient: someone unwilling to work and getting rich off of hard-working American taxpayers. Even after it was proven fictitious, Reagan continued to tell the story (Hill-

Collins 1990). Further, he continued to link public-assistance programs and lenient crime policies to rising crime rates—a clear 1980s example of the association of race, crime, and welfare discussed in chapter 1.

President Reagan stated in his first inaugural address, "Government is not the solution to our problem. Government is the problem" (1981). The American public had ample stories of excessive government spending and bureaucratic snafus as evidence. ABC's television program *20/20* provided compelling examples of what was wrong with government when it exposed the now infamous $435 hammer, $640 toilet seat, and $7,600 coffeemakers paid for by the Department of Defense. Reagan cited figures that put the cost of government waste and inefficiency at $50 billion in 1980, and he made reducing this a cornerstone of his campaign. The extreme cases of overspending circulated widely as they became the material of late-night talk show hosts (Thompson and Hays 2000).

Economists provided another source of the shifting ideology. They created the model later known as Reagonomics, which called for across-the-board tax cuts and widespread cuts in social welfare spending to jumpstart the economy. When George H. W. Bush (the elder) ran against Reagan for the presidency, he had criticized this approach as "voodoo economics," only to have a change of heart after being nominated as Reagan's vice president. The theory held that giving tax cuts to the wealthy would result in their spending and investing more, with benefits that would "trickle down" through the rest of society. Included in this package were large-scale tax cuts for corporations and decreased regulation. Spending cuts affected federally funded lunch programs, social security, and alternative criminal justice practices, like rehabilitation programs, which were seen as part of the lenient criminal justice system. Experts also argued that downsizing the U.S. government was necessary for economic recovery and pointed to the practices of conservative British prime minister Margaret Thatcher, who had overseen the large-scale sale of government-owned industries, like gas, electric, airline, and oil industries. Although Americans rarely look overseas to learn about how to run the United States, one of the lessons was that government should not be in the business of business. This came to mean that government should do nothing business could potentially earn a profit by doing.

The get-tough messages and practices that characterized the domestic front regarding crime were echoed by the plans for ensuring national security during the Cold War with Russia, which President Reagan referred to as the "Evil Empire." Like criminal justice, the military was one area of government spending not targeted for cuts. In fact, Reagan's philosophy was "peace through strength," which required a massive military buildup—just as "getting tough" required a massive expansion in the criminal justice system. The Cold War was not only a response to the Soviet nuclear threat but also a crusade to establish the superiority of the free market. In the final analysis, Reagan's beliefs contained the two elements important for privatization. First, it contained an antigovernment aspect by advocating for a smaller government. Indeed, the tax cuts, combined with increased spending for military and criminal justice, would create deficits of crisis proportions that would fuel a "need" to cut spending. Second, the belief system was pro-business in its embrace of the free market as the solution to America's problems.

While faith in the free market sometimes approaches the level of religious conviction, conservative economists and think tanks added theoretical sophistication to the arguments. Two related theoretical models came to underpin advocacy for privatization: the standard market model and public-choice theory. The standard market model asserts that the market comprises a large number of small buyers and sellers, each pursuing his or her own interests within a framework of "perfect competition." Because many sellers compete for buyers' dollars, they are forced to keep costs low and quality high enough to satisfy buyers. In addition, the model assumes that no significant barriers exist for either buyers or sellers against entering or exiting the market, so no concentration of market power can be established in the form of monopolies or oligopolies. In addition, all parties have complete information on all topics important for a transaction, an assumption known as perfect information. If all these conditions hold, a competitive market emerges, one in which the forces result in a quality and quantity of products that maximize both the satisfaction of consumers and the profit of producers (Schiller 2003).

Public-choice theory builds on the market model by assuming that without the profit motive and competition, public services are captured by "bureaucrats [who] look after their personal interests, not the interests of the public" (Boston 1991, 3). So, the existence of government monopolies in public service ultimately decreases the quality of service because there is a lack of incentive to be efficient, produce quality services, or respond in any way to the demands of consumers (the public). The addition of market dynamics supposedly helps with quality and efficiency in addition to facilitating citizens' expressing preferences from among available choices through the political process. Thus, proponents of privatizing public services argue that the debate centers not on the choice between public and private enterprise but rather on that between (government) monopoly and competition (Savas 2000). To E. S. Savas, government monopolies mean that goods and services become expensive and subject to "rampant waste, thoughtless consumption and possible exhaustion"(2000, 59). In the end, these can be controlled only by breaking the government monopoly and reintroducing the marketplace into the supply of goods and services.

Although such arguments sound reasonable at first glance, they contain some problematic assumptions—a common critique of economics. (How many economists does it take to change a light bulb? Two: one to change the bulb and one to assume the existence of a ladder.) For example, the authors of "The Autistic Economist," an article that ran in the *Yale Economic Review*, use the analogy of neurological disease to critique economics in many ways, including how the discipline "hangs on to its preconceptions, when serious analysis shows that they are untenable" (Alcorn and Solarz 2006). Simplifying assumptions are necessary to deal with complex phenomena, but economists hold on even to those that run counter to reality—including basic propositions about rational actors and perfect information. "Methodological acrobatics" (Alcorn and Solarz 2006) are then required to match reality and theory. (How many economists does it take to change a light bulb? Eight: one to screw in the light bulb and seven to hold everything else constant.)

Just as chapter 1 noted that Robert Martinson's "nothing works" research was used to justify rather than inform, the same can be said about a great deal of economic theory. Indeed, "Nobel Prize winner Joseph Stiglitz and others often complain that academics are largely ignored, that the advice of economists is only accepted when it confirms ideological positions" (Alcorn and Solarz 2006). With private prisons, later chapters will outline a number of factors that contradict assumptions built into these models, like having two private prison firms that tend to dominate and buy out smaller rivals, thus undercutting perfect competition. The business has high barriers to entry because of the large amounts of capital required to build prisons. Further, political favoritism undermines competition, as when private businesses hire former government officials to lobby government for favorable contracts. Maximizing profit not only becomes an exercise in business efficiency but also entails lobbying government for sweetheart deals that ultimately waste taxpayers' money—a process especially likely when competition is limited.

While the development of theory helped, Reagan's creation in June 1982 of the President's Private Sector Survey on Cost Control, also known as the Grace Commission, was an important, concrete step toward promoting the legitimacy of privatization. Comprising 161 executives from the private sector and headed by industrialist Peter Grace, the commission's task involved determining which government services the private sector could provide better and more efficiently and to determine the feasibility of privatizing a host of services. In 1983, the task force released a twenty-three-thousand-page report on government waste and inefficiency and made 2,478 recommendations that they said could save $424 billion over three years (Kennedy and Lee 1984). The report helped legitimize privatization as a solution because of the president's official recognition and the tendency of state governments to follow the lead of the federal government. Indeed, according to Charles Goodsell (1984) these recommendations represent one of the strongest initiatives ever taken by an administration toward reaching the goals of privatization. The task force's recommendations and the activities that followed helped elevate the idea of privatization and became a springboard for many other privatization efforts, including prison privatization. Citizens Against Government Waste, a spin-off of the Grace Commission, publicly promoted the commission's recommendations, taking out a full-page newspaper ad, buying spots on television, and providing toll-free numbers for citizens to call if concerned with government operations and waste. State and local governments established privatization commissions of their own.

The federal Office of Management and Budget formalized many privatization sentiments in 1983 with Circular A-76:

> In the process of governing, the Government should not compete with its citizens. The competitive enterprise system, characterized by individual freedom and initiative, is the primary source of national economic strength. In recognition of this principle, it has been and continues to be the general policy of the Government to rely on commercial sources to supply the products and services the Government needs. (1)

This circular establishes federal policy regarding the performance of commercial activities and sets forth the procedures for determining whether commercial activities should be performed under contract with commercial sources or in-house using government facilities and personnel. It states that "the government shall not start or carry on any activity to provide a commercial product or service if the product or service can be procured more economically from a commercial source" (Office of Management and Budget 1983, 1).

By 1985, the year that the recently founded CCA made its bid to take over the entire Tennessee prison system (see below), privatization had transcended its right-wing foundations and gained the acceptance of many liberal Democrats. New York governor Mario Cuomo stated, "It is not government's obligation to provide services, but to see that they are provided" (Tolchin 1985d, B12). And the former Social Security administrator under Jimmy Carter, Stanford G. Ross, advised, "Ideological concerns regarding private verses public sector approaches are less important than results" (Tolchin 1985d, B12). Lost in all the privatization discussion was an argument for using nonprofits and nongovernmental organizations, instead of more self-interested for-profit entities, to help bring change and innovation to the government.

Based on this history, privatizing prisons may seem like a done deal, but it has been argued that correctional services and punishment are fundamentally different from other goods or services (Sinden 2003, 39). Those interested in public policy, including conservatives like John Dilulio, question the legitimacy of privatized punishment and administration of justice. Stressing the moral implications, DiIulio poses the question, "Who *ought* to administer justice?"(1988, 72). This question gets at what Max Weber has described as a fundamental characteristic of the modern state—its claim to exercise a monopoly over the use of legitimate force. The delegation of the state's primary reason for being to private contractors delegitimizes both the practice and the message of punishment. DiIulio argues that criminal law is the one area where citizens have conceded to the state an almost unqualified right to "employ the force of the community" (1988, 89). Prisons are a public trust to be administered on behalf of the community in the name of civility and justice, not a private enterprise to be administered in the pursuit of profit (McDonald 1990, 176; Ryan and Ward 1989, 70), which is why even supporters of the death penalty might see privatized for-profit executions as inappropriate.

The nondelegation clause in the Constitution raises additional issues concerning the legality of delegating both the power to restrict liberty and the responsibility for doing so (Robbins 1988). It is possible, in Ira Robbins's view, that even though federal courts have allowed delegation of broad powers to private actors, they "may apply more stringent standards to delegations that effect *liberty* interests than they do to those that effect property interests" (1988, 34). The crux of Robbins's point is that private incarceration is fundamentally different because the power to incarcerate is "intrinsically governmental in nature" (1988, 43). On the state level, Robbins points out that the delegation of a state's administrative powers, while not barred by law, may also pose legal problems.

However, these concerns did not stop private prisons from taking root, and the next section looks at this process in more detail. It starts by noting the origins of the company and critically examines the for-profit health-care experience that they claim was a success to emulate. CCA spent its first year simply promoting privatization because it did not have a contract to actually run a prison, but that did not stop the company from bidding to take over the entire prison system of Tennessee. This event garnered CCA a great deal of media attention and, just as important, an opportunity to testify before congressional committees; so we examine both this event and the company's hearing testimony claims. The section concludes by reviewing the activities of another presidential commission on privatization that held hearings in which three of the four witnesses concerning prisons favored privatization. This commission then delegated the writing of the prison section of the main report to a supporter of privatization.

THE KENTUCKY FRIED PRISON SOLUTION

The expansion of the prison population and the fervor of privatization collided in 1983 when Thomas W. Beasley and Doctor R. Crants, two

Nashville businessmen and lawyers, envisioned a private prison business. At a Republican presidential fund-raiser, Crants and Beasley (Tennessee Republican Party chairman) hit upon the idea of privatized prisons during a conversation with an executive of the Magic Stove Company: "He said he thought it would be a heck of a venture for a young man: To solve the prison problem and make a lot of money at the same time" (CCA Source 2003).They created the Corrections Corporation of America, which proposed to design, build, and/or manage prisons for all levels of government. Prison management started as a per diem (daily) fee for inmates, with revenue based on the number of "compensated man days" and the highest profits coming from running the prison at close to maximum occupancy. This business logic is the same as that used by the hotel industry, which has the same concerns about food service and laundry (this is also one reason why Sodexho-Marriott would invest substantially in CCA).

Crants and Beasley later contacted a friend, the commissioner of corrections for the state of Tennessee. Beasley remembers, "I didn't think he would receive the idea very well, but he did. He picked up the phone and connected us to Don Hutto, who was the highest state corrections director in Virginia and had just been elected president of American Correctional Association (ACA). Don said he would be happy to be involved" (CCA Source 2003). (The ACA has been described as "a lobby, professional standards-setter, peer review group, public relations mill, seller of prison-related junk and a place where people pop-off and retire" [in Lilly and Knepper 1993, 157].) CCA lists Hutto as one of the company's founders (CCA 1995), and Hutto would spend the next several years as president of ACA pushing for privatization while also benefiting from it through his involvement with CCA—an obvious conflict of interest discussed more in chapter 3. Although the public record, in the form of a Supreme Court opinion, noted that the Arkansas attorney general had conceded that the Arkansas Department of Corrections in the 1970s under Hutto acted in bad faith for years regarding inmate suits over prison conditions (see box 2.1), Crants and Beasley knew Hutto's position with ACA could legitimate their business. Besides, neither one of them had any experience with prisons.

BOX 2.1   CCA FOUNDER HUTTO—A REFORMER?

Don Hutto had been director of corrections for Arkansas during the 1970s when there was considerable litigation over prison conditions (see chapter 1), a fact critics use to impugn Hutto while CCA defends him as a reformer (Wray 1986). A fair assessment would note Arkansas had significant litigation in 1965 and 1967; the first decision in the class-action prisoner lawsuits came down in 1969 (*Holt v. Sarver*, 300 F.Supp. 825 [*Holt I*])—two years before

Hutto arrived—and subsequent decisions extend through the 1970s. Thus, problems existed before he arrived, but so did major reform efforts.

The federal judge who heard the cases in the 1960s held extensive hearings in 1970 and retained jurisdiction of the case (*Holt v. Sarver*, 309 F.Supp. 362 [*Holt II*]) to have further hearings and file supplemental decrees in 1971–1973. This extensive background with Arkansas prison conditions gives the court an impressive basis for making determinations about Hutto's performance, such as in August 1973 (*Holt v. Hutto*, 363 F.Supp. 194 [*Holt III*]). The court says, "With some reservations as to particular individuals, the Court finds that Messrs Hutto, Lockhart, Britton and Boren are qualified for their jobs, and the Court finds that up to a point at least they are trying to do good jobs and to run an efficient, reasonable humane, and constitutional prison system" (363 F.Supp. 194, at 201). If that seems like faint praise, it is because "the Court is convinced that today it is dealing not so much with an unconstitutional prison system as with a poorly administered one. However, unconstitutionality can arise from poor administration of valid policies as well as from policies that are constitutionally invalid themselves" (363 F.Supp. 194, at 202).

The circuit court noted reports of progress but had enough concerns that it ordered the district court to retain jurisdiction of the case. The next year, the federal district court noted that "Commissioner Hutto issued his policy memoranda prohibiting 'physical abuse of inmates' in December of 1971. Nevertheless, there is evidence as of January 1973 that excessive force, verbal abuse and various forms of torture and inhumane punishment continue" (*Finney v. Arkansas Board of Correction*, 505 F.2d 194, at 206 [1974]). The court concludes, "The effort to make *some* amelioration of those conditions will simply not suffice. The fact that an individual has violated the criminal law, is generally uneducated and in poor health is no justification for inhumane treatment and brutality. Segregation from society and loss of one's liberty are the only punishment the law allows" (505 F.2d 194, at 215, emphasis in the original).

After further hearings in 1975 the district court filed another opinion in 1976 (*Finney v. Hutto*, 410 F.Supp. 251) noting both progress and problems. One issue was that "the court is not satisfied that Commissioner Hutto and others connected with recruiting prison personnel have really exerted themselves to the fullest extent possible or have exhausted their resources as far as hiring responsible blacks is concerned" (410 F.Supp. 251, at 268). Also, the court had some concerns about administrative segregation that required "substantial changes" to be made "within the immediate future" (410 F.Supp. 251, at 275). But most important is the court's decision to award attorney's fees from 1973 to the present case—a time when Hutto was clearly responsible for the Department of Correction: "The court thinks that in a legal sense respondents and their predecessors in office and employment have acted in bad faith and oppressively" (410 F.Supp. 251, at 284). The court notes a "hardening of Departmental attitudes and an unwillingness on the part of the prison administrators to go much if any farther than they have gone, and as has been seen, the progress that has been made to date is still insufficient" (410 F.Supp. 251, at 284–85). Finally,

> At practically every stage of the litigation evidence has brought to light practices of
> which those in higher prison authority were ignorant, and which they eliminated
> when the facts were disclosed. It seems to the court that the prison authorities
> should have discovered at least some of those conditions and practices for them-
> selves and corrected them without waiting for them to be developed in the course
> of evidentiary hearings in this lawsuit (410 F.Supp. 251, at 285).
>
> The court of appeals upheld the award of attorney's fees because "the record
> fully supports the finding of the district court that the conduct of the state
> officials justified the award under the bad faith exception" (*Hutto v. Finney*,
> 548 F.2d 740, 742n6). The Supreme Court agreed and noted that "although
> the [Arkansas] Attorney General argues that the finding of bad faith does not
> overcome the State's Eleventh Amendment protection, he does not question
> the accuracy of the finding made by the District Court and approved by the
> Court of Appeals" (*Hutto v. Finney*, 437 U.S. 678, 689).

Alluding to the changes described in this chapter, Beasley commented, "We knew the era of big government was over. We could sell privatization as a solution, you sell it just like you were selling cars, or real estate, or hamburgers" (CCA Source 2003). This reasoning must have made sense because the new business received the support of venture capitalist Jack Massey, who helped build Kentucky Fried Chicken, the Hospital Corporation of America (HCA), another company that was a leading franchisee of Wendy's hamburgers, and Mrs. Winner's Chicken & Biscuits. Massey is legendary in investment circles for being the only person ever to take three companies to be traded on the New York Stock Exchange—KFC, HCA, and Mrs. Winner's (now called Volunteer Capital Corporation). (Although he backed CCA financially, he was a consultant rather than a principal, so his involvement in CCA rarely appears in his biographies.) Beasley modeled the private prison business on HCA: "CCA will be to jails and prisons that are owned and managed by local, state and federal governments what Hospital Corporation of America has become to medical facilities nationwide" (Mattera, Khan, and Nathan 2004, 11). It's not clear exactly what elements of HCA Beasley meant, but the controversial leader in for-profit health care provides a colorful introduction to the equally controversial history of CCA.

The Hospital Corporation of America was founded in the late 1960s by the medical and political Frist family of Tennessee, whose members include former Senate majority leader Bill Frist. During the 1980s, HCA grew rapidly by aggressively acquiring a series of nonprofit hospitals—a trend that accelerated after its 1994 merger with Columbia, when it became "the PACMAN of the marketplace" (Martin 2000). CEO Richard Scott led a public relations campaign against public hospitals and believed that "nontaxpaying hospitals shouldn't be in business" (Kuttner 1996b, 448).

Robert Kuttner describes the campaign as "portray[ing] nonprofits as social parasites" (1996b, 448), even though "historically they have embraced a social ethic, serving uninsured patients, taking Medicaid losses, not insisting that every admission or procedure be profitable, and spending money on research, teaching, and public health as part of a broader mission of service to the community" (1996a, 363). But public health has no value to a for-profit hospital company, and Columbia/HCA's chief operating officer even commented, "We are not in the health care business. We are in the sick care business" (Kuttner 1996a, 363).

While HCA achieved some efficiencies, like economies of scale and purchasing power, other strategies involved cutting back on staffing levels, especially nurses (Berens 2000; PBS *NewsHour* 1997), and "they were accused of cherry picking profitable admissions, cream skimming and patient dumping" (Martin 2000; see also Mokhiber and Weissman 1997). HCA's aggressive billing of the government's Medicare and Medicaid programs ultimately triggered a ten-year investigation of Columbia/HCA that found evidence of billing fraud dating back to 1984 (U.S. Department of Justice 1998). The results were announced in the headline of the Department of Justice's press release: "Largest Health Care Fraud Case in U.S. History Settled: HCA Investigation Nets Record Total of $1.7 Billion" (2003). Critics contended that HCA built its profits on fraud and "MacMedicine" (Martin 2000; Mokhiber and Weissman 1997). More systematic evaluations of for-profit chains "generally found that the for-profits had slightly higher average costs and charges than nonprofits, that they provided below average rates of uncompensated and charity care, and that their clinical outcomes [quality of care] were not significantly different from those of comparable nonprofits" (Kuttner 1996a, 365; see also PBS *NewsHour* 1997).

This history is important because CCA legitimated private prisons partly based on the "success" of for-profit health care. CCA also became the largest private prison company through ongoing acquisitions, though not so much of government prisons and more of other for-profit companies in the same field. The company did deride the cost and quality of government services, at least until it experienced significant problems itself with abuse, riots, and a near bankruptcy—at which point its rhetoric turned to public-private partnerships (see chapter 4). Along the way, there were accusations of understaffing and of cherry-picking inmates whose backgrounds and health would most likely be profitable given the per diem rate. Further, Florida would accuse CCA of $12 million in overbilling, and chapter 4 explores whether CCA (and other private prisons) has engaged in the equivalent of what Columbia did, that is, if they got business by appearing to price low but expected to find additional ways to increase revenues.

Of course, as CCA got its start, the problems with HCA and its privatization model had yet to unfold. And while CCA would have a number of challenges, one of the first is most significant: to seed the idea of widespread prison privatization *and* convince leaders to contract out to a company that had just started up and had little operating history. The three enterprising men who founded CCA had social and economic status that afforded them access to decision makers, but two of them had no background in corrections. They correctly recognized that their solution, privatization, fit with the attack on the government's handling of public service, the fervent belief in the power of free markets, and the dominant discourse suggesting that more incarceration was the only answer to the crime problem. By appealing to societal concern over big-government waste and framing the prison problem as a further example of it, they were poised to take advantage of conditions ripe for private entry into the operation of prisons, which would concurrently allow the get-tough policies to remain intact.

A close examination of the industry's early claims reveals a script that over the coming years would be repeated and manipulated to fit political, economic, and societal concerns about imprisonment. To be certain, the early script's main theme was economics: cost savings and efficiency. However, the industry also aligned itself with the positive aspects of privatization—volunteerism and professionalism—and separated itself from the negative aspects—prison labor and convict leasing. Private corrections thus became redefined in a way that aligned with many of the dominant cultural values, such as entrepreneurialism, innovation, and the get-tough mentality. Offering to purchase and run the Tennessee prison system gave CCA the national spotlight and the forums through which its founders could build legitimacy for their idea and fledgling company.

BUYING THE TENNESSEE PRISON
SYSTEM AND GAINING ATTENTION

Private industry had made some minor inroads into the prison business during the late 1970s and early 1980s via various low-security facilities and less visible regions of the penal systems by providing services at the federal level. For example, 70 percent of all federal contracts to place inmates sentenced to community treatment centers were with private providers (Logan 1990, 16). Federal officials in what was then the Immigration and Naturalization Service (INS) utilized private contractors to build new detention facilities chiefly because they could accomplish the task much more quickly than the federal government (McDonald 1990). In 1979, the INS began contracting with private firms to detain illegal immigrants pending hearing or deportation, and in 1980 it awarded the first facility-management contract via competitive bidding to Behavioral Systems Southwest.

States would sometimes contract out drug treatment, certain rehabilitation services, or programs for juvenile offenders. According to the 1982–1983 census, of 808 juvenile institutional facilities nationwide, 123 (23 percent) were private (Logan 1990, 17).

While these developments went relatively unnoticed and provoked little controversy, this emerging market, especially at the federal level, was critical to the private prison companies of today. It provided a foundation upon which later claims could piggyback and was the principle financial seedbed for the wave of private companies that would become involved in the imprisonment of adult inmates in the 1980s and beyond (McDonald 1990). For example, Ted Nissen, president of Behavioral Systems Southwest, commented in 1984 that "the work done in the public sector in the last 30 years has been a dismal failure" (Tolchin 1985d, B12). Nissen had been a guard at San Quentin prison, where he became convinced that "no convict would be ready for the outside world after doing time [there]" (Anrig and Crouch 1986, 57). After he worked as a parole supervisor, California let him set up a program for heroin addicts with money from a federal grant. The program was a success, but funding was cut in 1976 after five years because of federal budget cuts, so the project became a nonprofit organization. His partner later incorporated it as a for-profit company while Nissen was on vacation; she said, "Ted was irate because he didn't want to make money off inmates and addicts" (Anrig and Crouch 1986, 57), but he finally came around.

At this point, private operation of prisons appeared destined to remain at the federal level and in the and less visible parts of the correctional system. Then a crucial event occurred: CCA placed a bid to take over the entire prison system for the state of Tennessee. In 1985, Tennessee governor Lamar Alexander was forced to call the legislature back into a special session to deal with a federal court order that placed a cap on the state's prison population. Tennessee, like other states across the country in the late 1970s, began its own crusade to lower crime rates through the get-tough sentencing policies such as mandatory minimum sentencing. Predictably, this created all the associated problems described in chapter 1: riots, overcrowding, and federal court intervention. When conditions in the state's oldest prison were declared in violation of the Eight Amendment, Tennessee found itself immediately in need of at least seven thousand additional prison beds and called for an additional $380 million to build six new prisons (Select Oversight Committee on Corrections 1995). CCA offered to buy the Tennessee prison system for $50 million down, $50 million over the next twenty years, and promised to invest $150 million in improvements and new buildings. For operating the prisons, CCA was to be paid from the state treasury a sum not to exceed the $175 million annual operating budget of the state's corrections system, and the company would be granted a ninety-nine year lease (Cody and Bennett 1987). Tom Beasley, CCA's CEO, said,

> Our proposal is simple—we will pay the State for the right to manage the system under the state's supervision; we will spend private capital to improve the system and draw our profit out of more efficient use of the State's regular operating budget. That's a $250 million—one quarter of a billion—dollar turn around in the state budget—without a tax increase! We believe this is absolutely a win/win situation and an unprecedented opportunity to make Tennessee a leader in this most difficult area. (Hallett 2004, 8)

Whether it was strategically planned or just luck, the timing of the offer could not have been better. The offer was made September 12, 1985, at the same time that the National Association of Criminal Justice Planners, representing prosecutors, judges, corrections officers, sheriffs, and criminal justice planners in seventy-five large urban areas, was holding its annual conference. The offer quickly became the chief topic of conversation at the conference after Governor Alexander's press secretary stated, "Governor Alexander plans to recommend that the Legislature consider privatization" (Tolchin 1985a, A12). The *New York Times* headline, "Company Offers to Run Tennessee's Prisons," further pushed the idea of private prison operation into the national spotlight. CCA cofounder Don Hutto later commented, "One of the things that happened as a result of the bid was that it forced everyone to take us seriously. The offer ran on a full front page of the afternoon paper. We were a national story" (CCA Source 2003).

Two months later, the National Association of Counties held the Fourth National Assembly on the Jail Crisis. Promoters of prison and jail privatization addressed the audience of more than eight hundred county commissioners who are responsible under the law for the operation of jails (which hold people awaiting trial and those sentenced to less than one year). Among the chief promoters was Commissioner John B. Hutt of Bay County, Florida. "The sheriff's proposed budget for operating the jail was $3.2 million, but after soliciting bids we signed with Corrections Corporation of America for $2.5 million. That's a $700,000 savings. The prisoners are happy; we have not had a riot or a single stuffed commode" (Clendinen 1985). Hutt also noted that the county was facing two lawsuits involving a death and a coma, but now he stressed, "We are buffered by the corporation in case of future injuries" (Clendinen 1985). The push and sell of privatization to local-level correctional decision makers at this meeting was taking place exactly at the same time that in Washington, D.C., privatization promoters were selling the idea at the federal level, which, as noted earlier, played an important role because other government entities generally followed the federal government's lead (Hallett and Lee 2001).

The Committee on the Judiciary's Subcommittee on Courts, Civil Liberties, and the Administration of Justice was scheduled to meet on November 13, 1985, with the expressed goals of (1) reviewing recent developments in corrections (privatization), (2) examining their advantages and disadvantages, (3) exploring what action the federal government should take, and (4) raising further questions, if appropriate (Serial 40 1986, 1). According to Blane Merritt, then counsel for the House Committee on the Judiciary, one comes to testify at a subcommittee hearing in one of two ways: by receiving an invitation or submitting a request. Either way, Merritt added, "Committee members come to know who the players are through various media sources, business, industry and professional journals, word of mouth, etc., and base their selections on that. The idea is to cull as much information so that appropriate policy recommendations can be made" (personal communication 2004). Given the media coverage in the *New York Times* and *Washington Post*, advertisements, and articles in industry and professional journals regarding CCA and its "ambitious, audacious, shocking, incredible" (Tolchin 1985a, A12) bid, it was not surprising that CCA vice president Richard Crane was one of the three invited "distinguished witnesses" to testify before the subcommittee. This opportunity to testify as a member of the "expert" panel nationalized and elevated the legitimacy of not only CCA but operational privatization in general. On this stage, operational prison privatization became a permanent part of the national corrections agenda.

The primary technique used to sell the privatization of prisons was the claim of cost savings. For the INS, CCA offered to house illegal aliens at a cost of $23.84 per inmate per day, a savings of more than $10 per inmate per day at the time. In addition, CCA offered to provide the $5 million in capital expenditures for the land and construction, saving the government from having to borrow the money (Serial 40 1986, 29). Before the House of Representatives Committee on the Judiciary, Crane stated, "We can do it less expensively, our construction costs are about 80 percent of what the government pays for construction" (Serial 40 1986, 29). Intricately woven into the claims of cost effectiveness were criticisms of the public prison system, tapping into a major goal of the political administration: identifying and eliminating government waste and inefficiency. Crane continued, "Contractors, it appears, will generally bid higher on government work because of the red-tape and the delays and so forth, and our experience thus far is to say we can do it for 80 percent" (Serial 40 1986, 29).

The claims of cost savings need to be evaluated critically, which we will do later in this book. For now, S. J. Brakel (1988) provides important context for evaluating both claims and performance during this initial period:

> CCA is the leading best-endowed company in the field. It is operating in a context of heightened public scrutiny, at a time when it hopes to convince the

public—corrections bureaucrats, other law and policy makers and executors, academics, etc.—of its capacity to do the job and at the same time to capture a sizeable share of the market. This creates the specter of halo-effect performance, and out-of-the-ordinary effort on the part of the entrepreneur to put his best foot forward (Brakel 1988, 244).

It is not uncommon for businesses, in any industry, to bid low or even operate at a loss to establish market share and thereby ensure their longer-run viability. Indeed, the August 1986 prospectus for the initial public offering (IPO) of shares notes that "from inception in 1983 through June 30, 1986, the company had an accumulated deficit of $5,850,450" (CCA 1986). For the full year of 1985 and the six months ending June 30, 1986, total revenues were less than facility and administrative expenses. CCA had additional expenses for interest on its debt and the development of new contracts (see chapter 5 for further discussion of overhead costs).

Crane continued his criticism of the public system and claimed superior service provision for CCA in other areas as well: "Across the country the turnover rate of correctional officers is 30 percent; ours is about 15 percent. The cost of training is very, very high. We are able to, by retaining employees, avoid those additional training costs" (Serial 40 1986, 29). Whether or not this statement was true at the time is difficult to ascertain, but later private prisons did have high turnover rates that in one case led directly to a prison riot (Carceral 2005). Generally, the compensation package at a private prison is less than those offered by states, resulting in higher turnover.

In addition, privatization promoters' claim of service superiority addressed the problems arising from the mounting court orders surrounding constitutional violations. Crane promised CCA would "meet the American Correctional Associations standards in our facility. The Supreme Court has said on at least two occasions that those standards by the ACA go beyond those that would be required by the Constitution" (Serial 40 1986, 29). Alluding to the apparent inferiority of public prisons, he commented that "these standards go beyond the Federal Standards, INS standards. We are not just going to be on the cutting edge of constitutional rights of inmates, we are going much further" (Serial 40 1986). By this time Don Hutto had been both president of ACA and a senior vice president of CCA for several years. Hutto no doubt highlighted the importance of accreditation for legitimacy and at a minimum helped CCA negotiate the ACA accreditation process. However, in spite of embracing accreditation, CCA would have its share of problems with unconstitutional prison conditions and inmate rights violations (Mattera, Khan, and Nathan 2004).

Having obtained the authority not only to build and own but also to operate a federal detention facility, CCA and the promoters of privatization increased the legitimacy of privately owned and operated prisons by constructing privatization as both "nothing new" and as "something new." On the one hand, they argued that "the concept of contracting with private companies to provide government services is not new. For the first 100 years or so of this country's existence, most public services were provided or performed by private companies, fire protection and transportation for example" (Serial 40 1986, 32). The promoters demonstrated this ongoing practice by pointing to the fact that governments in more recent times are

> now turning to private professional engineering firms to manage water and waste treatment services, airports and public transit systems. . . . There has been a history of involvement of the private sector in owning and managing halfway houses, pre-release residential programs and the like. . . . Private providers of healthcare, food service, education, rehabilitation programs and transportation have been welcomed into public jails and prisons. (Serial 40 1986, 32)

Continuing the theme of history and adding the appeal of professionalism, Crane stated, "We have over 160 years of management experience in the operation of every type of facility" (Serial 40 1986, 48). It was later pointed out that CCA had not been in the business for 160 years; rather Crane was referring to the number of years the company's various employees spent working in the public system added together. Indeed, CCA was incorporated on January 28, 1983, but its first facility management contract did not become operational until a year later, according to the prospectus for their IPO. Given this lack of operating history, the company describes itself as "the primary developer of the *concept* of privatization of prisons" (CCA 1986, emphasis added). Cofounder Beasley's background was in insurance, and cofounder Crants was president of Tennessee Media South, Inc., doing consulting for the broadcast industry before joining Beasley in Tri Insurance (CCA 1986).

Opposition to the private operation of prisons further thrust the idea into the national spotlight. In rural Pennsylvania, a small, privately operated facility arranged with the District of Columbia to transfer fifty-five inmates from the District's jails to relieve overcrowding. Local residents, fearing escapes, organized themselves and patrolled the streets with shotguns. Public officials, at the behest of the American Federation of State, County, and Municipal Employees (AFSCME), challenged the action, arguing that the private facility was not state certified, which prompted a judge to order the inmates returned to Washington, D.C. (Bivens 1986). Within a month of this event the subcommittee met again. This time, however, the push and sell of operational prison privatization was conducted not by an official representative of the industry but by Norman Carlson, the director of the Federal Bureau of Prisons (BOP), who would later became a member of the board of directors of Wackenhut Corrections Corporation (now GEO Group, the second-largest private prison company in the country).

Robert Kastenmeier, the subcommittee chairman, called the event in rural Pennsylvania "a real legal quagmire" and asked if the same problems could potentially arise at the federal level. Carlson responded, "The district situation is not our responsibility. . . . We use private control for halfway houses exclusively and our experience has been generally positive" (Serial 40 133). Carlson added further, "In the face of the extreme overcrowding we are confronting today I personally would like to have the flexibility to use privatization or private sector operations for lower security inmates" (Serial 40 133). Carlson's testimony and the later memos sent to the subcommittee included references to "success" with contracting and the commitment to expanding the use of private contracts where they best meet the government's needs.

The hearing never directly engaged the questions presented earlier about whether privatization delegitimizes punishment or whether prisons are a public trust to be administered on behalf of the community in the name of justice rather than a private enterprise to be administered in the pursuit of profit. The closest they came was to address the narrower question of whether the Federal BOP had statutory to contract with private vendors for prison operation. Carlson tried to put this question to rest by submitting the statement of the general counsel: "We conclude that there is authority to contract with private facilities based both on the legislative history to [18 USC] Section 4082 and on the need to read Section 4002 so as to make meaningful the language of Section 4082 which allows designation to non-federal facilities, including private facilities" (Serial 40 1986, 150–62).

Although Carlson and the BOP claimed authority, the American Bar Association proposed a moratorium on privatization "until the complex constitutional, statutory and contractual issues are developed and resolved" (Serial 40 1986, 113). This position is similar to that of the American Civil Liberties Union, which argued that "privatization must be examined more closely before permitting public monies to be committed, contracts awarded and prisoners confined" (Serial 40 1986,14). The subcommittee concluded that there was "no need to write additional statutory language in terms of authorization or anything else given the sort of minimum interest the Federal Bureau of Prisons has at the moment" (Serial 40 1986, 158). This left the door open to operational privatization in the future.

In the aftermath of these events, prison privatization emerged as one of the most discussed issues in correctional circles. Most organized bodies in the criminal justice field took a stand on the issue. In 1986, the ACA took a more guarded stance than its president, Hutto. AFSCME opposed privatization of federal prisons on philosophical, ethical, legal, practical, and economic grounds and urged the subcommittee to do the same (Serial 40 1986, 16). The National Sheriffs Association reiterated its 1984 resolution placing the organization on record as "being opposed to the private operation of adult local detention facilities" (Serial 40 1986, 58). Even though the National Sheriff's Association took an official position against operational privatization, individually many sheriffs found the private option economically and politically attractive because it allowed them to remain tough on crime while appearing fiscally conservative. Sheriff Tom Mylander of Hernando County, Florida, suggested turning the keys to the new county jail over to CCA, saying, "I do not want to run the jail any longer. I'd prefer to devote our energies to law enforcement" (Sutton 1987, 3). Mylander also mentioned that the expense of opening the new jail would adversely affect his law enforcement budget (Sutton 1987).

Tennessee eventually turned down CCA's offer but passed the Private Prison Act of 1986, which ensured that at least two state facilities would be privately owned and operated in the future. Of far greater importance, though, was the exposure that came from making the offer to take over the entire prison system in terms of appearing before the committee, giving media interviews, and making privatization a topic of conversation among government officials. Still, the congressional hearing brought forth many sides of the debate and also gave attention to the detractors of private prisons. Proponents of privatization in general, and of prison privatization in particular, needed an explicit endorsement. The opportunity to achieve one arose during the closing years of the Reagan administration with the establishment of the President's Commission on Privatization.

ANOTHER PRESIDENTIAL COMMISSION ON PRIVATIZATION

In 1987 Reagan established the President's Commission on Privatization, which released its report in 1988, Reagan's final year in office. The commission's goal was "to review the appropriate division of responsibilities between the federal government and the private sector, and to identify those government programs that are not properly the responsibility of the federal government or that can be performed more efficiently by the private sector" (Executive Order No. 12607). Included in the commission's review of government activities were low-income housing, housing finance, air traffic control, educational choice, postal service, federal asset sales (Amtrak, Naval Petroleum Reserves), Medicare, urban mass transit, and the contracting out of both military commissaries and prisons. For private prisons, the success lay in the commission's recommendations, which helped the industry overcome many of the challenges to its legitimacy.

The first of these challenges entailed the legality of contracting out an "inherently governmental function." In its 1986 prospectus for the initial public stock offering, CCA noted that "it is unclear whether governmental agencies have the authority to delegate their custodial functions to private organizations." The commission, citing 18 USC Section 4082, recognized the federal government's authority to enter contracts for the operation of federal prisons. Citing the earlier testimony of the general counsel for the Federal BOP during the subcommittee hearings (discussed above), the commission concluded that the legislative history of Public Law 89-176 was "clearly meant to extend to adult inmates the kind of authority the Attorney General already has in contracting with private agencies" (Linowes 1988, 149). This historical precedent, combined with the observation that "no state has enacted legislation specifically prohibiting privately operated correctional facilities, most state statutes are silent on the subject and a few states have passed specific legislation authorizing contractual prison operations" (Linowes 1988, 149), led the commission to firmly dismiss challenges to further privatization of prisons at all levels.

While not specifically cited, a broad interpretation of the Office of Management and Budget's Circular A-76, which refers to inherently governmental functions, was used to counter the claims that incarceration was an "inherently governmental function" and could not be turned over to private industry. The commission stated that by contracting for operation and management of prisons and jails at any level of government, the "government does not relinquish its authority or abdicate its ultimate responsibility" (Linowes 1988, 149). Because prisons remain subject to the supervision and regulation of the government and are subject to the rule of law, privatization promoters argued, operational privatization of prisons is a service in support of an inherently governmental function rather than performance of the function itself. Thus, the commission recommended that "contracting should be regarded as an effective and appropriate form for the administration of prisons and jails at the federal, state and local levels," and "proposals to contract for the administration of entire facilities at the federal, state or local level ought to be seriously considered" (Linowes 1988, 149–50).

The second challenge to privatization involved the issues of accountability and liability, specifically the fact that contractors are insulated from the public and not subject to the same political controls as government officials. However, citing the testimony of CCA's Tom Beasley, the commission concluded that this was not necessarily the case: "Some operators are contractually bound to the standards of the American Correctional Association, the field's primary professional association" (Linowes 1988, 159). The commission continued the themes Richard Crane stressed in the earlier subcommittee hearings, noting the professionalism of the industry while criticizing the publicly run facilities: "Several facilities have been accredited by the Commission on Accreditation for Corrections, a private organization that applies ACA standards in a voluntary program of accreditation. Most government correctional facilities are not accredited" (Linowes 1988, 150).

To address privatization detractors' claim that contracting may cost the government more by increasing its liability exposure, the commission drew upon the claims-making technique of typifying stories. By stating that "liability issues have not proved to be an insurmountable obstacle in jurisdictions where contractual operations have been established," the commission implied that liability in general was a nonissue (Linowes 1988, 151). Once again the commission drew upon the strategy established earlier to counter the liability claims of critics of private prisons: it criticized the public system by citing current and past litigation. The commission pointed out that the public system had encountered liability litigation in the past and went on to suggest that privatization could reduce the amount of litigation and liability by the development of "model prison contract provisions." Thus, Commission Recommendation 12 stated, "Problems of liability and accountability should not be seen as posing obstacles to contracting for the operation of confinement facilities. Constitutional and legal requirements apply, and contracted facilities may also be required to meet American Correctional Association standards" (Linowes 1988, 161).

The third challenge to privatization involved data about both cost and quality. At the time of the commission's hearings and final report, no research compared the quality of operational private prisons to government-managed facilities, but various groups (including AFSCME) charged that quality suffered as a result of privatization. The commission relied upon data provided from a 1984 National Institute of Corrections (NIC) study, which preceded the move to operational privatization in the core adult prison population. This study's primary concern and findings, however, related to private-sector involvement in prison services rather than operation. Nonetheless, the commission used a creative interpretation of the findings to counter the claim of low quality, pointing out that "responding administrators cited more benefits than liabilities" (Linowes 1988, 150). Further, the commission effectively countered cost-control concerns with quality issues. Citing the same study, the commission reported that while "three-quarters of the agencies reported some savings, even agencies not reporting savings concluded that the operational benefits more than outweighed the cost factor" (Linowes 1988, 151).

The committee noted that "most available figures on the costs of government prison operations are incomplete" (Linowes 1988, 152), which in the political context of the time implied that the government was not doing a good job of tracking its expenditures, and there was a strong likelihood of fraud, waste, and abuse. Further appealing to the administration's general theme of ferreting out and doing away with fraud, waste, and abuse, the commission recognized that "a contractor's fee tends to capture more of the costs of running a prison and to clarify which costs remain with the government" (Linowes 1988, 151). (As chapter 4 notes, successive contracts tend to push more costs back on the government.) Therefore, Commission Recommendation 13 stated,

> The Bureau of Prisons should be asked to prepare an analysis of total government costs for an existing federal correctional institution. The General Accounting Office [GAO], the Office of Management and Budget, and the National Institute of Justice [NIJ] should be asked to cooperate with the Immigration and Naturalization Service (INS) in preparing cost studies that compare currently contracted detention facilities with those run directly by the INS. (Linowes 1988, 152)

Recommendations 14 to 16 all urged increased use of private operation. Using the history of privately operated facilities housing the less visible prison populations as support, the commission recommended expanding privatization of a federal correctional institution or penitentiary: "The Bureau, as an experiment, should contract for the private operation of one new facility comparable to at least one government run facility, and cooperate with outside researchers in an evaluation of the results" (Linowes 1988, 153).

The language supporting these recommendations perhaps best demonstrates the techniques used to dismiss the claims of privatization opponents. Although the commission earlier recognized no complete cost comparisons existed, the commission nevertheless reasoned "that private companies are more likely to design for efficient operation, build faster, at better prices and can usually pay off debt faster than governments can" (Linowes 1988, 154). Therefore, the commission urged pursuit of lease-purchase agreements (Linowes 1988, 154). Recommendation 17 tied the prior recommendations together: because state and local governments needed more information to help them identify what administrative reforms and conditions were best for the administration of prisons, continued research was needed, and because research was needed, experimentation was needed.

The commission's recommendations are problematic in several ways. First, it reasoned that because contracting was already being done and no law prohibited it, it must be legal, which completely disregarded the consideration that the law had simply not caught up with changes in society, as is so often the case. This argument also failed to persuade the GAO, which in 1991 released a report, *Private Prisons: Cost Savings and BOP's Statutory Authority Need to Be Resolved*, indicating that body's ongoing concerns with this conclusion. Second, the new definition of "inherently governmental function" put forth by the commission neglected the importance of turning the restriction of liberty into a service. With private companies building prisons and running them, the distinction between performing the essential government function and being a service in support of an essential government function is not clear.

Further, the recommendations encouraged states to continue the practice as policy, while at the same time they pointed out that state contracts are not under the purview of the federal government. Indeed, the report carried a contradiction by recommending that the federal government continue the practice based on the developments in state and local facilities while simultaneously noting that federal facilities are different from those state and local facilities. On the one hand, the commission encouraged states and localities to continue their practice for jails and prisons, while on the other hand it addressed the objections of privatization as state and local issues and not relevant to the considerations of the commission (Linowes 1988, 154).

Given that operational privatization was already moving forward at the local and state levels, some see the formal impact of the commission as relatively small. As Charles Logan has put it, "The President's Commission did not have much impact; it received little media attention and most of the research on privatization that NIJ supported was initiated by James Stewart, the director of NIJ who already believed in privatization before the commission was formed or issued its report" (personal communication 2004). However, and perhaps more important, the commission's activities and final report played a significant symbolic role in operational privatization. The mere fact that the federal government was discussing the issue and recommending privatization, local and state correctional decision makers now had support for their decisions in that direction. Further, the commission legitimated the promoters of operational privatization as the authority on the subject.

Charles Logan, a known supporter of operational privatization, was invited to write the section of the commission's report dealing with prisons: "They asked me to write a draft, then they reworded it some and added their recommendations after some discussion. I was nominated for that purpose, I think, by James Stewart, Director of NIJ at the time" (personal communication 2004). In addition, of the four people who testified at the hearings on prisons, three were supporters of operational privatization. Norman Carlson's replacement at the BOP, Michael Quinlan, expanded his predecessor's view that privatization was a needed and successful option for the Federal BOP. (Quinlan also argued with the GAO that the BOP did have authority to privatize, then he would leave the government to become an executive of CCA.) James Stewart, director of NIJ, not only testified himself about the positives of privatization but also nominated Logan as the writer of the commission's justifications for their recommendations. Tom Beasley of CCA testified to the successes of operational privatization.

The lone voice in opposition to operational privatization was Ira Robbins representing the American Bar Association. Robbins's testimony focused on potential legal issues surrounding operational privatization. As noted above, the commission dismissed these claims as "not insurmountable" and acknowledged that the American Bar Association was "currently working to develop model contract provisions to guide resolution of issues related to future prison contracts" (Linowes 1988, 151). Noticeably absent from these hearings were representatives from AFSCME, the leading opponents to operational privatization. The commission's recommendations for operational privatization can thus be viewed as predetermined. The selection of commission members and experts and of the ideas that would be brought to the forefront were heavily skewed in favor of operational privatization. In the end, the Reagan administration's fiscal 1989 budget proposed two pilot projects. One would focus on federal prison industries and the other on private operation of federal minimum-security prisons.

Although the commission recommended experimenting with private prisons in order to gather systematic data, the outcome was contracts for private prisons without data collection. A 2007 study by the GAO noted that it is "not currently feasible to conduct a methodologically sound cost comparison of BOP and private low and minimum security facilities because these facilities differ in several characteristics and BOP does not collect comparable data to determine the impact of these differences on cost" (2007, 4). The GAO report also noted that BOP does not collect the data because "federal regulations do not require BOP to do so when selecting among competing contractors," even though these data are key to evaluating quality of service and include "data on the number of inmates attended to by health care professionals due to misconduct, staff turnover rates, and the experience level of the staff" (2007, 5).

CONCLUSION

The United States is unique among countries in the world in that its founding documents so clearly emphasize the centrality of liberty. Much of the development of the prison thus happened in America because the deprivation of liberty seemed like such a fitting punishment for a "free" country. The privatization of such a function developed out of an incarceration binge—where the "land of the free" has the highest incarceration rate in the world—and a period whose ideology was both antigovernment and pro–free market. Indeed, these forces were strong enough that a company with political connections but little history operating as a business could testify before Congress and have a stock offering. And, just as for-profit hospitals are about "sick care" rather than public health, the debate over private prisons included no discussion of alternatives to incarceration; nor did the congressional hearings or the commission's final report include the word "rehabilitation."

CCA's bid to take over the Tennessee prison system was a crucial event in the emergence of operational prison privatization and the subsequent assumption of power, even though the company ultimately lost the bid for the entire state system. As then senator of Tennessee Robert Rochelle (D) put it, "I think the CCA proposal was made for bargaining purposes, giving CCA the opportunity to alter its proposal and still end up managing at least part of the Tennessee system. Offer to take it all, settle for what you can get" (Vise 1985). CCA ended up with several facilities and gained valuable exposure for future developments. This exposure and the bid's timeliness pushed not only CCA but other private companies into the legitimate public market for criminal justice decision makers at every level across the country. In addition, CCA and operational privatization gained legitimacy through the company's recognition as "expert" in the field by local, state, and federal officials, as evidenced by its participation in subcommittee hearings and its effect on the recommendations set forth by the President's Commission on Privatization.

The timing of CCA's bid on the Tennessee system and the congressional hearings also coincided with another crucial event in the emergence of private prisons: CCA's "going public"—having an IPO of stock and becoming a company traded on the stock exchange. Joel Dyer comments on one aspect of this event: "Anyone—anyone with money, that is—can now profit from crime" (2000, 11). On another level, the IPO helps CCA raise capital, which it will use for acquisitions, building prisons, and project development. All of these activities help increase cash flow, which boosts the stock price, which allows the company to sell additional shares and raise more capital, and so forth. Seeing the initial success of this strategy encourages other private prison companies to go public and sell shares.

Chapter 3 explores the IPOs in more detail and starts to explore some financial aspects of the private prison industry. It also looks more systematically at some issues raised above, like the political connections of CCA's founders, venture capital, and the movement of government officials into the private prison business. It also adds in elements like the industry's hiring lobbyists and those who accumulate shares working in the interests of the industry. In short, the rise of private prison IPOs leads to a close examination of their part in the larger criminal justice–industrial complex and how Wall Street financiers, behind billions of dollars in debt lines for private prison firms, seek to guard against some of the risks associated with the business.

II

UNDERSTANDING THE OPERATIONS OF PRISON, INC.

3

The Prison-Industrial Complex

Profits, Vested Interests, and Politics

At the same time that private prisons started to gain traction in the 1980s, lawmakers were changing regulations about the use of inmate labor. Laws passed during the Great Depression sought to protect scarce jobs by prohibiting the interstate shipment of goods made in prison, thus limiting the market for them. The Justice System Improvement Act of 1979 and later the Justice Assistance Act of 1984 created the Prison Industry Enhancement Certification Program, which ultimately allowed prison-made goods to trade across state lines if certain conditions were met. Of course, many other prison industries exist outside of this certification program and have also experienced significant growth, often because they allow employers to take advantage of low-wage labor and keep a "Made in the USA" label on their products. According to the General Accounting Office (GAO), in 1998 the Federal Bureau of Prisons' (BOP) annual correctional-industry income was $568 million; the nineteen states that responded to the GAO survey had another $515 million in correctional-industry income, making for a total of more than $1 billion based on old and very incomplete data (GAO 1999).

"Prison industry" conjures up the notion of factory work and inmates stamping license plates or making office furniture. However, any jobs that can be outsourced to low-wage countries can also be moved to prisons, so inmates do data entry, operate call centers (frequently for state tourism information), and serve as telemarketers (GAO 1999). Some states have prohibited prison-based telemarketing, not just because of concerns about personal information but also because people usually do not want law-abiding citizens bothering them with calls, let alone convicted criminals. When the Federal Trade Commission (FTC) created rules on abusive telemarketing—the regulation that included the creation of the-do-not-call registry—it received several comments requesting that prison-based telemarketing be banned or that people be informed when they are speaking with an inmate (whether an inmate initiates or answers a call). The Corrections Corporation of America (CCA) opposed such rules, and the FTC included no language regarding inmates in its final rule (FTC 2003).

While many people think about inmate labor in terms of rehabilitation—giving the inmate marketable skills and a work ethic—fully understanding this issue also requires "following the money" (the more than $1 billion in sales each year from prison-based businesses). Examining the business aspects of inmate labor involves looking at who has an interest in turning a captive population into low-cost employees for everything from building office furniture to telemarketing. More generally, it means going beyond discussions of just deserts, rehabilitation, and deterrence to exploring who has a vested financial interest in particular policies, what that interest might be, and who is profiting from current arrangements.

Inmate labor and the associated prison industries form a small but visible aspect of business interests that influence public policy. Following the money means coming to understand the term *prison industry* in a larger sense, as referring to businesses that make a profit through their connection with the corrections system. While our focus remains on private prisons, our analytical lens is the *prison-industrial complex*, which in turn is part of a larger *criminal justice–industrial complex*. These terms derive from the idea of the *military-industrial complex* that President (and former general) Dwight D. Eisenhower warned of in his Farewell Address. He was concerned that the businesses with which the military contracted, increasingly outside of public scrutiny and accountability, were driving defense policy.

Eisenhower stated that until World War II, "the United States had no armaments industry," and other businesses converted to manufacture them as necessary. Having a permanent armaments industry of "vast proportions," which exists along with "three and a half million men and women directly engaged in the defense establishment" and substantial military spending, was new. He said that the "economic, political, even spiritual" influence of these interests was

> felt in every city, every Statehouse, every office of the Federal government. We recognize the imperative need for this development. Yet we must not fail to comprehend its grave implications. Our toil, resources, and livelihood are all involved. So is the very structure of our society.
>
> In the councils of government, we must guard against the acquisition of unwarranted influence, whether sought or unsought, by the military-industrial complex. The potential for the disastrous rise of misplaced power exists and will persist. We must never let the weight of this combination endanger our liberties or democratic processes. We should take nothing for granted. Only an

alert and knowledgeable citizenry can compel the proper meshing of the huge industrial and military machinery of defense with our peaceful methods and goals, so that security and liberty may prosper together. (Eisenhower 1961)

Eisenhower saw the military-industrial complex as a new phenomenon and warned that allowing it to acquire too much influence could threaten democracy and liberty. Similarly, while prisons and the criminal justice system have had contracts with businesses for supplies and consultants for much of their history, the nature of these relationships and the amount of money involved have reached a critical mass because of the war on crime that started in the 1970s. Chapter 1 noted that the United States spends upward of $68 billion on corrections each year, which has created Las Vegas–style conventions for businesses selling goods and services. Further, because the size of the prison system has grown, the related businesses have also grown in size so that they now include firms with publicly traded stocks and billions of dollars in loans brokered by Wall Street investment banks. Basically, the increases in spending from the wars on crime and drugs have created a new type of permanent industry with "grave implications" for criminal justice policy.

As more companies generate revenue from corrections, there is increasing concern that misplaced power in the multi-billion-dollar prison-industrial complex leads to distorted sentencing policy: the interests of corporate shareholders become increasingly important, causing increasing corporate lobbying, while public safety and public accountability have less import. For the businesses involved, the goal is profit; basic free market principles dictate that companies with shares traded on a stock exchange have the duty to make money for shareholders. Herbert Stein, a former chairman of the President's Council of Economic Advisors, argues that corporations "discharged their social responsibility when they maximized profits" (1996). Under this widely accepted analysis, businesses involved in incarceration have no duty to balance their desire for ever-increasing profits with, say, crime-prevention funding or money for schools. They are acting in socially responsible ways when they lobby for policies to further expand the world's highest incarceration rate. Indeed, sentencing reform and declining crime rates are "risk factors." Eric Schlosser summarizes the issues:

Three decades after the war on crime began, the United States has developed a prison-industrial complex—a set of bureaucratic, political, and economic interests that encourage increased spending on imprisonment, regardless of the actual need. The prison-industrial complex is not a conspiracy, guiding the nation's criminal-justice policy behind closed doors. It is a confluence of special interests that has given prison construction in the United States a seemingly unstoppable momentum. It is composed of politicians, both liberal and conservative, who have used the fear of crime to gain votes; impoverished rural areas where prisons have become a cornerstone of economic development; private companies that regard the roughly $35 billion spent each year on corrections not as a burden on American taxpayers but as a lucrative market; and government officials whose fiefdoms have expanded along with the inmate population. (1998)

Schlosser correctly identifies the prison-industrial complex as being substantially larger than private prisons. It includes all those who supply goods and consulting to jails, prisons, parole, and probation—see below and conclusion (GPS tracking of parolees). The *Corrections Yellow Pages* provides a starting point for conceptualizing the prison-industrial complex and includes some companies originally part of the military-industrial complex that now provide electronic monitoring and related services for parole and probation. The criminal justice–industrial complex includes the prison-industrial complex plus all those who supply goods or consulting to police departments and private security firms. (This is also sometimes referred to as a "commercial" rather than an "industrial" complex [Lilly and Knepper 1993].) Some of these firms were also part of the military-industrial complex that transformed into the criminal justice–industrial complex following the end of the Cold War and the escalating wars on crime and drugs, a transformation facilitated by a 1994 memorandum of understanding between the Departments of Defense and Justice "for interagency collaboration in developing and sharing dual-use technologies for law enforcement agencies and military operations other than war" (National Institute of Justice 1995).

Schlosser also identifies politicians as part of these industrial complexes, but this group does not include merely those who deployed the fear of crime to get votes. Politicians receive campaign contributions from businesses that make up the prison- and criminal justice–industrial complexes. They sit on committees that draft legislation and can become part of a "subgovernment," which exists when the "decision making within a given policy arena rests within a closed circle or the elite of government bureaucrats, agency heads, interest groups or private interests that gain from the allocation of public resources" (Lilly and Knepper 1993, 151). Like the military-industrial complex, the prison- and criminal justice–industrial complexes interweave private business and government interests. This arrangement is also referred to as an "iron triangle" because each of its three sides—government bureaucracy, key members of legislative bodies, and private business interests—protects itself as well as the others from external influence, regulation, and public accountability. When the three components and their respective powers are combined, a subgovernment is created that has the potential to determine public policy free from scrutiny with far-reaching economic, political, and social consequences (Adams 1984).

In order to provide a better explanation of the interests of private prisons and the prison-industrial complex, this chapter's first section starts following some of the money. As such, the discussion focuses on the business dynamics of private prisons and how they communicate with investors about the desirability of their business. For those coming to this book with a criminal justice background, some of this material may be unfamiliar, but it is essential to achieving a fuller understanding of our contemporary criminal justice system and policy. In the second section, we look specifically at private prison companies' initial public offerings (IPOs). IPOs enable companies to raise money by selling shares to the public, which requires them to disclose a great deal of information about their operations, including their finances, general business strategy, and risk factors. The private prison IPOs also bring in a number of banks, Wall Street investment firms, nationally recognized accounting and auditing firms, lawyers, lobbyists, consultants, and former government officials. After providing an overview of the IPO process, we review the IPO of the Corrections Corporation of America, the first private prison company to go public. Our write-up presents a summary using the words of company spokespeople wherever possible in order to give the reader a sense of the IPO document as a tool for investors. Following the write-up of CCA's IPO, we highlight some key aspects of the private prison business model by including statements from other private prison IPOs and link those statements back to the idea of the prison-industrial complex. Finally, we analyze the iron triangle that developed and the lobbying private prisons do.

IPOS: PRIVATE PRISONS "GO PUBLIC"

An initial public offering is the first time a private company issues shares to the public and becomes traded on a stock exchange. This is also known as "going public." A widely circulated quote of unknown origin describes this process: "Going public is like planning a child. Your life becomes more complicated. It will cost you a lot of money. And it can be a very, very rewarding experience."

Before the IPO, the company may have shares owned by the founders and key employees. The company can also raise money by issuing shares to venture capitalists or private financiers. For example, before its IPO, CCA had 6.6 million shares outstanding, with Massey Burch Investments (founded by Jack Massey and discussed in chapter 2) being the single largest holder because of its willingness to provide start-up money and consulting. Pre-IPO shareholders also included Vanderbilt University, where Thomas Beasley received a law degree (and which has done some research favorable to private prisons). The IPO allows a company to raise significant sums of money by selling partial ownership (a "share") to anyone interested in investing in the company. After the IPO, those who want to buy shares of the company and those who want to sell them arrange transactions through the stock exchange, and the company can also sell additional shares (secondary offerings) once it is listed with the exchange.

The IPO also means that a great deal of information must be disclosed to the public and to potential investors through filings with the Securities and Exchange Commission (SEC). Created after the 1929 stock market crash and the ensuing Great Depression, the SEC's purpose was to restore investors' faith in publicly traded U.S. businesses. SEC regulations require what is known as a prospectus before stocks can be issued, then regular reports once a company goes public. A few of the items required in the prospectus include recent financial data presented according to generally accepted accounting principles (GAAP); a summary of the business strategy; a list of key executives, their pay, and any other agreements the company has with them; and a list of risk factors. (See the appendix for information on researching private prison companies through the SEC website.)

The anonymous quote above notes that going public costs a lot of money, and this cash flow represents an important aspect of the prison-industrial complex. Earlier, we stated that government prison systems had always contracted with businesses for certain services, but, as with the military-industrial complex, there was something "new" to it. The arrival of publicly traded companies is a key aspect of the critical mass that changes the policy environment because the sums of money increase dramatically and the publicly traded private prison companies bring in their wake a growing legion of lawyers, accountants, and bankers. For example, as part of the IPO process or at some point afterward, companies frequently switch from a local accounting firm and auditor to a nationally recognized firm. (Many of the later private prison IPOs used the now defunct Arthur Anderson.) They believe this will help with investor confidence and reduce the likelihood of an error that could result in a class-action shareholder lawsuit. Companies need to hire a law firm that can advise them in securities law, which includes preparing all the SEC filings: quarterly reports, annual reports, and documents related to "material events," to name a few. They also frequently need to engage in corporate restructuring before going public. Finally, companies need to hire an underwriter—an intermediary for transferring stock between a company and those who want to purchase shares of the IPO. Underwriters agree to buy a specified number of shares from the company, which they will then resell. As compensation for the work of selling the shares and taking on the risk that people will not buy them, they buy shares from the company for less than the underwriter charges the public. The IPO may also include guaranteed payments to the underwriter and/or consulting payments for reorganization, refinancing debt, and so forth.

In the early 1990s, "there [were] approximately 24 companies operating approximately 71 private correctional facilities" (Esmor 1993), although a small number of those went public with IPOs. Table 3.1 summarizes private prison IPOs, and box 3.1 describes several unusual IPOs that did not start off as being related to a criminal justice–industrial complex but ended up getting pulled in. The column on the far right in table 3.1 starts to quantify some of the fees associated with the IPO and why private prisons' prospects excited Wall Street. These fees just for the IPO include "underwriting discounts and commissions, and fees for registration, legal, accounting, transfer agent, printing and other miscellaneous fees" (Wackenhut 1994). Because of inconsistent reporting, the issue fee amount is not necessarily a total; at times it includes only underwriting fees.

Even though the number of private prisons that went public is relatively small, the IPO prospectus is a rich source of material to better understand the business operations of private prisons. All the IPO documents explain the business operation in similar terms, and the business model described there will generally apply to companies operating in the private prison sector even if they did not have an IPO. (In fact, many of the companies that had IPOs raised cash and later acquired smaller, privately held prisons.) The documents also provide insight into the potential rewards and risks for capital looking to invest in this part of the prison-industrial complex. Readers can get outside of a criminal justice or public policy perspective on private prisons and see them from the vantage point of investors who have provided private prisons with billions of dollars.

The size of the IPOs listed in table 3.1 may seem inconsistent with the statement that billions of dollars have been pumped into the criminal justice–industrial complex through private prisons. Some of the early IPOs were not large because they represented new businesses venturing into a controversial area. IPO documents disclosed that contractual authority to delegate prison management—the whole foundation of the business—was less than clear (see discussion in chapter 2). More important, the IPO is merely the first time the company issues shares to the public, and companies regularly do "secondary" offerings to raise additional capital. We are focusing on the IPO because it marks the emergence of the prison-industrial complex and discloses important information about the industry, but the secondary offerings, especially of CCA and Wackenhut Corrections Corporation (now GEO Group), involve much larger sums of money. For example, CCA's IPO was about $18 million. In 1996, however, it issued $30 million in shares to Sodexho (which would partner with Marriott hotels in 1998) and also "completed a public offering of 3,700,000" shares at a price to the public of $138.8 million; "the proceeds of the offering, after deducting all associated costs, were $131.8 million" (Prison Realty Trust 1997). Recently, the GEO Group noted the results of a secondary offering where "the aggregate net proceeds to us from the offering (after

Table 3.1. Private Prison Initial Public Stock Offerings by Company, Date, and Dollar Amount

Company	Year of IPO	Size
CCA	1986	$18 million sales price to public; $1.2 million in issue costs
		See this chapter for a full discussion of CCA's IPO
Pricor	1987	$7.7 million sales price to public; $985,894 in issue costs
		Pricor's prospectus describes the company as emphasizing youth and juvenile services. A substantial portion of the revenue comes from consulting with government entities, including a two-year contract with Tennessee "to assist and advise in developing a master plan for the state's correction's system" to comply with a 1985 district court order (see chapter 2 on CCA's bid for the entire correctional system). The company reports a cumulative loss of $2.3 million on revenue of $4.4 million for the period July 1, 1985, to March 31, 1987. Massey Burch Investment Group provided financial consulting and is the largest single pre-IPO shareholder.
Esmor Correctional Services	1993	$5.4 million sales price to public; $1.3 million in issue costs
		Esmor describes itself as engaging in private management and operation of facilities, including a center for illegal aliens, intermediate (nonsecure) sanction facilities, and "a shock incarceration facility, which is a military-style 'boot camp' for youthful offenders. The company believes that boot camps for youthful offenders are gaining widespread acceptance and that it is positioned to be a leader in this new concept." Esmor started operations in 1989 and at the time of its IPO operated six facilities or programs with a total of 829 beds. In 1992, the company recorded a profit of $793,000 on revenues of $10.3 million.
Wackenhut Corrections Corporation	1994	$19.7 million sales price to public; $2 million in issue costs
		Wackenhut Corrections Corporation (WCC) was a subsidiary of Wackenhut Corporation, "a leading provider of professional security services," formed "to capitalize on emerging opportunities in the private correctional services market." The self-description notes that WCC provides a "comprehensive range of prison management services from individual consulting projects to integrated design, construction and management" of facilities. WCC was founded in 1984 and entered into its first contract in 1986 (it now operates under the name GEO Group). At the time of the IPO, the company had 7,670 beds under management. It made a profit of $795,000 on revenues of $62.8 million in 1993. WCC says the IPO proceeds will be used to pay off indebtedness to parent company of $11.4 million and "to repay bank debt incurred to fund a special dividend to Parent" of $4.5 million. (Thus, of the $17.6 million net from the IPO, $14.4 went to parent Wackenhut company.)

Cornell Corrections, Inc.

1996

$37.4 million for the company; IPO document noted expectation of $4.15 million in issue costs

According to its self-description, Cornell "is one of the leading providers of privatized correctional, detention, and pre-release services in the United States." The Cornell Cox Group was cofounded in 1991 by David Cornell, a former Bechtel executive; it received its first contract in 1993. (Current corporate history notes that "through predecessor entities, [Cornell] began juvenile operations in 1973, adult community-based programs in 1974, and adult secure operations in 1984.") In 1994, Cornell purchased Eclectic Communications, which began developing prerelease facilities in California in 1977; International Self-Help Services, Inc., for $10 million; and MidTex, a private prison operator in Texas, for $22.7 million. Cornell had contracts to operate twenty facilities with 3,349 beds and reported a loss of $989,000 on revenue of $20.7 million in 1995.

Prison Realty Trust (CCA)

1997

$446.8 million sales price to public; $34.1 million in issue costs

CCA's Prison Realty Trust was created "to capitalize on the opportunities created by the growing trend toward privatization in the corrections industry." It is a real estate investment trust (REIT), a vehicle created by federal tax law for owners of land and buildings that has some important tax and investor advantages if certain conditions are met (see the explanation in this chapter and see chapter 5 for more on subsequent problems). CCA is to receive $308 million for nine prisons from the IPO proceeds, and Prison Realty has options for more in the future. The company's "primary business objectives are to maximize current returns to shareholders through increases in cash flow available for distribution and to increase long-term total returns to shareholders through appreciation in the value of the Common Shares." To fulfill this objective, "the Company intends to pursue a growth strategy which includes acquiring correctional and detention facilities" and is thus looking for "acquisition opportunities."

Correctional Properties Trust (Wackenhut)

1998

$142.6 million sales price to public; $11.9 million in issue costs

Like Prison Realty Trust, this is an REIT. Wackenhut formed Correctional Properties Trust in February 1998 "to capitalize on the growing trend toward privatization in the corrections industry by acquiring correctional and detention facilities from both private prison operators and governmental entities." The company plans to use $113 million of proceeds to acquire eight prisons with a total capacity of 3,154 beds. Seven of these will be purchased from WCC for 122% of their initial cost.

Sources: CCA 1986 and 1987; Pricor 1987 and 1988; Esmor 1993 and 1994; WCC 1994 and 1995; Cornell 1996, 1996, 1997, and 2009; Prison Realty Trust 1997 and 1998; Correctional Properties Trust 1998 and 1999. The companion website for this book contains a file with more detailed descriptions of all the IPOs; see PaulsJusticePage. com > Punishment for Sale.

deducting underwriters' discounts and expenses of $12.8 million) were $227.5 million" (2009b). Those are only two of several offerings for particular years. The cumulative total of secondary offerings and changes in the stock price led to CCA's reporting in 2009 that the value of common stock held by investors other than management was approximately $3.3 billion as of June 30, 2008, based on the closing price of shares that day multiplied by the number of shares outstanding. (This number is also known as a firm's market capitalization.) The GEO Group (2009b) stated that the market value of its shares held by investors other than management was approximately $1.1 billion.

One important aspect of table 3.1 is Prison Realty Trust and Correctional Properties Trust, the last two IPOs in the table and by far the largest. Both are real estate investment trusts (REITs), a structure created by federal tax law for owners of land and buildings. Because profits are exempt from federal corporate income taxes and 90 percent must be paid out to shareholders, REITs can be quite popular. The Prison Realty Trust IPO noted an intention to pay 8.1 percent based on its IPO share price. The share price can rise or drop, but this substantial dividend is attractive to investors because there should be an 8 percent return even if the share price does not change. An REIT's income can only come from rent of land and buildings, so Prison Realty used $308 million to buy nine facilities from CCA, which it would lease back to CCA to manage; Correctional Properties Trust did the same with Wackenhut. Prison Trust (1997) stated that it must rely on tax counsel to negotiate "the application of highly technical and complex Code provisions" to qualify as an REIT; eighteen pages of the Correctional Properties Trust IPO (1998) summarized that company's REIT qualification and tax status.

Ultimately, the REIT arrangement caused significant problems, and CCA had to deal with class-action investor lawsuits, a reorganization, and near bankruptcy (see chapter 5). For now, the point is the amount of money and escalation of the prison-industrial complex. Indeed, the Correctional Properties Trust IPO had eighteen underwriters for the 6.2 million shares, including Smith Barney, Prudential Securities, Lehman Brothers, Merrill Lynch, and Morgan Stanley (1998)—most of the big investment banks that existed at the time. The Prison Realty Trust (1997) IPO involved more than fifty underwriters for the proposed 18.5 million shares, including Lehman Brothers, PaineWebber, Bear Sterns, Credit Suisse First Boston, Goldman Sachs, Merrill Lynch, and Morgan Stanley. The underwriters and others associated with this IPO made $34.1 million (CCA 1998b).

BOX 3.1   FROM COWS AND
SNEAKERS TO CRIMINAL JUSTICE

We did research for this chapter by identifying a number of companies within the prison-industrial complex that had been traded on the stock exchange, then put in a request with the SEC for paper copies of older IPO documents that were not available on the SEC's website (see the appendix). Two of the documents were unusual in that they were not about criminal justice but did show the power of the prison-industrial complex to attract additional money.

BI Incorporated described itself in its annual report as "the leading manufacturer and provider of electronic monitoring equipment and services, and community correctional services to the criminal justice market worldwide" (2000). However, the company's 1983 prospectus says it "currently designs, manufactures, assembles and markets electronic identification systems and components. The Company's products are presently used to automatically identify individual dairy cattle and regulate their feeding, as well as to monitor milk production." The $2.25 million IPO is to help it develop new products, including a "complete dairy farm management computer system" (BI Incorporated 1983). A check of the central identification key (CIK) used by the SEC to keep track of all a company's filings showed the filings to be by the same company. Soon after its IPO, the company entered into the home-arrest-products market and in 1990 expanded through an aggressive series of acquisitions, including the rights to an automated case-load-management service, monitoring service centers, community correctional services, and two correctional service centers specializing in treatment and drug court services (BI Incorporated 2000).

While Avalon Enterprises did not start off dealing with cows, its 1991 IPO was an unusual "blank check" offering. According to the prospectus, the company has no product or business and it "*intends* to participate in at least one business venture considered to be potentially profitable" (Avalon Enterprises 1991, emphasis added). Basically, investors buy shares with the expectation that the company can find a suitable target for acquisition or merger. Potential companies need to be able to provide certified financial statements, but outside of that requirement, "investors will be entrusting their funds to the virtually unlimited discretion of management."

Avalon believes that its "status as a publicly-held entity will enhance its ability to attract and develop" opportunities. Since this was a small IPO— $110,400 gross proceeds—the business venture "may involve an acquisition or merger with a corporation which does not need substantial additional capital but which desires to establish a public trading market for its securities." The corporation may be interested in a venture with Avalon because it "may desire" to "avoid what the corporation and its principals may deem to be the adverse consequences of undertaking an initial public offering (including factors such as time delays, significant expenses, loss of voting control and the inability or unwillingness to comply with various federal and state laws enacted for the protection of investors)." When a deal with Innovation Athletics fell through because the company could not furnish audited financial statements, Avalon acquired Southern Corrections Systems, Inc., a private prison operator in Oklahoma that "intends to pursue additional facilities in the future" (Avalon Enterprises 1992).

CORRECTIONS CORPORATION OF AMERICA GOES PUBLIC

The body of CCA's IPO was 63 pages and the total filing comprised 1,352 pages, which included a variety of exhibits presenting the documents about reincorporation in Delaware, bylaws, employment agreements with executives, stock ownership plans for executives and employees, loan agreements with banks, the consulting agreement with Massey Burch, stock option details, and all contracts CCA had with governments. The self-description in its prospectus stated that CCA

> manages prisons and other correctional facilities for governmental agencies. The Company is the leader in the privatization of these facilities, and currently owns or leases nine facilities containing a total of 1,646 beds. The Company has more beds under management than all of its competitors combined. CCA provides a full range of services to governmental agencies including managing, financing, designing and constructing new facilities, and redesigning and renovating older facilities (CCA 1986).

In a subsequent section titled "Proposals," CCA noted that it "has entered into a joint venture agreement with two individuals in order to develop a proposal to privatize a portion of the penitentiary system of France, where there has been increased interest in privatization."

The financial information indicated that from its inception on January 28, 1983, to December 31, 1983, CCA reported a loss of $531,000 with no revenue. For 1984, it lost $2 million on revenue of $2.5 million; for 1985, it lost $2.3 million on revenue of $7.6 million. CCA's revenues were based on payments from governments "in negotiated amounts per inmate per day ('compensated man-days')" that varied depending on the type of facility and extent of services. The company broke expenses down into several categories, the largest of which relates to operating the prisons. Within this category of facility operating expenses, two-thirds of the cost entailed salary and employee benefits, and "substantially all other operating expenses consist of food, insurance costs and supplies" (CCA 1986). Contracts require the company to maintain insurance, so at this point CCA has $5 million in general liability and $21 million to cover property and casualty risks. The prospectus noted that each facility is fully staffed when it opens but might have few inmates, so the company has experienced a loss due to high expenses and low compensation. As the occupancy rate increases, revenues rise while expenses (for food, supplies, etc.) increase by very little comparatively.

The next largest expense is "general and administrative," which "consists of salaries of officers and other corporate headquarters personnel, legal, accounting and other professional fees, travel and entertainment expenses and rental for the Company's executive offices" (CCA 1986). The next largest expense is for "development," which consists of "promotional and marketing expenses incurred in the general promotion of the concept of the privatization of prisons" and in the process of working with specific governmental authorities on identified projects. CCA notes that it "engages in extensive promotional and marketing efforts and has incurred substantial development costs." The final and smallest category is interest expenses related to borrowing money.

The prospectus heading "Prisons and the Corrections Industry" starts by noting that Bureau of Justice Statistics (BJS) reports "indicate that greater numbers of people are being incarcerated in the United States than in any previous period" (CCA 1986). The per capita incarceration rates for state and federal inmates rose 45 percent from 1980 to 1985. Between 1984 and 1985, state and federal prison capacity expanded by forty-five thousand beds, but the prison population increased by sixty-eight thousand, an increase of "8.4% over the prior year and 67.9% from 1977. At December 31, 1985, federal and state corrections facilities operated at 123% and 105% of capacity, respectively. At June 30, 1985, the corrections systems, in whole or part, of 34 states were under court order to improve conditions." (See the discussion in chapter 1 for more on this background.)

In this environment, the prospectus continues, "CCA believes that the private sector can offer a solution to the corrections problems currently facing governmental agencies. Privatization of services has been accepted in many other contexts, including hospital management and refuse collections, in which the private sector has demonstrated its ability to offer improved services at a lower cost than the private sector" (1986). CCA asserted it "is able to achieve reduced costs by better management and planning." For example, "the Company designs and constructs new facilities or redesigns and renovates existing facilities to reduce the number of security personnel required to staff a facility properly." It also tried to reduce overtime, utilize central purchasing to buy items for all its prisons at better rates, and claimed it could complete capital projects (construction and renovation) in less time than the government. It also believed "the Company can reduce its exposure to civil rights claims by having the Company's facilities satisfy ACA [American Correctional Association] standards" (CCA 1986).

When it received inquiries from governments about its services, CCA determined "whether the legal and political climate in which the inquiring party operates is conducive to serious consideration of privatization" and responded "to the most promising of these inquiries with personal meetings and political and educational efforts" (the development costs mentioned above). In the meeting, CCA "help[s] the agency further define its needs and . . . explain the requirements and details of the request for proposal ('RFP') or request for qualification ('RFQ') process." This process is similar for other private prison operators, as well government contractors in general, and the prospectus provides an overview:

> In the case of an RFP, a bidder submits a proposal that describes the services to be provided by the bidder, its experience and qualifications, and the price at which the bidder is willing to provide services, which may include the renovation, improvement, or expansion of an existing facility or the planning, design and construction of a new facility. In the case of an RFQ, the requesting agency selects a firm believed to be the most qualified to provide the requested services and then negotiates the terms of the contract with that firm, including the price at which the services are to be provided. (1986)

The time between first inquiry and granting a contract can be fifteen to twenty-four months. (Chapter 4 provides a more detailed analysis of contracts.)

An important aspect of the prospectus and many other reports for investors was a listing of risk factors. We have mentioned elsewhere that private prisons see declining crime rates and sentencing reform as risks, but CCA's IPO document does not contain this language. In 1986, crime was increasing, and sentencing patterns were only likely to get tougher. So, CCA saw the real challenge simply as successfully signing contracts with governments. At this point, the prospectus (1986) listed four items under the heading of risk factors:

- "From inception in 1983 through June 30, 1986, the Company had an accumulated deficit of $5,850,450. No assurance can be given that the Company will not continue to experience operating losses."
- "Both the purpose for which the Company was founded and the Company's method of operations are innovative. The Company's success depends largely on its ability to convince various governmental entities to contract with a private enterprise for a service that has historically been a governmental function and to overcome opposition of a variety of interest groups that campaign against the Company's contract proposals." Elsewhere in the document, CCA noted, "It is unclear whether governmental agencies have the authority to delegate their custodial functions to private organizations." Some states have passed legislation granting such authority to their departments of corrections, but such laws may be challenged.
- CCA must acquire property on which to build prisons and "therefore anticipate[s] legal actions and other forms of opposition from residents" in areas surrounding each proposed site. "The Company expects to incur significant expenses in responding to such opposition and there can be no assurance of success."
- CCA stated that the development and operations of its "business are materially dependent upon the active participation" of Thomas Beas-

ley, Doctor Crants, and Don Hutto. Elsewhere, the prospectus noted that the company paid for a $3 million "key man" life insurance policy on Beasley, chairman of the board and president, and Crants, vice chairman of the board, treasurer, and secretary; there is a $5 million policy on Hutto, the executive vice president. Part of the proceeds were assigned to "Dominion Bank as security for amounts drawn under the Company's bank line of credit."

CCA also disclosed its status as a Delaware corporation that is the successor to a Tennessee corporation, and "the sole purpose of the merger was to change the domicile of the Company from Tennessee to Delaware, primarily to obtain the advantages of the Delaware General Corporation Law and the judicial decisions thereunder." In its first annual report filed with the SEC, CCA noted that as of March 1987 there were 8.6 million shares outstanding (compared with 120 million in February 2009). The company disclosed that it "employ[s] registered lobbyists" in states that are considering legislation about privatization (CCA 1987).

PRIVATE PRISONS AND THE PRISON-INDUSTRIAL COMPLEX

The CCA prospectus focused for obvious reasons on investors' concerns, but we must explore certain broader implications by examining all the private prison IPOs. Specifically, these documents help inform the analysis of what vested interests the private prison business has and what threats its continued growth likely poses. An important starting point is the observation that the CCA prospectus described the increasing incarceration rate not as a social problem but as a business opportunity—or in Schlosser's words, "not as a burden on American taxpayers but as a lucrative market" (1988). All the other private prison IPOs share this trait. The first substantive page of Pricor's prospectus is a map of the United States with shading to indicate correctional departments under court order. The company also noted the overall size of the operating budgets for state prisons, in addition to which "approximately $3.0 billion was allocated for capital expenditures for 299 major new projects and 157 major renovation projects" (Pricor 1987).

Further, Esmor Correctional Services' IPO document states that "the increase in federal and state prison populations for 1992 translates into a nationwide need for approximately 1,143 new prison bedspaces per week" (1993), up from 981 per week in 1991. The prospectus quotes BJS reports to show that "at the end of 1992 twenty-one jurisdictions reported a total of 18,191 state prisoners held in local jails or other facilities because of overcrowding in state facilities." In terms similar to those we discussed in chapter 1, Esmor states that "this back-up has prompted many localities to initiate lawsuits against their state correctional systems for not accepting convicted offenders" (1993). Cornell's IPO document contains an "industry and market" section, which noted that "the number of adult inmates in United States federal and state prison facilities increased from 503,601 at December 31, 1985, to 1,104,074 at June 30, 1995, an increase of more than 119%" (1996).

Given that CCA's founders' stated aim was to solve the overcrowding problem and get rich (see chapter 2), such statements are perhaps expected. The problem is that companies need the current elevated rates of incarceration and overcrowding to continue indefinitely. Consider the statement in the GEO Group's 2008 annual report:

> The demand for our correctional and detention facilities and services could be adversely affected by changes in existing criminal or immigration laws, crime rates in jurisdictions in which we operate, the relaxation of criminal or immigration enforcement efforts, leniency in conviction, sentencing or deportation practices, and the decriminalization of certain activities that are currently proscribed by criminal laws or the loosening of immigration laws. For example, any changes with respect to the decriminalization of drugs and controlled substances could affect the number of persons arrested, convicted, sentenced and incarcerated, thereby potentially reducing demand for correctional facilities to house them. Similarly, reductions in crime rates could lead to reductions in arrests, convictions and sentences requiring incarceration at correctional facilities. Immigration reform laws which are currently a focus for legislators and politicians at the federal, state and local level also could materially adversely impact us. (2009)

CCA uses similar language in its 2008 annual report, which states that the company's

> possible growth depends on a number of factors we cannot control, including crime rates and sentencing patterns in various jurisdictions and acceptance of privatization. The demand for our facilities and services could be adversely affected by the relaxation of enforcement efforts, leniency in conviction or parole standards and sentencing practices or through the decriminalization of certain activities that are currently proscribed by our criminal laws. For instance, any changes with respect to drugs and controlled substances or illegal immigration could affect the number of persons arrested, convicted, and sentenced, thereby potentially reducing demand for correctional facilities to house them. Legislation has been proposed in numerous jurisdictions that could lower minimum sentences for some non-violent crimes and make more inmates eligible for early release based on good behavior. Also, sentencing alternatives under consideration could put some offenders on probation with electronic monitoring who would otherwise be incarcerated. Similarly, reductions in crime rates could lead to reductions in arrests, convictions and sentences requiring incarceration at correctional facilities. (2009b)

Readers will have a variety of reactions to the types of reforms listed above based on notions of just deserts, public safety, and government accountability to taxpayers. But these debates over mandatory minimums, alternatives to incarceration, and immigration now happen in a policy environment where a multi-billion-dollar industry wants to maintain existing policies and increase incarceration rates simply for its own profit. Nils Christie, a Norwegian criminologist, claims that companies servicing the criminal justice system need sufficient quantities of raw materials to guarantee long-term growth: "In the criminal justice field, the raw material is prisoners and the industry will do what is necessary to guarantee a steady supply" (2000, 87). Logically, for the supply of prisoners to grow, the "socially responsible," profit-maximizing company will work to ensure a sufficient number is incarcerated regardless of whether crime is rising or incarceration is necessary.

CCA stated that such policies, and certainly crime rates, are beyond its control. But the company can influence a wide variety of policies through lobbying, even if it does not dictate the end result. In its 2008 annual report, CCA states it has a "significant amount" of debt: "As of December 31, 2008, we had total indebtedness of $1,192.9 million," or almost $1.2 billion (2009). Those who hold this debt—along with CCA, its shareholders, and all those similarly situated with the GEO Group—have too much at stake to leave criminal justice reform to chance. Equally disturbing is that companies have at times noted explicitly that "changes in dominant political parties in any of the markets in which the Company operates could result in significant changes to previously established views of privatization" (Wackenhut 1994). Cornell's IPO (1996) used similar language, and even if private prison companies no longer use language this direct, the sentiment is still true today.

Another significant point is the business model of "compensated man-days" and occupancy rates. Under virtually all of the early contracts, private prisons received a set amount per inmate per day. A fee per day is called a per diem, and the per diem for one inmate is a unit called a compensated man-day. Revenue, and thus profits, for their prisons are highest when the prisons are full or at least have high occupancy rates. (Conversely, empty beds in a publicly run facility decrease the cost to taxpayers.) Wackenhut's IPO explicitly states, "Under a per diem rate structure, a decrease in occupancy rates could cause a decrease in revenue and profitability" (1994). The business model resembles that of the hotel industry, which is one of the reasons Sodexho-Marriott became a major investor in CCA. Many of the IPOs note that revenue and profits are negatively affected during the start-up phase. Esmor, for example, notes that if a contract is awarded, the company's start-up costs include "recruitment, training and travel of personnel and certain legal costs." From the first day of operations, the prison is fully staffed, but "residents" (prisoners) arrive over the course of one to four months. If revenues are based on a per diem fee, the company is likely to experience an operating loss until high occupancy rates are reached (Esmor 1993). Cornell discusses the same problem and explains that "a minimum fixed number of employees is required to operate and maintain any facility regardless of occupancy levels." Because of this cost structure, the company experiences a loss when it initially opens or expands a facility, and "to the extent that the Company can increase revenues at a facility through higher occupancy or expansion of the number of beds under contract, the Company should be able to improve operating results" (Cornell 1996).

However, the logic of the per diem fee or compensated man-day model of the private prison industry means the concern with occupancy rates extends beyond the start-up phase to ongoing operations. For example, Cornell's 2008 annual report states that "because revenue varies directly with occupancy, occupancy is a driver of our revenues. Our industry experiences significant economics of scale, whereby as occupancy rises, operating costs per resident decline . . . and we are mindful of the need to maintain such occupancy levels" (2009). Being "mindful" really means lobbying government, as private prisons depend on government for inmates. Cornell stated in an earlier filing that its contracts had a per diem structure, so

> a decrease in occupancy rates would cause a decrease in revenues and profitability. The Company is, therefore, dependent upon governmental agencies to supply the Company's facilities with a sufficient number of inmates to meet the facilities' design capacities, and in most cases such governmental agencies are under no obligation to do so. Moreover, because many of the Company's facilities have inmates serving relatively short sentences or only the last three to six months of their sentences, the high turnover rate of inmates requires a constant influx of new inmates from the relevant governmental agencies to provide sufficient occupancies to achieve profitability. (Cornell 1996)

Put more concisely, the company depends on governmental agencies "to supply the facility with a sufficient number of inmates to meet and exceed the facility's break-even design capacities" (Cornell 1996). And a "failure of a governmental agency to supply sufficient occupancies for any reason may cause the Company to forego revenues and income." Further, contracts have terms of one to five years, after which the governmental agency can renew or rebid the contract. Cornell can give "no assurance" that contracts will be renewed or that the company will prevail if the government agency puts the contract out for open bidding.

The picture that emerges from the business model and risks described above involves not just lobbying and campaign contributions but the creation of a subgovernment where influence works outside the sphere of public scrutiny. As noted earlier in this chapter, subgovernments comprise key legislators, government bureaucrats or agency heads, and private interests that gain from the allocation of public resources. In a seminal article on the corrections-commercial complex, R. Lilly and P. Knepper (1993) note that actors outside of the iron triangle have a difficult time exerting influence when the major participants are united. The subgovernment becomes stable over time when there is a "steady flow of information, access, influence, personnel and money" (Lilly and Knepper 1993, 153). As the subgovernment becomes stable, "the line between the public good and private interest becomes blurred as governmental and nongovernmental institutions become harder to distinguish" (Lilly and Knepper 1993). Further, because much policy making is routine, "decision making is normally invisible" and "the closed, low-profile operations of a subgovernment are not noticed by the public, the media, or other governmental agencies" (Lilly and Knepper 1993). Finally, subgovernment participants "work to isolate the mutually beneficial alliance from other arenas"—thus creating the notion of the iron triangle—especially as "policymakers and private participants come to share the assumption that they are not only acting in their own interests, but the general interest as well" (Lilly and Knepper 1993, 153–54).

Writing in 1993, Lilly and Knepper sought to call attention to the extent to which businesses were already involved in corrections and raised a number of questions about subgovernments. Despite some ups and downs for private prisons, it is clear now that a prison-industrial complex exists, and private prisons are involved in subgovernments. To help illustrate this concept, we will examine CCA's (1) early history, (2) lobbying and political donations, and (3) participation in professional policy-advocacy groups. The discussion below is not meant to be comprehensive on all these points but rather to convey a sense of how policy making around prisons and criminal justice policy is done and why it threatens democracy. Further, to the extent that a subgovernment has a low level of visibility, its functions are not noticed and reported, so the accounts we draw on for this book are themselves incomplete records of subgovernmental activities.

The relationship between politicians, industry leaders, and agency heads started with the inception of the idea of operational privatization by CCA's founders and its funding by venture capital. As head of the Republican Party in Tennessee, Tom Beasley had access to politicians. Cofounder Hutto remarked on the importance of these connections: "We have said this was a good idea and that there was a need and that the investors were there. But the fact is that a good idea has to be sold, enthusiastically and untiringly. Without Tom Beasley's ability to talk to governors, legislators and commissioners, to persuade them to listen, this company would have never succeeded" (CCA Source 2003). Cofounder Doctor R. Crants, a respected, successful businessman and a partner in several large corporate ventures, had connections to Sodexho-Marriott Services, the largest supplier of food services to correctional facilities, which became for a time the largest investor in CCA. Finally, cofounder Don Hutto was the president of the American Correctional Association (ACA) and the director of corrections in Virginia. According to Beasley, Hutto gave them the federal connections the company needed: "Don's national reputation gave us an advantage with the federal government. He was involved in a tier of all of the top management on the federal side" (CCA Source 2003). Further, CCA (and Pricor) was backed by Massey, whose partner in Kentucky Fried Chicken, John Brown, went on to become governor of Kentucky. As a multimillionaire Massey was well known in political circles, and came to the Tennessee State Capitol to lobby for CCA's bid to take over the entire state prison system (Carey 2005, 172).

As time passed, private prisons recruited key former government employees to become executives or members of the board of trustees. Chapter 2 noted that Norman Carlson, a director of the Federal Bureau of Prisons, would later become a member of Wackenhut's board of directors. Carlson's replacement at the BOP, Michael Quinlan, became a CCA executive. Benjamin Civiletti, U.S. attorney general from 1979 to 1981, joined Wackenhut's board. The GEO Group's board currently includes Anne Foreman, a former undersecretary of the U.S. Air Force, general counsel of the Department of the Air Force, and the associate director of Presidential Personnel for National Security. John Perzel served as a Republican representative in Pennsylvania's House of Representatives, including four terms as majority leader before becoming Speaker of the House.

CCA's executive vice president and general counsel is Gustavus (Gus) Adolphus Puryear IV, a legislative director for former Tennessee senator and later majority leader Bill Frist. (Puryear apparently helped Vice President Dick Cheney prepare for the 2000 and 2004 vice presidential debates. President George W. Bush appointed him to a federal judgeship in Tennessee, but as the Senate had not confirmed him before Barack Obama became president, the nomination is likely dead.) CCA's CEO and board chairman, John Ferguson, was the commissioner of finance for the state of Tennessee and on the Governor's Commission on Practical Government for that state as well. CCA board member Donna Alvarado served as deputy assistant secretary of defense for the Defense Department. Three-term Arizona senator Dennis Deconcini joined CCA's board in 2008. CCA board member Thurgood Marshall, son of the late Supreme Court justice, served as an aide to President Bill Clinton and director of legislative affairs and deputy counsel to Vice President Al Gore. In a further attempt to expand the company's network of resources, Michael Quinlan established an advisory committee. It, too, consists of former leaders from the government side of the triangle: Bob Brown, former director of corrections for the state of Michigan, and Rick Seiter, former director of corrections for the state of Ohio and former

BOP assistant director. In addition, the company hired Mike Grotefend, the former national president of the Council of Prison Locals, one of the industry's leading adversaries, and Hardy Rauch, the former director of accreditation for the ACA.

This list is by no means exhaustive, as many other executives throughout the ranks have come from federal, state, and local governments where private prisons do business or hope to enter a market. We can expect attempts to strengthen the triangle through the co-opting of former government officials and donations to privatization-friendly politicians and decision makers to continue in the future and even to escalate as the private prison business grows larger. However, expect also to see more former industry executives and managers appearing in state- and federal-level decision-making positions. This happened in 2004, when John D. Rees became the commissioner of the Kentucky Department of Corrections. A former vice president of CCA (1986–1998), Rees also owned stock in the company until his 2004 appointment in Kentucky. After a riot in the CCA-operated Lee County facility, Rees recommended the company pay a miniscule $10,000 fine. A state investigation revealed that the facility had been violating a host of contract requirements: staffing levels were inadequate, educational programs were lacking, and substance-abuse programs had been cancelled. The company responded by firing (scapegoating) the warden. Meanwhile, Rees continued his support for awarding a contract for the new 941-bed Elliott facility to a private operator (Cheves 2004b). Rees's deputy commissioner of support services in Kentucky, J. David Donahue, had been a senior vice president and chief operating officer for U.S. Corrections Corporation until 1998, when he took the job in Kentucky. In January 2005, he was appointed commissioner of Indiana's Department of Corrections.

CCA reinforced the influence of its executives and had seven registered lobbyists in the state of Tennessee alone by 1997. The Speaker of the House in the Tennessee General Assembly was married to CCA political lobbyist Betty Anderson, and Governor Donald Sundquist's former chief of staff owned CCA stock while she was advising the governor on prison privatization. From 1994 to 1996, Crants and Beasley donated $60,491 to Tennessee lawmakers, including $38,500 to Governor Sundquist's reelection campaign. Shortly after the donation, Governor Sundquist endorsed a controversial arrangement whereby CCA could contract to build and operate a 1,540-bed jail, funded with $47 million in state bonds. The arrangement circumvented a Tennessee statute that allows only one privately managed prison to operate in the state at a time. In addition, Senator Robert Rochelle received campaign contributions from CCA board members and later sponsored a bill to permit privatization of any newly built state prison. He also sponsored—and the Tennessee state legislature passed—a bill that exempted from state training requirements private-prisoner transport guards employed by CCA subsidiary TransCor America, which transports prisoners nationwide. Beasley and Crants also donated to Senator Jim Kyle, chairman of the Select Oversight Committee on Corrections (Friedman 1997).

An examination of the political contributions and corrections-related legislation in 2000 reveals that private prison companies managed to maintain their contracts despite adverse budget pressures and to repel efforts to reduce state reliance on private prison companies (Bender 2002). In the 2000 election cycle, private prison companies contributed more than $1.1 million to 830 candidates in fourteen southern states overall and another $96,432 to political parties. CCA alone made six hundred contributions, totaling more than $443,300 to candidates and $36,568 to state political-party committees (Bender 2002). In several states, lawmakers considering corrections policy received campaign contributions from the companies that stood to profit from their decisions. In 2000, for example, North Carolina lawmakers who heard reports of poor staffing and management practices, escapes, and violence in private correctional facilities imposed limits on the construction of new private prisons. They also banned the importation of out-of-state prisoners to private facilities, a common practice to help increase occupancy rates. However, by 2001, the state's move away from private correctional services had been reversed, and lawmakers had authorized the state to contract with private-prison-building firms for up to three new one-thousand-bed prisons, which the state would then buy back using a complicated purchase-and-lease process. This agreement, Senate Bill 25 (SB25), signed by Governor Michael Easley, committed the state to a twenty-year contract with an estimated total cost of $246.6 million, about $100 million more than the facilities would have cost in a straight-purchase agreement. Supporters of the build-and-lease proposal contributed more than $250,000 during the 2000 election cycle to candidates that would later vote on SB25. CCA, its lobby representatives, and executive Tom Beasley gave to forty-four different candidates (Bender 2002).

In December 2004, CCA CEO John Ferguson donated $100,000 to then U.S. House majority leader Tom DeLay's (R-TX) charity DeLay for Kids. Texas, under DeLay's leadership, signed a lucrative contract with CCA for the management of eighty-three hundred beds in seven state prisons. The fund-raiser at which the donation was presented took place at the home of Kelly Knight, finance chairwoman of the Kentucky Republican Party. The fund-raiser, which also yielded $113,000 for DeLay's defense fund (against charges of money laundering and illegally using corporate money to influence Texas elections) took place shortly *after* CCA bid for the contract, but *before* it was awarded, to run Kentucky's newest prison. According to Rick Cohen of the National Committee for Responsive Philanthropy, "These political foundations have become methods for well-heeled corporate executives, lobbyists and others to purchase influence and face-time with top politicians and without the limits or disclosure required of campaign donations or lobbying" (Cheves 2004b).

Louisiana governor Kathleen Blanco collected more than $1 million from private corporations and individuals to spend on her inauguration activities and transition to the governor's office. CCA and Wackenhut, which both ran prisons in Louisiana, made donations (Maggi 2004). California governor Arnold Schwarzenegger, who rejects donations from the state prison guards' union, accepted $53,000 from Wackenhut in 2003. The money came as the state prepared to close a 224-bed Wackenhut Corrections Corporation facility (Morain 2003). By July 2004, Governor Schwarzenegger had put private prisons back on the table, stating, "It is a priority of my administration to reform the California prison system. Reform options will include the use of privatization" (Segal 2004).

The private prison industry has also effectively killed legislation that would limit or impose penalties on the industry. For example, Georgia House Bill 456 (HB 456) responded to increasing problems with privately built prisons importing out-of-state inmates, who could then escape. The bill would have banned future private facilities without the approval of the state and local authorities. It also proposed to ban the importation of sex offenders or other violent criminals and required private prison companies to reimburse the state for costs associated with the capture of escaped inmates. This measure came in response to several examples in which private prisons had taken inmates from other states to help fill the facility, and the local community only found out what type of inmate had been imported after there had been an escape, which the local police were called in to deal with. The Georgia House of Representatives approved the measure 116–54. However, by the time it reached the Senate Corrections Committee, corrections industry lobbyists had made 149 donations totaling $56,650 to the committee chairman and other members. CCA's lobbyists funneled $25,950 and contributed more than $12,500 to the Democratic Party of Georgia (Bender 2002). HB 456 died in committee.

Between 2004 and 2008, CCA spent at least $10 million on lobbying, based on a review of public records (Martin 2009). Lobbying and elections laws mandate keeping records of lobbyists and donors as part of a larger effort to prevent money from totally corrupting the election system. However, corporate contributions to certain trade associations are not included, and the corporation itself does not disclose political contributions made on its own behalf or through executives individually. Further, private prison companies do not disclose the process by which they decide how much to spend on candidates. To address some of these issues, an activist group of shareholders submitted a proposal to shareholders of CCA, Wackenhut, and Cornell to provide for the release of such information. All three companies argued against it (see box 3.2), and shareholders of all three companies voted it down. Cornell stated in its filing, "The Board does not believe any significant incremental shareholder value is created by the adoption of this proposal" (2008b).

In addition to strengthening their relationship with policy makers via campaign contributions and hiring former government officials and registered lobbyists, CCA became involved with professional organizations that play a major role in criminal justice policy making. The American Legislative Exchange Council (ALEC), founded in the early 1970s, describes itself as "a bipartisan membership association for conservative state lawmakers who share belief in limited government, free markets, federalism and individual liberty" (2005). Others, however, charge that it is "one of the nation's most powerful and least known corporate lobbies" (Ollson 2002). At best, its members gather to swap ideas and form model legislation; at worst, industry leaders pay the council dues for the privilege of ghostwriting legislation to benefit their businesses. Tommy Thompson, former Wisconsin governor and Bush administration health and human services secretary, as well as an early member of ALEC, explains, "Myself, I always loved going to these meetings because I always found new ideas. Then I'd take them back to Wisconsin, disguise them a little bit, and declare that 'It's mine'" (Biewen 2002).

ALEC's corporate members include at least a dozen companies that do prison business: the drug companies Merck and Glaxo Smith-Klein, the telephone companies that compete for lucrative prison contracts, and CCA. The payoff for membership, according to CCA's vice president Louise Green, is that it gives the corrections corporation a chance to explain the benefits of privately run prisons to state lawmakers. Critics, however, point out that this is where the problem lies; business executives who stand to gain from stricter sentencing policies advise state lawmakers behind closed doors. This then becomes the basis on which criminal justice decisions are made.

On top of its membership dues and contributions to help defray the costs of ALEC meetings, CCA pays for a seat on ALEC's Criminal Justice Task Force. That panel, which a CCA official cochaired for a period, writes the group's "model" bills on crime and punishment. For years, ALEC's criminal justice committee has promoted state laws letting private prison companies operate and has pushed a tough-on-crime agenda. The lawmakers on the task force, according to it's director Andrew LeFevre, led the drive for increased incarceration by going back to their home states and "talking to their colleagues and getting their colleagues to understand that if, you know, we want to reduce crime we have to get these guys off the streets" (Biewen 2002). Among ALEC's model bills were mandatory-minimum-sentencing laws, three-strikes laws, the Truth-in-Sentencing Act, the Habitual Juvenile Offender Act, and the Shock Incarceration Act. The Truth-in-Sentencing Act and three-strikes laws have been among the most widely adopted (Bender 2000). As of 2000, the Criminal Justice Task Force listed prison privatization as one of its major issues (Bender 2000).

Private prison executives claim that they do not push for longer sentencing policies. "You don't see CCA advocating for longer sentences; that's not true. If government, through its elected representatives, identified that, well, we are going to need to provide for public safety by incarcerating individuals—that is not a vendor-driven issue," says James Ball, CCA's vice president of customer relations (Biewen 2002). Others are skeptical (Ollson 2002; Biewen 2002). The proposals to incarcerate more people for longer benefit these executives, and given the various risk factors and disclosures from SEC documents noted earlier, it is difficult to believe that private prison companies limit their advocacy through ALEC to privatization issues only. ALEC's reports were credited for the 1998 passage of truth-in-sentencing legislation in Wisconsin (Biewen 2002), a CCA customer, which resulted in overcrowded facilities in that state, increasing the use of private prisons. And CCA would like everyone to believe this is just a coincidence.

BOX 3.2. GEO GROUP ARGUES AGAINST GREATER DISCLOSURE OF POLITICAL CONTRIBUTIONS

As owners of the company, shareholders can introduce proposals that can become company policy if approved by a majority of the company's shareholders. Usually, proposals do not become policy without the support of management, which owns a large numbers of shares and whose support or opposition guides the voting of many large shareholders. In 2008, an activist group of nuns introduced a resolution to shareholders of the GEO Group to advocate greater disclosure of political contributions in the name of transparency and accountability for corporate spending on political activities. Management of GEO opposed the measure, and shareholders voted against it. Here is their resolution and rationale, along with management's response, taken directly from GEO's 14 DEF filing with the Securities and Exchange Commission (GEO Group 2008b).

Shareholder Proposal Requesting Semi-Annual Disclosure of Political Contributions
The Mercy Investment Program, 205 Avenue C, #10E, New York, New York 10009, which is the beneficial owner of 360 shares of GEO stock, has filed the following shareholder proposal:
"Resolved: that the shareholders of The GEO Group hereby request that our Company provide a report, updated semi-annually, disclosing our Company's:

1. Policies and procedures for political contributions and expenditures, both direct and indirect, made with corporate funds.
2. Monetary and non-monetary political contributions and expenditures not deductible under section 162(e)(1)(B) of the Internal Revenue Code, including but not limited to contributions to or expenditures on behalf of political candidates,

political parties, political committees and other political entities organized and operating under 26 USC Sec. 527 of the Internal Revenue Code and any portion of any dues or similar payments made to any tax exempt organization that is used for an expenditure or contribution if made directly by the corporation would not be deductible under section 162(e)(1)(B) of the Internal Revenue Code. The report shall include the following:

a. An accounting of our Company's funds that are used for political contributions or expenditures as described above;

b. Identification of the person or persons in our Company who participated in making the decisions to make political contribution or expenditure; and

c. The internal guidelines or policies, if any, governing our Company's political contributions and expenditures.

This report shall be presented to the Board of Directors' audit committee or other relevant oversight committee and posted on our Company's website to reduce costs to shareholders.

Supporting Statements

As long-term shareholders of GEO Group, we support transparency and accountability for corporate spending on political activities. These activities include direct and indirect political contributions to candidates, political parties or political organizations; independent expenditures; or electioneering communications on behalf of a federal, state or local candidate. Disclosure is consistent with public policy, in the best interest of our company and its shareholders, and critical for compliance with recent federal ethics legislation. Absent a system of accountability, company assets can be used for policy objectives that may be inimical to the long-term interests of and may pose risks to the company and its shareholders.

The GEO Group contributed at least $744,916 in corporate funds since the 2002 election cycle. (National Institute on Money in State Politics: http://www.followthemoney.org/index.phtml)

However, relying on publicly available data does not provide a complete picture of the Company's political expenditures. For example, the Company's payments to trade associations used for political activities are undisclosed and unknown. In many cases, even management does not know how trade associations use their company's money politically. The proposal asks the Company to disclose all of its political contributions, including payments to trade associations and other tax exempt organizations. This would bring our Company in line with a growing number of leading companies, including Pfizer, Aetna, Dell and American Electric Power that support political disclosure and accountability and disclose this information on their websites. The Company's Board and shareholders need complete disclosure to be able to fully evaluate the political use of corporate assets. Thus, we urge your support for this critical governance reform."

Recommendation of the Board of Directors

GEO's board of directors recommends a vote "AGAINST" the adoption of this proposal for the following reasons:

The GEO board believes that this proposal is unnecessary and duplicative because various federal, state and local campaign finance laws already require us to disclose political contributions made by GEO, and GEO fully complies with these disclosure and reporting requirements. As a result, the board believes that ample public information exists and is available regarding GEO's political contributions adequate to alleviate the concerns cited in this proposal. In addition, with respect to political contributions by GEO, we note that current law prohibits corporate contributions to federal candidates or their political committees. However, GEO is able to make corporate contributions to state and local candidates or initiatives where permitted by law. Various members of GEO's management decide which candidates, campaigns, committees and initiatives GEO will support based on a nonpartisan effort to advance and protect the interests of GEO and our shareholders and employees.

GEO also sponsors non-partisan political action committees (the "GEO PACs"). The GEO PACs allow our employees to pool their financial resources to support federal, state and local candidates, political party committees and political action committees. The political contributions made by the GEO PACs are funded entirely by the voluntary contributions of our employees. No corporate funds are used. A committee comprised of appropriate members of GEO's management decides which candidates, campaigns, committees and initiatives the GEO PACs will support based on a nonpartisan effort to advance and protect the interests of GEO and our shareholders and employees. The GEO PACs file reports of recipients and disbursements with the Federal Election Commission (the "FEC"), and appropriate state reporting authorities, as well as pre-election and post-election reports. These detailed, publicly available reports identify the names of candidates supported and itemize amounts contributed by the GEO PACs, including any political contributions over $200. Given these existing reporting requirements, we do not believe that posting the requested information on our website would provide shareholders with additional meaningful information. Instead, we believe that it would impose unnecessary costs and administrative burdens on us while often requiring duplicative disclosure of already public information.

The board also believes that the expanded disclosure requested in this proposal would place GEO at a competitive disadvantage. GEO is involved on an ongoing basis with a number of legislative and political initiatives at the federal, state and local levels that could significantly affect its business and operations. While the public disclosure of contributions relating to these efforts is often required on a jurisdiction-by-jurisdiction basis, reporting them in one medium on GEO's website could reveal valuable information regarding GEO's long-term business strategies, business development initiatives and business priorities. Because third parties with adverse interests also participate in the political process for their own business reasons, any unilateral expanded disclosure by GEO which is not required of such third parties could benefit these parties to the detriment of GEO.

In short, we believe that this proposal is unnecessary, burdensome and duplicative because a comprehensive system of reporting and accountability for political contributions already exists. In addition, we believe that, if adopted, the proposal would cause GEO as a reporter of the requested information to be exposed to potential competitive harm, without commensurate benefit to our shareholders. For these reasons, the board of directors recommends that you vote AGAINST this proposal.

CONCLUSION

A 1994 *Wall Street Journal* article reported,

Americans' fear of crime is creating a new version of the old military-industrial complex, an infrastructure born amid political rhetoric and a shower of federal, state and local dollars. As they did in the Eisenhower era, politicians are trying to outdo each other in standing up to the common enemy; communities pin their economic hopes on jobs related to the buildup; and large and small businesses scramble for a slice of the bounty. These mutually reinforcing interests are forging a formidable new "iron triangle." (Thomas 1994, A1)

The article quotes a securities analyst who had spent the weekend reading the Violent Crime Control and Law Enforcement Act of 1994 crime bill and put together a list of "theme stocks for the 1990s" with CCA at the top. It also quoted a New York assemblyman as saying prisons have become "the juiciest pork in the barrel." A member of the prison-industrial complex reflects that "it's easier for us to build prisons than to look at the causes of crime" (Thomas 1994, A1).

Diverse sources from more than a decade ago point to a prison-industrial complex and an iron triangle that drives policy. The prison-industrial complex differed from the criminal justice contracts of the 1980s only in scale, the privatizing of actual prison management, and private-prison-related IPOs. Without the IPOs, private prisons would have remained smaller, and states would have had to confront the results of their tough-on-crime rhetoric more directly. With the IPOs, billions of dollars from America's investor class flowed in to building prisons privately, which facilitated the construction of more prisons for America's poor and created a larger criminal justice–industrial complex to lobby for building even more.

Of course, the expansion of private prisons revealed a number of problems with their operations—riots, escapes, and human rights violations to name just a few. In response to these events and the media coverage of them, private prisons toned down their rhetoric about how poorly the government ran prisons and their own claims about superiority. The new talking points emphasized public-private partnerships and focused criticism on the contracts they had negotiated with government agencies. This implicitly put the blame on government when the companies tended to have the upper hand because they had more expertise with contracts than government did. Chapter 4 explores these issues through an analysis of many actual contracts and a bailout given to the industry during its darkest hour when CCA almost had to declare bankruptcy.

4

Confronting Problems

Blame Prisoners and Contracts, Then Get a Bailout

Even as Wall Street was hyping private prisons and raking in millions of dollars in underwriting and advising fees, problems started mounting with private prisons: financial overruns, prisoner escapes, escalating inmate violence, guard brutality, and a multitude of human rights violations. Promoters of operational privatization nonetheless managed to maintain their existence and growth. Perhaps the most famous incident in operational prison privatization is what Alan Mobley and Gilbert Geiss (2001) describe as the Youngstown Debacle, which occurred in 1998. The prison had been built on an abandoned industrial site sold to the Corrections Corporation of America (CCA) for $1. The city also offered the additional incentive of 100 percent tax abatement for three years to attract the company to the economically depressed area. Court and financial pressures on the District of Columbia led to the decision to transfer seventeen hundred medium-security inmates to the CCA prison operated in Youngstown, Ohio. Within fourteen months of the facility's opening, there were two fatal stabbings, forty-seven assaults, twenty of them involving knives, and six escapes.

CCA employees' various responses to these incidents are revealing and contradict the initial claims made by promoters of operational privatization. First, a CCA board member commented, "The idea was to move folks to a much safer environment than Lorton. That's all we had to do" (Shichor and Gilbert 2001, 214). CCA spokesman Peggy Lawrence added, "The company does not believe the Youngstown prison is less safe than other facilities. Prisons are violent places and this facility is being run the way it needs to be run" (Eyre 1998). Yet information from Virginia's Corrections and Criminal Justice Coalition (CCJC) revealed a different story. Overall, Ohio State prisons had forty-eight thousand inmates, with twenty-two stabbings in the past year and no murders; CCA's Youngstown prison had seventeen hundred inmates, twenty stabbings, and two murders. In other words, the early claim that private prisons are of better quality turned into a claim of equal quality. A CCA board member further commented, "We had some problems early on that we have addressed and will continue to address, but we will never be a problem-free facility" (C. Montgomery 2000, A1). He added that "glitches were to be expected, [as] this is relatively new" and referred to the incidents as the normal "growing pains" of an institution in its start-up phase (C. Montgomery 2000, A1). But most prisons starting-up operation do not have such problems, and this event occurred more than ten years after CCA's congressional testimony claimed 160 years of prison-management experience (see chapter 2).

Promoters of operational privatization pointed to the nature of prisons as violent, drawing upon the accepted stereotypical image of prisons and thus deflecting fault from the company and privatization. In addition, the company further deflected charges of mismanagement by scapegoating individual employees. For instance, CCA warden Jimmy Turner told lawmakers in a later investigation that what had happened the day of the escapes "was human error. The decisions that people made that day were wrong" (Morse 1998, 5). Turner told the lawmakers a female employee helped the inmates get the wire cutters used to cut through the fences, one guard was in the restroom, and other guards were out of position. The promoters' initial claims of professionalism and experience were under attack, but again the company successfully maintained those claims in an inventive twist. CCA board member Thompson told the *Washington Post* regarding the events at Youngstown that CCA officials had replaced the warden with Turner, who had ten years' experience. Turner pointed to the innovative practices implemented by CCA following the escapes: "Additional razor wire and more sensors are being installed, along with a watch tower. The number of perimeter guards is being doubled and disciplinary action is pending against the guards who weren't at their assigned posts" (Morse 1998, 5). Adding the needed expert opinion to boost this rationale, Charles Logan (1990) pointed out, "In no area have I found any potential problem with private prisons that is not at least matched by an identical or a closely corresponding problem among prisons that are run by the government. It is primarily because they are prisons, not because they are contractual, that private operations face challenges" (1990, 5). Finally, a besieged CCA put out a press release denouncing its critics and insisting that privately managed prisons pose no greater a safety risk than publicly run facilities (Trevison 1998).

When it was later suggested that the violence at Youngstown was in part a result of moving prisoners so far from their families, CCA officials denied this was the case. However, the company went on to use that charge to gain support for a proposal with the Federal Bureau of Prisons (BOP) (which has jurisdiction over D.C. prisoners) to house D.C. inmates after Lorton's court-ordered closing. Then D.C. mayor Marion Barry supported CCA's proposal to build on the forty-two-acre site formerly owned by the National Park Service. "It's not close to anybody's house. It's not close to anybody's neighborhood," commented Barry (C. Thompson 1998a, A8). Ward 8 resident Wanda Lockridge, leading the group supporting the new prison, pointed out the logic: "I have family members in the system, and I certainly don't want to travel across country to see them. I support it and I support it in Ward 8" (C. Thompson 1998a). For its part, CCA officials invited Mayor Barry to conduct motivational speeches in its facilities and promised the residents of Prince George County Ward 8 a $1 million fund for minority business loans, a vocational training institute, and a satellite campus for the University of the District of Columbia (*Washington Post*, June 13, 1998). CCA's new marketing strategy began to emerge: private corrections as a public-private partnership. A CCA board member said, "I think what a community like Ward 8 needs is a partner like we want to be to help them with jobs. It's good for us and the system" (C. Thompson 1998a, A8).

Despite the claim of partnership, the BOP would ultimately decide on CCA's proposal for Ward 8. The only city-level decision makers that had any say in CCA's plan for the new prison were the members of D.C.'s Zoning Commission. Concurrently, the findings of the D.C. corrections investigation of the events at Youngstown were being revealed. The four-month review found an array of problems. The District's contract with the facility was flawed from the outset; it imposed weak requirements on the corporation and contained minimal provisions for enforcement. Both the District and the company improperly classified inmates, mixing medium- and maximum-level prisoners, and "almost all staff of the jail, especially supervisors, lack[ed] correctional experience. In spite of the commitment and enthusiasm of line staff as a group, they [were] not yet sufficiently experienced and trained for their duties" (C. Thompson 1998b, B7). Finally, the report addressed the lack of responsibility shown by D.C. corrections officials: until it was under the political spotlight and in federal court, "the department took little responsibility for its role of monitoring the operations at the Northeast Ohio Correctional Center (NOCC)" (King 1998, A23). Midway through the investigation, CCA officials announced that the company would no longer comment on its operations and would focus instead on their "safety and security."

In a further attempt to manage the claims-making activities of opponents, CCA sought a federal court gag order. Asked by CCA's lawyers to bar public comment by inmates or their attorneys, a U.S. district court judge denied the order. However, CCA was likely able to control inmate comments informally. Testimony of Alex Friedman, a former inmate in a CCA facility, before the Ohio House State Government Committee reveals the techniques of inmate comment control: "When I tried to voice complaints I was subjected to cell searches, a retaliatory transfer and a guard tried to recruit other inmates to beat me down because I refused to withdraw a grievance" (Schroeder 2001). Friedman, after appearing in a cover story in *The Nation* criticizing CCA operations, was abruptly transferred to another facility after being accused of "a deliberate effort to disseminate material which is negatively oriented to the prison operating company" (Bates 1998, 13). Silencing inmates who were detractors became corporate media-access policy (Palmer 2001).

When it was revealed that official company reports seriously underreported the number of violent attacks in the Youngstown prison, Cincinnati civil rights attorney Alphonse A. Gerhardstein and Jonathan Smith, executive director of the D.C. Prisoners' Legal Services Project, pointed out, "We've been screaming for months for someone to do something about this. We've been ignored. And because we've been ignored, people died" (C. Thompson 1998d, J1). Furthermore, the complaints about operational privatization were ignored from the very beginning. Despite detailed testimony about the horrific conditions in the CCA prison presented by prisoners' rights advocates and by prisoners' family members prior to the D.C. council's approval of the contract with CCA to house the district prisoners in Youngstown, the council approved the contract without a single dissenting voice (*Washington Post* 1997). Despite the Youngstown debacle, multiple violations of health and safety regulations, and numerous reports of staffing problems and escapes, Wall Street analysts continued to praise CCA. "It's revenues are expected to grow at a 40 to 50 percent pace through 1999. CCA is the Mercedes Benz of private prison companies" (Tatge 1998e, 1A).

CCA was not the only private prison company experiencing problems. Within a year of opening two prisons in New Mexico (1998), Wackenhut Corrections Corporation's facilities were the site of riots, nine stabbings, and five murders, one of a guard. A Wackenhut spokesperson explained the reason for the troubles: "New Mexico has a rough prison population" (Palast 1999). Pointing out that prisons across the country are violent places whether private or public, Wackenhut managed to obtain two additional contracts following the guard's murder. State Senate president Manny Aragon had once fiercely opposed proposals that sought to privatize the state's prison system. However, in 1998, he signed a consulting deal with Wackenhut and simultaneously reversed his opposition, leading the way for the two additional contracts (Center for Public Integrity 1999).

All of these incidents caused private prisons to backtrack on their claims of superiority. Running prisons, they now claimed, was difficult, and they had no more difficulties in this environment than governments did. Private prisons maintained this claim even in spite of evidence, like with Youngstown, that they did have more difficulties. Further, and luckily for them, questions never surfaced in the right places about how their business model makes them more susceptible to problems. For example, because of overhead costs (see chapter 5), private prisons need to pay labor less than governments do, which leads to higher turnover and thus less experienced staff. Further, private prisons are more aggressive than government in replacing people with technology like cameras, so they are more likely to experience disturbances that result from pushing this strategy too far.

The other major damage-control talking point was the claim that private prisons are bound by the terms of their contracts. In other words, if there are problems, they result from the contracts' restrictions; thus government mismanagement is indirectly to blame. Therefore, we turn to an examination of the contracts. The first section below places the contracts in context, and a second section reports on the results of our analysis of a number of contracts obtained (with difficulty) under the Freedom of Information Act. Examining the terms of the contracts is a lucrative lesson in the ongoing operations of the facilities and the opportunities for corruption, abuse, and neglect; it is also a necessary step in our endeavor to follow the money. Finally, this chapter looks at the "bailout" of the troubled industry by the federal government by way of lucrative contracts and an escalating number of detained immigrants.

A BETTER WAY: PUBLIC-PRIVATE PARTNERSHIPS

In response to problems at CCA facilities, spokesperson Susan Hart suggested, "Let's all be working together to come up with the best solution" (J. Thompson 1996). Apparently, the problem was not low wages, high turnover, and minimal staffing; what was needed was "a better way to privatize." When the hype about superiority and managing an entire state prison system (see chapter 2) was no longer tenable, the rhetoric became about public-private partnerships. This framing accomplished two very important tasks for operational privatization. First, the problems encountered or created by operational privatization, including those at Youngstown, became the result of a lack of communication or cooperation between government and the company. Thus, the cause was not company mismanagement, and the company was not at fault. Rather, the problems were of a shared nature that could be fixed if the government would do its part. Second, because the problem was of a shared nature, the cost for fixing it, either through contract monitoring or passing legislation, was the responsibility of government. In other words, operational privatization was only in need of tweaking on the part of the government. The CCA was suggesting that if the contracts were written better or legislation was in place, these problems would not happen.

This redefining of the problem promoted by industry executives prompted some state-level activity, yet in the end perpetuated the use of private prisons. Ohio passed a state law requiring that contracts contain a provision specifying that criminal offenses in the facilities be reported to authorities. Similarly, following escapes in Houston in 1996, State Senator John Whitmire proposed legislation that included provisions for billing private prisons for law enforcement help received during escapes or uprisings. Wisconsin established the Contract Monitoring Unit of the Department of Corrections (DOC) two years after it began contracting with CCA to house its prisoners out of state. The unit, according to Senator Gwendolyn Moore, was established to ensure that the company complied with the tenets of the contracts. In 1998, two years after it started doing business with the company, the state hired six inspectors and two medical monitors in response to the multitude of complaints from inmates and their relatives. According to the senator, the company was in violation of numerous contractual agreements, including safety and health requirements. By 2000, Senator Moore was calling for an independent compliance audit of the $45-million-a-year contracts. Although the monitors found a multitude of serious contract violations and had spoken to the company about them, the company continually failed to make any necessary changes. "Contract monitors do not appear to *require* that private prisons change their behavior. Instead, monitors merely encourage changes in the way in which the prison is managed," Moore commented (Special Report on Wisconsin's Prisoners 2000). Furthermore, added Moore, "Despite the numerous violations, the DOC has never fined or threatened to cancel contracts with any of these facilities over their failure to fulfill their contracts. Failing to respond to these violations only encourages the private facilities to further disregard their contractual obligations." Finally, Moore pointed out what had been one of the early concerns about state dependence on the private prison industry: "Currently, it would be impossible to place the 5,000+ inmates housed in private prisons into Wisconsin facilities since Wisconsin's prisons are already overcrowded" (Special Report on Wisconsin's Prisoners 2000).

In 1997, the release of a videotape of guards abusing Oklahoma and Missouri inmates housed in a Texas county jail operated in part by Capital Correctional Resources, Inc., prompted Oklahoma and Missouri to cancel their contracts with the company—but not to end contracting with private prisons all together. In fact, Oklahoma moved its inmates from the Texas facility to a CCA prison in Oklahoma. Legislators in Oklahoma reasoned that they could effectively deal with or prevent any problems by keeping their inmates in their own state and by carefully writing and thoroughly monitoring contracts. In 1998 Oklahoma House Bill 1053 (HB 1053) specified facility location restrictions (not near schools) and eligibility criteria for inmates. HB 1053 also provides evidence of the effectiveness with which the public-private partnership idea was taking hold in so far as it allowed for the DOC to train the private guards: "The DOC shall charge a reasonable fee for such training, not to exceed the cost of the training" (Beutler 1999).

The state thus subsidized expenses that should appear on the cost side of the private company's balance sheet by providing the service at or below its own cost. Further, Oklahoma, Louisiana, and Missouri have added an additional contract requirement that is a result of framing the cause of violence in prisons as the mixing of prisoners from different states. These states now require that companies separate inmates from different states.

In August 2000, two inmates escaped from a CCA facility in Bartlett, Texas. According to investigators, doors had been left unlocked, and no one was watching the closed-circuit monitor. When the alarm sounded, staff turned it off and did nothing. Following that, Texas began including language in its contracts pertaining to staff training. After more than ten years of doing business with CCA, the state of Tennessee passed legislation requiring all vendors to create contract bids that were at least 5 percent less than the cost for the government to incarcerate its own prisoners (Herron 2004). Ohio added the 5 percent savings requirement statute in 1999 following the events at Youngstown (Hallett and Hanauer 2001). Texas has required at least a 10 percent savings since it began using private prisons. However, calculating cost savings has proven difficult, if not impossible (Fox 1998).

The private prison industry had been claiming—and continues to claim—savings of 10 to 15 percent. However, research on the cost savings as a result of operational privatization raises questions about the level of savings and where they are. According to an Abt report, "Some proponents [of privatization] argue that evidence exists of substantial savings as a result of privatization. Indeed, one asserts that a typical American jurisdiction can obtain economies in the range of 10–20 per cent. Our analysis of the existing data does not support such an optimistic view" (McDonald et al. 1998, iv). In a 2001 report for the U.S. Department of Justice's Bureau of Justice Assistance, James Austin and Garry Coventry concluded that "there are no data to support the contention that privately operated facilities offer costs savings; similarly no definitive research evidence would lead to the conclusion that inmate services and the quality of confinement are significantly improved in privately operated facilities" (2001, 7). In August 2000, state officials in Utah abandoned a plan for that state's first fully privatized prison after concluding that it would be cheaper to rent space in county lockups (Gehrke 2000). The studies contradicted the most compelling rationale for prison privatization: the promise of big savings. But the industry leader dismissed the importance of these studies by insisting that it had not tried very hard to save tax dollars. "When you're in a race and you can win by a few steps, that's what you do," said CCA's Doctor R. Crants. "We weren't trying to win by a great deal" (Bates 1998, 13).

When critics of the industry raised complaints about prisoner idleness and the failure to achieve early claims of employing inmates, the industry countered with the suggestion that it was the government's fault. "We follow the directives of the states, but ultimately it is the states that decide, when setting contracts, how much is offered" (Smalley 1999b). In other words, blame for failure to meet early claims of innovative practices did not lie with the company; rather the company was a victim of the state's constricting contracts. At this point we turn to an examination of the components of the contracts and how, during the litany of troubles, efforts were made to tweak them. The end result of these efforts reveals two important conclusions. First, early contracts were quite vague to give the industry room to "innovate"; more restrictive language entered the contracts only after serious problems arose. Second, the industry is quite creative in proposing language that allows it to generate revenue above and beyond the basic cost for inmates.

Understanding Contracts

Obtaining contracts to analyze for this chapter was difficult, time-consuming, and expensive (see box 4.1). We ultimately reviewed twenty-one contracts private firms made for local jails and state prisons; we have waited several years for contracts signed by the Federal BOP, which had not been delivered at the time we finished writing this book. While the main point here is to review the content of the contracts themselves, it is worth noting that the process of obtaining them exposes the lack of transparency in this process. Citizens who want to know the terms on which their government is entering into contracts and spending state money may find obtaining this information an up-hill battle, often won long after it is too late to take action. Someone hoping to learn more about a private prison in his or her area will also have difficulties.

BOX 4.1 USING THE FREEDOM OF INFORMATION ACT TO OBTAIN CONTRACTS

The quest to obtain copies of private prison contracts began with a simple question: What is in them? What does a contract involving the deprivation of liberty look like? We had no idea that question would lead us down a costly, frustrating, and time-consuming path. We began with a phone call to the industry leader requesting a copy of one specific contract. We were told to make a formal request. We did. The response was disappointing but not unexpected: the company denied our request and said, "These are corporate documents that are not likely to be shared with the general public." But the contract is only partially a corporate document; it is also a government document. So, an enterprising graduate assistant called the county clerk's office and requested a copy of the contract. We received it one week later—at no charge! The next two years were not quite so easy.

After making multiple phone calls to no less than fifteen government agencies, spending tens of hours in electronic phone directories, and being placed on hold, redirected, and ultimately denied, we began filing Freedom of Information Act (FOIA) requests. FOIA is a federal law that requires the production of many government documents requested by citizens. While state laws differ from the federal FOIA in their titles and language, most are similar regarding what is exempt and how information requests get processed. We submitted a request to the Texas Department of Criminal Justice for copies of contracts with Corrections Corporation of America. We were denied. While a straightforward request for "contracts the State of Texas has with the Corrections Corporation of America" allows the agency to readily identify relevant documents, we were informed that processing required specific contract numbers. We were caught in a catch 22: without copies of the contracts, we could not get the numbers, and without the numbers we could not get the contracts.

The American Federation of State, County and Municipal Employees, a leader in the opposition to private prisons, supplied us with the much needed contract numbers. We submitted our requests again. This time we received an acknowledgement that our requests had been received. However—and this is important for anyone attempting to obtain information—the law requires a timely response to the *request* for documents but does not require the actual requested information be provided in a timely fashion. We called to check on our request every week for months. First, we were told our request had "gone back into the queue" because of staff turnover. Months later we were informed that the documents were being reviewed to redact confidential information. Finally, we were sent an invoice for $145.00, prepayment required. Approximately eighteen months after we made our initial inquiry, we received the contract.

We continued to submit information requests in the hope that at least some of the agencies would not have that requirement. Several agencies responded that they would supply the information requested provided we pay copy costs and mailing up front, a standard aspect of FOIA. Ultimately, we were able to obtain twenty-one contracts, for eight different facilities including county jails, state prisons, and youth facilities: Hamilton County Jail (TN) 1984; Hernando County Jail (FL) 1988 and 2005; Bay Correctional Facility (FL) 1998 through 2005; Otter Creek, Marion, and Lee (KY) 1990 and 1992; Bartlett State Jail (TX) 1998 through 2006; and State of Utah, Division of Youth Corrections 1996. We are still waiting for contracts from the Federal Bureau of Prisons.

One issue of major importance regarding the future of similar research is the status of the Private Prison Information Act. This legislation would require prisons and other detention facilities holding federal prisoners or detainees under a contract with the federal government to make the same information available to the public that federal prisons and detention facilities are required to do by law. Introduced in 2005 and again 2007, this bill never became law. However, in July 2008 a Tennessee judge ruled that CCA was "essentially acting as a government entity and is subject to public records laws" as required by the state constitution (Associated Press 2008). The company promised an appeal. It is still too early to determine what effect, if any, this ruling will have on the ability of the public to obtain information.

Examining the contracts made us aware that the past and ongoing research regarding the cost savings of private prisons usually focuses on the daily cost of housing an inmate, so there is a glaring omission in that the legal costs associated with crafting a contract are not taken into account. This process starts with the cost of preparing the requests for proposals (RFPs, see chapter 3), which range from a few pages to several hundred; then there is the time the state needs to review the proposals submitted by private prisons, the resulting contract negotiations, and the review of the contract terms by legal teams. As an indication of the bulk of material that an RFP may generate, nine responses to a design-build-operate proposal in one state filled more than eighty file boxes and produced more than eighty rolls of drawings (W. Collins 2000). The earliest contracts were thirty-five- to fifty-five-page legal documents. These costs to government are not calculated in the simplistic cost savings estimates of privatization proponents and naïve researchers.

Beginning with one of the earliest (1988) through more recent contracts (2005), major items emerge that are directly related to cost and quality. Compensation and the provision of adjustments to compensation are most directly related to cost. However, maintenance requirements, staffing, and the provision of contract monitors emerge as contractual categories that serve as an avenue to boost industry profits and directly impact the quality of services. The sections below review these topics.

Compensation

The area of compensation is fraught with guarantees for private prisons and adjustments that can be costly to government. The contracts specify a per diem rate of pay (see chapter 3), calculated based on the average daily census for the month. For example, the 1988 Hernando County contract specifies a rate of $28.75 per inmate per day. It also guarantees payment for at least 160 inmates regardless of whether or not the inmates are actually there. As time passes, the guarantee of payment for a minimum number of inmates, regardless of their actual existence, becomes standard language of the contracts. For example, the 1998 contract with Bay County, Florida, guarantees $53.50 per inmate per day and promises to pay as if the facility is 90 percent full regardless of the actual number of inmates. The result is payment for nonexistent inmates, referred to as ghost inmates. In addition, over time the contracts add a clause that significantly increases the per diem if the facility is one person over 90 percent full; for each inmate over 90 percent capacity the company is paid $74.97 per inmate per day. This structure encourages governments to keep the number of inmates below the 90 percent they are paying for, thus boosting company profits. Paying for a certain capacity, regardless of the number of inmates, is defended on the basis of the "flexibility" it allegedly gives to government (although it likely has more to do with lobbying and campaign donations). Someone concerned about wasting the taxpayers' money should ask for a more thorough explanation of the benefits, especially when accompanied by high costs for a single inmate over the 90 percent capacity (which seems to undermine "flexibility").

This guaranteed minimum payment becomes particularly problematic for comparative cost analysis. When a state or local facility has an empty bed, taxpayer costs are reduced, but when that government entity contracts out under a system of guaranteed payments, taxpayers foot the bill for empty beds. If a state pays $40 per inmate per day with a guarantee of 300 inmates but only houses 250 inmates, then the correct cost figure should be $48 per inmate per day ($40 per day times 300 inmates equals $12,000 total cost, divided by the 250 inmates actually being housed). The logic of this contractual language sets up two striking and costly situations. First, it is possible that it reduces the use of alternatives to incarceration insofar as states may say, "We have room, and we are paying for it anyway, so lets use the prison." The second is equally troubling as it raises larger questions of sentencing policy. As long as the company maintains capacity over 90 percent, profit margins increase in addition to supporting the argument that more prison space is needed.

Contract adjustments are an additional component of compensation that results in substantial profit increases. The earliest contracts spanned a period of two to three years. Each year the compensation rate increased at no less than 2.5 percent and no more than 6 percent. This increase was determined through the use of the implicit price deflator (IPD), a measure of the change in prices of all new, domestically produced, final goods and services in the U.S. economy. There was no guaranteed drop in per-inmate price if the IPD indicated a move in the negative direction. By 1994 the use of IPD and other economic measures to set price increases had all but disappeared from the contracts and was replaced with guaranteed increases ranging from 3 to 4 percent. Contract durations also changed to an average of five years. In 2004, CCA received a per diem increase of 4 percent each year regardless of the fact that the IPD for that year was 2.76 percent. In 2005, the Office of the Inspector General (Florida) determined that even though the law required that per diem rates be set on an annual basis, this was not done. As a result the state could not even begin to determine whether private prisons were meeting the legal requirement that they save the state a minimum of 7 percent (Internal Audit Report 2005, iii). Further, the auditor concluded that the state had overpaid CCA and GEO Group a total of $13 million (James 2005). Ultimately, GEO agreed to pay back some of the money, about ten cents on the dollar for its part of the overpayment.

Initial contracts allowed the company to contract with other governments to fill empty beds. The 1988 Hernando County contract even guaranteed that the government would assist the company in inmate shopping (again, this is a taxpayer cost not included in the cost-savings calculations). For its effort in selling beds, the county received 80 percent of the proceeds from bed rental. By 2005 there was a pronounced shift in the distribution of rental proceeds in the contract. Instead of the county's receiving 80 percent of rental proceeds, the company would retain 85 percent of the rental income. On the downside, if the county housed inmates in its own jails, a 100 percent per diem clause kicked in: if the local sheriff opted to use his own jail, even for an overnighter, and there was room for that inmate in the CCA facility, the county would have to pay the company as if every single bed in the company's jail were occupied (regardless of the number of inmates actually in the facility). As early as 1988, contract language protected the company from competition either from governmental agencies or other private companies. This clause remains constant through 2005: "The County agrees it will not house inmates eligible for commitment to the CCA, so long as the Detention Facility operated by CCA is not at capacity. . . . If additional Detention facility capacity is constructed by or for the County, both CCA and the County shall have the option to add the management of such additional capacity to this contract" (1998, 2005).

Facility Maintenance

Contractual language regarding facility use and maintenance has changed dramatically over time; however, the changes are not in the taxpayers' favor. As with the compensation-adjustment clauses, this area provides opportunities to increase the bottom line by shifting those costs to the government agency. Frequently, those costing out contracts only look to the per diem fee and do not add in these expenses.

For example, the 1998 contract between CCA and Florida to operate the Gadsden facility called for a per diem maintenance fee of $2.80 per inmate, or about $645,000 per year for routine facility maintenance and repair. However, the company records, when audited, revealed that the company only spent about $170,000 per year on maintenance and repairs. Over the five-year contract term, the state was billed and (it is important to note that the company overbilled them) overpaid the company by about $2.85 million. The company has yet to pay back the funds. It is important to remember that this overpayment is for only one facility and one contract. In 2005 Florida had largely privatized its juvenile detention system and had six privately operated prisons (Internal Audit Report 2005–6, 4–7).

Contract language regarding facilities maintenance is at the very least confusing. Take for example this from the 2005 Hernando County/CCA contract:

> CCA takes possession of the Detention Facility in an "as-is" condition, and CCA shall be liable for all costs of repairs, improvements and maintenance, including appropriate preventative maintenance, of the Detention Facility. The COUNTY shall not be obligated to make any repairs whatsoever to the Detention Facility or Movable Equipment except for major repairs or replacements of major components of the Detention Facility. (2005, 7)

Thus, the county is responsible for all major repairs to the facility. Remarkably, there is no process by which the county has a say in determining what constitutes a major repair. Moreover, this language is boilerplate; it appears, with a few minor changes, in a significant number of contracts and is not part of the cost-savings calculation so often touted by the industry and naïve researchers. Equally problematic is the lack of oversight regarding the contractual routine-maintenance responsibilities of the company. If a private prison company manages a government-owned facility and does not perform maintenance, the facility is returned to the government in poor shape and requires an infusion of money for maintenance and repairs. This occurred in 2005 when Tulsa County ended its contract with CCA for management of the county jail. The facility, according to the sheriff, had been neglected for the five-year period to the point that a minimum of $250,000 in repairs were needed (*Tulsa World* 2005). This was money over and above that already paid (unrecoverable) to the company, even though the contracts called for the submission of maintenance logs.

Governments that decide to contract out need to factor in all costs, and maintenance is a major item. Definitions of what the government is responsible for should be explicit. Maintenance logs and receipts should be required, with fines and penalties for noncompliance. Contracts should have "clawback" clauses allowing recovery of money given for maintenance but not expended by the company.

Contract Monitors

As mentioned above, most contracts require a contract monitor. However, this provision does not ensure contract compliance and often opens the door to additional problems. In most cases the government entity and the company agree on the selection of the contract monitor. In some cases (Texas) the monitor is on-site, while in others (Kentucky) he or she periodically visits the facilities. Both scenarios set the stage for potential problems. In Texas, for example, the Coke County prison (a juvenile facility), operated by GEO Group, won the "Texas Contract Facility of the Year" award in 1999 and 2005. In 2007, Coke County's four on-site contract monitors submitted their annual report, rating the facility a 97.8 out of 100 and thanked the Coke County staff and administration for the "positive work they do with the TYC youth" (McGonigle 2007, 2). A short six months later the Texas Youth Commission (TYC) ombudsman visited the facility and reported to the governor the facility's deplorable conditions, concluding that the juveniles were enduring squalor and deprivation. He reported a high degree of fear and intimidation, bug infestation, overreliance on pepper spray, and young inmates being kept in "malodorous and dark" security cells for five weeks. He found dirty mattresses lying on cell floors and a large infestation of spiders, beetles, and crickets crawling around the facility. Inmates told him their sheets and clothes had not been laundered in weeks or months. "Most of what I had seen had to be pre-existing for months if not years" (McGonigle 2007, 3).

Ultimately, the governor canceled the $8-million-per-year contract and transferred the youth to other facilities. The four contract monitors, having given the facility stellar ratings for the past several years, were fired. Per the contract, these monitors were state employees, paid by the state, and agreed upon by the company and the TYC. However, it was later revealed that three of the four contract monitors were former GEO Group employees. The state had hired two directly from GEO Group, and the third was a previous employee. Thus, the contract requirement of having monitors in place does not insure contract compliance.

This contract language does not prohibit, but rather encourages, the close relationship between the monitors and the company they are supposed to be monitoring. Given the rural location of most prisons, on-site monitors likely live in the same community, and off-duty social interactions probably make it difficult for them to report wrongdoing on the part of their friends and neighbors. This is the case even if they have an office "across the street from the facility" to lessen the possibility of their sympathizing with the company, as CCA's Richard Crane (2000) suggests in a publication on contract monitoring. For example, the Coke County prison, located in a one-stoplight town, was the town's second-largest employer after the school district. One-third of the school district's $6 million budget was tied to programs at the prison. Two of the fired TYC employees lived in the town; the former supervisor of the monitoring unit had two children in the schools, and her clerk was married to a member of the school board (McGonigle 2007).

Requiring periodic visits by off-site monitors is also problematic and costly. Crane's monitoring manual states that "the usual course is to advise the company of the monitor's schedule and purpose of the visit" (2000, 19). Given the remote location of facilities, monitors often schedule their visits in advance, which allows facilities to alter conditions and day-to-day operations prior to a visit. Agencies must be careful to calculate into the contract this cost. Alaska, for example, can only estimate the cost at $64,000 per year, while Oklahoma reports the cost is approximately $100,000 per year (Crane 2000).

Brian Gran and William Henry argue that "through the contractual components of formation, maintenance and liability, accountability may be enforced, social groups protected and justice pursued" (2007, 175). Further, they point out that contracts can be used to compel private companies to function like the government with respect to service provision. This "publicization"—the use of contracts to hold private firms accountable to public standards—they maintain, is one way to insure a proper public-private balance in the privatization of prisons. While that may be the case in an ideal setting, the current state of privatization does not lend itself to a proper balance. The mere existence of a monitor does not guarantee compliance. In fact, even the *How to Monitor* manual was written by an industry insider, Richard Crane, former legal counsel to CCA and current director of Cornell Companies. It is also significant that this industry was established and grew on the idea and promise that private companies could run prisons better than government. Clearly, if contracts are needed to "compel companies to function more like government" at the very least, then one of the primary arguments for opening the prisons to private industry has proven faulty.

The introduction of contract monitors and ombudsmen and the establishment of privatization commissions could have served as what Laura Dickinson (2007, 149) calls a necessary component in public-private partnerships: public participation. Allowing people affected by an activity input into how that activity is carried out, she argues, can be a mechanism for either accountability or constraint. However, Crane's recommendations on behalf of the Association of State Correctional Administrators directly oppose this idea. For example, Crane asserts that "interviews with inmates and staff are usually the least effective means of monitoring a facility" (2000, 16). He goes on to suggest that a monitor should refer inmate complaints to the inmate grievance system for resolution. This suggestion is based on the faulty assumption that inmates have access to a grievance process. The TYC Coke County incident discussed above demonstrates that inmates can possibly be denied this process.

Contract monitors are crucial parts of the process, even though there are problems with existing models. At minimum, monitors should not be close friends of those they are monitoring or immediate former industry employees. Employment contracts could stipulate a period after leaving the job during which the monitor would be ineligible for employment with private prisons. That should help prevent monitors from "going easy" on firms in the hopes of securing jobs. Monitors should be allowed to make surprise visits or to give minimal notice. Finally, significant fines need to be in place for contract violations. Having dutiful contract monitors does little good if a company faces few consequences for noncompliance. At minimum, the fine should be greater than the profitability of the contract violation—certainly higher than the $5,000 maximum penalty for any violation of the CCA/Kent contract in Kentucky.

Staffing

It is customary that RFPs or the resulting contracts contain language regarding staffing levels. At a minimum, staffing requirements state the ratio of staff to inmates. More developed contracts include language on types of staff (supervisors, shift commanders, line officers), including the number of staff on duty at specific times of day. Others include minimum training standards for officers, usually on par with American Correctional Association standards. More recent contracts include background-check specifications. On the surface, these contract developments appear to increase the standards according to which a privately run facility operates, or at least to raise them to a level comparable with those of publicly run facilities.

However, this too has become a profit-generating area that allows for cost shifting to the public. Billing for "ghost employees," similar to the ghost-inmate scenario described above, cost the state of Florida an estimated $4.5 million between 2001 and 2004 (Office of Inspector General 2005). This situation included billing the state for vacant positions. In addition, there remains some question as to overbilling with regard to overstating staff experience levels, so governments may be billed as if a supervisor were present rather than a line officer. Several contracts allow for companies to alter staffing requirements when necessary and bill the government at a lower rate, for instance, by replacing a registered nurse (RN) with a licensed practicing nurse (LPN). Predictably, this alters the level of care, but it also requires that the company report the replacement and make the necessary reductions in billing.

Where contracts include specific language regarding staff background checks, that language should also include specifics about what types of arrests, convictions, or other issues will eliminate an applicant from consideration for a position. Moreover, simply including language in a contract requiring a background check does not ensure compliance. For example, in 2008 federal prosecutors charged a GEO Group prison administrator with "knowingly and willfully making materially false, fictitious, and fraudulent statements to senior special agents" (Rosa 2009). An audit found that over a period of more than two years ending in 2005, GEO hired nearly one hundred guards without performing the required criminal background checks. The GEO employee responsible pleaded guilty. According to the plea agreement, the employee falsified documents "because of the pressure she felt" while working at the GEO lockup to get security personnel hired at the detention center "as quickly as possible" (Rosa 2009).

CONTRACTS ARE NOT THE PROBLEM FOR PRIVATE PRISONS

Neither carefully crafted contracts nor the addition of monitors, ombudsmen, and commissions resulted in more cost-effective, safer prisons. The idea that private-public partnerships would eliminate the industry's troubles was illusionary at best, costly and dangerous at worst. As government agencies took on the additional costs associated with contracts, private industry was able to turn the changes in contracts into profit opportunities by shedding costs, controlling monitors, and engaging in corruption, fraud, waste, and abuse. Ironically, early privatization proponents argued that these very same practices would be eliminated if only prisons were operated by private companies.

TROUBLES, BAILOUTS, AND
PROFITS FROM THE IMMIGRANT "CRISIS"

Negative media coverage about escapes, riots, human rights violations, and poor management, combined with the declining crime rate, slower growth in state prison populations, and the budget squeeze brought on by a stagnant national economy, all contributed to stalled growth in privatization. (This helps explain some of the creative adaptations to contract language.) Some states around the country overcame their capital shortages and started building their own prisons and filling those first. Other states revisited costly sentencing and parole practices. Georgia prison official Scott Stallings put it this way: "We don't have pressure on us now. We're not in crisis" (Slevin 2001, A03). In Oklahoma, corrections official Scott Hauck explains, "Incarceration rates are way down. We fill our own beds first and we've got quite a bit of space" (Slevin 2001, A03). Between 2000 and 2001, ten states reduced prison populations (Bureau of Justice Statistics 2002b). From 2000 to 2001, not a single state solicited private contracts (Greene 2001).

By late 2000 private firms were losing customers. California cancelled plans for four new five-hundred-bed prisons. New York failed to enter into contracts with CCA. Roughly two thousand privately owned beds sat empty in Colorado. CCA built two facilities in Georgia in the hope that prisoners would come, but the state of Georgia was not interested. North Carolina cancelled contracts with two CCA prisons out of frustration with staffing levels. Overall, CCA had about nine thousand beds sitting empty. Adding to these problems, fines and lawsuits were mounting. In March 1999, the company agreed to pay $1.6 million to prisoners and $756,000 in legal fees to settle the class-action lawsuit brought on behalf of the prisoners at Youngstown (Mattera, Khan, and Nathan 2004). A South Carolina jury ordered CCA to pay $3 million in punitive damages because CCA guards had abused the youth in their juvenile prison with use of force "repugnant to the conscience of mankind" (Mauer 2002, 101). North Carolina fined CCA over $1 million for chronic failure to meet contract requirements, followed by that state's terminating two contracts with the company. Finally, the company settled a $120 million lawsuit with investors angry about restructuring after problems with the Prison Realty Trust real estate investment trust arrangement (see chapters 3 and 5). A Louisiana judge ordered that the Wackenhut-operated Jena juvenile facility be shut down after it was determined that the youths in the facility were treated no better than animals. The justice department charged that conditions there were "life threatening," and Wackenhut eventually lost its contract. Texas officials fined Wackenhut $624,000 for chronic staff shortages and eventually terminated the contract with the company to run the Travis County jail amid indictments of guards for sexual abuse of prisoners. Arkansas took over two Wackenhut facilities after the company was criticized for sanitary conditions and prisoner idleness (Mauer 2002).

Clearly, operational privatization of prisons was at a pivotal moment in its history, with CCA near bankruptcy (see chapter 5) and Wackenhut losing contracts both nationally and internationally. Then, in what has been described as "a private prison bailout" (Greene 2001, 01), CCA was selected in 2000 for two new BOP contracts to house 3,316 inmates, with guaranteed payment for 95 percent occupancy regardless of the actual inmate population. CCA/Prison Realty stated that revenues from these contracts for the three-year initial term and seven renewal options of one year would be $760 million, "not including award fees." Further, "the facilities are eligible to receive a bonus of up to 5 percent of annual revenues for superior performance" (Prison Realty 2000a). J. Michael Quinlan, the former Federal BOP director, had been an executive of CCA, then Prison Realty, and became president when the companies combined again (see chapter 5).

By the end of 2001, $4.6 billion was pending in government projects with private prison companies. Private prison company executives were claiming that these federal contracts could result in billions of dollars. Wall Street analysts agreed. "My fundamental belief is that this is a growth industry," said Douglas McDonald, who works for First Analysis in Chicago (Zahn and Jones 2000). In 2002, CCA was rewarded again with a $103-million BOP criminal-alien contract to fill its struggling McRae Correctional Facility in Georgia (CCA Source 2003).

The industry, thanks to its relationship with and access to federal agency heads (see chapter 3's discussion of the iron triangle), found its savior in the Federal BOP and another marginalized population: "the criminal alien." Nearly three quarters, or 72 percent, of the growth in prisoners held in private prisons in 2000 occurred in the federal system (Ziedenberg and Schiraldi 2001). Between 1985 and 2000, the percentage of noncitizens in federal prisons increased from 15 to 29 percent, making immigrants the fastest-growing sector of the federal prison population (Bureau of Justice Statistics 2002a and b). And, as of 2000, 54 percent of noncitizen inmates had been convicted of a drug charge, 35 percent of an immigration offense, and 11 percent of other offenses. At the same time, the incarceration rate of those convicted of immigration offenses increased from 57 to 91 percent between 1985 and 2000, and the average time spent in jail increased from 3.6 months to 20.6 months. (The 1996 Immigration Act requires that foreigners facing deportation be jailed while awaiting a trial and verdict.) Once again, race and drugs were linked.

Both for government and privately operated prisons, the rapid growth in the number of noncitizens in U.S. jails, prisons, and detention centers for immigration and drug offenses contributed to the health of the prison economy in the United States. For example, in 1995 when Wicmico County, Maryland, needed to raise $65,000 in three days, the county jail warden "picked up the phone and called the INS [Immigration and Naturalization Service] and said, 'send me 70 inmates.' And it was done" (L. Montgomery 2000). And when jails run short on inmates, wardens can often depend upon the INS to fill empty beds, ensuring the fiscal solvency of the growing prison system. In 2000, the INS spent just over one-third of its $800 million detention budget renting beds in 225 jails throughout the country (L. Montgomery 2000). The private prison industry describes the Federal BOP as its favorite client. As John Ferguson, CEO of CCA, put it, "We treasure the Bureau" (Hallinan 2001). It should.

Perhaps the most shocking of all contracts was awarded on December 24, 2004. The Federal BOP awarded CCA $129 million to house twelve hundred criminal-alien prisoners at its facility in Youngstown, Ohio. (The same facility shut down in 2001.) U.S. Senator Mike DeWine (R-OH) described the deal, which guaranteed a 90 percent occupancy rate for the next four years, as "a great Christmas present for the Mahoning Valley" (Vindy.com 2004). Youngstown mayor George McKelvey (the same mayor who had called CCA deceitful just three years before) explained his yearlong effort to reopen the facility as the only way the region was going to get back the jobs lost when it closed. Another clear example of the corrections-commercial complex and the access to decision makers is Senator DeWine's membership on the Senate Appropriations and Judiciary Committee. He led the fight to secure the federal contract for CCA by speaking to high-ranking

BOP officials about the need for the federal government to consider using current prison facilities rather than build new ones. According to Mayor McKelvey, the contract could not have been awarded without the support of DeWine, U.S. Senator George Voinvoich (whose brother owns the VGroup, CCA's design and construction partner), and President George W. Bush, "who gave a big thumbs up to Youngstown" (Vindy.com 2004).

The panic over criminal aliens exploded after the September 11 attacks and added people of Middle Eastern descent to the list of marginalized populations on which the private prison industry feeds. The country's focus on the war on terror did for private prison companies in the 2000s what the war on drugs did for them in the 1990s: it provided raw materials, or what Angela Davis calls "bodies destined for profitable punishment" (1999, 2). The war on terror created a buzz in the private prison industry. Less than three weeks after September 11, a *New York Post* story on the for-profit private prison industry stated, "America's new wall of homeland security is creating a big demand for cells to hold suspects and illegal aliens who might be rounded up" (Tharp 2001, 35). Cornell Corrections CEO Steve Logan welcomed this new "business opportunity" in a 2001 conference call with analysts:

> I think it's clear that since September 11 there's a heightened focus on deten-
> tion. . . . More people are gonna get caught. So I would say that's positive. . . .
> The other thing . . . is with the focus on people that are illegal and also from
> Middle Eastern descent in the United States. There are over 900,000 undocu-
> mented individuals from Middle Eastern descent. . . . That's, keep in mind, half
> our entire prison population. That's a huge number, and that is a population,
> for lots of reasons, that is being targeted. So I would say the events of 9/11 . . .
> let me back up . . . the federal business is the best business for us. It's the most
> consistent business for us and the events of September 11 is increasing that
> level of business. (Choudry 2003)

As CCA noted in a 2002 annual report,

> We believe that recently proposed initiatives by the federal government in
> connection with homeland security should cause the demand for prison beds,
> including privately managed beds, to increase. The proposed funding [for
> homeland security] is intended to support the agency's efforts to prevent illegal
> entry into the United States and target persons that are a threat to homeland
> security. We believe that these efforts will likely result in more incarceration
> and detention, particularly of illegal immigrants, and increased supervision of
> persons on probation and parole. (CCA 2002a)

The growth in the number of immigrants behind bars stems directly from the 1996 Immigration Reform Act, the failed war on drugs, the Patriot Act, and fear of "criminal aliens," which together have subjected documented and undocumented immigrants convicted of minor offenses to long sentences followed by deportation. (President Barack Obama's administration has not shifted course on the federal criminal-alien solicitations for private prisons during the early months of his term; see the conclusion.)

By the summer of 2002, after the publication of "Federal Government Bails Out Failing Private Prisons" (Greene 2001) and a front-page story in the *Wall Street Journal*, the BOP cancelled four contract solicitations that were to be awarded in late 2002 and temporarily stopped awarding criminal-alien requirement (CAR) contracts. Cornell's stock price plummeted from $17.75 to $7.75 following the elimination of CARs. However, industry leaders expected growth. Cornell Corrections's Steve Logan stated that the federal government had asked the company to retain existing sites, especially around the border area. Also, industry representatives implied that new RFPs would be issued through the INS, Office of the Federal Detention Trustee (OFDT), and Department of Homeland Security (DHS) as soon as the dust settled from the current restructuring proposals (Carrillo 2002). By the time the dust settled in September 2003, Cornell was back in the money, and stock prices rose to $16.25.

During Wackenhut Corrections's 2002 second-quarter conference call for analysts, George Zoley explained that the restructuring of the INS and the creation of the DHS and OFDT would speed the pace of contracting for detention beds by providing greater flexibility to procure detention beds and services. The reorganization of the INS into the Immigration and Customs Enforcement Division (ICE), housed in the DHS, has been a boon for the private prison industry. The Office of Detention and Removal, a division of ICE headed by former BOP procurement executive Craig H. Unger, has a yearly budget of $615 million for contracting out immigrant-detention beds.

CONCLUSION

The industry's specific strategies for maintaining and perpetuating its existence from the mid-1990s to 2003 have evolved with changing political, economic, and societal conditions. The privatization script, which in the beginning touted its superior quality, now claimed equal quality. The industry that had sold itself by claiming, "We can do it cheaper and better" than government now claimed "We can do it just as well as" government. No longer were the proponents of operational privatization talking up the industry's innovative management. In fact, the innovation claim had also morphed into a claim of similarity: "Virtually everything in our institutions is run exactly as they are in our governmental customer institutions" (Land 2000). Again stressing the similarities in private and public prisons, Edwin

Meese III, a former U.S. attorney general and distinguished fellow at the conservative Heritage Foundation, told *National Journal*, "There have been problems, but these incidents are similar to things that go on in public prisons" (Smalley 1999b).

When its claims of high-level professionalism and experience came under attack, the industry saved face by scapegoating individuals and pointing out that problems should be expected in such a "new" area—even though they had earlier emphasized the long history of private contracts to argue that privatization was nothing new. At the same time, prison-privatization promoters highlighted their own flexibility to utilize innovative practices to deal with problems after the fact. These practices were not, however, innovative at all and were, in fact, identical to the responses to troubles in publicly run facilities. Advocates dealt with this contradiction by stressing that prisons by their very nature are violent, be they private or public, and that private industry was doing just as good a job as government. Additionally, the industry charged that many of their problems were similar to those of public facilities due to the constrictive nature of doing business with inefficient governments. The solution was to employ a better way to privatize the public-private partnership. This maintenance strategy of shifting rhetoric aided the perpetuation of prison privatization. The industry shifted the blame for the problems and therefore the attention to the contracts. An examination of the contracts reveals, however, that the industry was able to turn changes in the contracts into avenues for profit.

Despite such evidence, government agencies will have no choice but to use the services of firms such as CCA because prison overcrowding persists. For example, a 2002 report by a Jefferies & Company analyst, stated,

> Although the growth rate in incarcerations has slowed in recent years, the absolute number of inmates continues to swell. Unfortunately, facilities at both the state and federal level are overextended, making placement of new prisoners much more difficult. With state budgets lacking sufficient resources to fund the development of new prisons and jails and the federal government ramping up drastic homeland security efforts, something needs to be done. While lighter or alternative sentencing can alleviate short-term budget constraints, it does not address the outstanding overcrowding issue. Instead, increased utilization of private prison capacity and services appears to be a logical choice. (Jefferies & Company 2002, 3)

Indeed, throughout its substantial troubles and nearly fatal, self-inflicted wounds, the industry remained a major player and a permanent fixture in American corrections. On the local level, the industry continued to align itself with criminal justice decision makers through the use of campaign donations. However, the courting of decision makers became more aggressive in the form of consulting and lecture fees. In the face of financial difficulties, the industry relied on its connections, the political side of the corrections-industrial complex, its ability to influence federal legislation through access to agency heads, and the high levels of racialized fear in American society for its much-needed raw materials. We examine the ongoing search for raw materials among marginalized populations and the strategies to secure them in light of current economic downturns in the conclusion.

Although the reality is that the use of private prisons will continue, we believe it important to think critically about the rationales given for privatizing. In particular, the deep-seated idea that business is more "efficient" than government generates skepticism toward research that finds no evidence that private prisons save money. So, chapter 5 examines some of the overhead costs incurred by private prisons to raise questions about how they can provide the same service as government and turn a profit. We focus on costs that governments do not incur, like mergers, acquisitions, corporate restructurings, and executive pay.

5

A Critical Look at the Efficiency and Overhead Costs of Private Prisons

One important argument in favor of privatizing holds that business is more efficient than government, which has too many rules and regulations; government means "red tape," and private business cuts through it. At times, that belief becomes ideological conviction with an almost religious fervor. The belief can also be considered a mere assumption open to investigation as to whether private prisons are truly more efficient than public departments of corrections. "Efficiency" is a general term that can have a variety of meanings, but an important element would involve having lower overhead costs. Costs are "overhead" when they do not relate directly to producing a good (like a car) or a service (like managing a prison) and thus have to do with upper-management and administration. Executive salaries are part of overhead, as are transaction costs and delays involved with accomplishing tasks related to the business.

In general terms, the Corrections Corporation of America (CCA) states that

> the Company's general and administrative costs consist of salaries of officers and other corporate headquarters personnel, legal, accounting and other professional fees (including pooling expenses related to certain acquisitions), travel expenses, executive office rental, and promotional and marketing expenses. The most significant component of these costs relates to the hiring and training of experienced corrections and administrative personnel necessary for the implementation and maintenance of the facility management and transportation contracts. (1998b)

While both public and private prisons publicize jobs and careers, a state's department of correction does not need to engage in promotion and marketing; any advertising aims to deter people from committing crimes rather than to fill prison beds. State departments of correction also do not engage in acquisitions in the same way corporations do with mergers; nor do they need to pay the fees for such activity. Ironically, among the biggest costs in contracting out to the more-efficient private sector is the high pay for the person who writes the contracts—and the state must also devote resources to the contract process (see chapter 4).

Further, chapter 3 noted that "going public" for private prisons involves many costs, from corporate restructuring to underwriting fees. Then, there are increased costs for having publicly traded stock. At the time Cornell Corrections went public more than ten years ago, the company stated that it had increased "general and administrative expenses of $300,000 for the year ended December 31, 1995, and $150,000 for the six months ended June 30, 1996, to reflect estimated cost increases associated with the Company becoming publicly held" (Cornell 1996). The private prison business requires responding to requests for proposals (RFPs, see chapter 3), which involve costs to prepare—and some will not successfully secure revenue. Back in 1993, Esmor Correctional Services noted the out of pocket cost to respond to an RFP can "range from $50,000 to $100,000" (1993). A year later, Wackenhut Corrections Corporation stated that "the Company incurs costs, typically ranging from $10,000 to $75,000 per proposal." Further, "the Company may incur substantial costs to acquire options to lease or purchase land for a proposed facility. In the past, the Company's option costs in responding to RFPs have ranged from approximately $20,000 to approximately $200,000" (Wackenhut 1994). If the contract is not awarded, the costs for the RFP and options to buy land for developing a prison become losses. Then, there are all the lobbyists and campaign contributions needed to persuade the government to write the contract.

All of the costs listed above are unique to private prisons as the state, before contracting out, does not have to deal with RFPs and the related activities. This chapter further explores the overhead costs and efficiency of private prisons. In some areas, like salary, we present comparisons between state departments of correction and private prison executives. We chose executive pay because the data were available and more easily understood than other measures of indirect costs and efficiency. CCA and GEO Group have compensation committees that hire consultants to help them benchmark executive salary at a sample of publicly traded peer companies of similar size and within the services industry classification. So, executive pay at CCA and GEO Group is comparable to other executive pay, but the amount of pay difference in excess of a government salary is overhead cost—and requires much lower overhead elsewhere or impressive efficiencies, or both, just to recoup that difference and turn a profit. The first section below focuses only on the top two positions in state bureaucracies and private prisons, so it doesn't aim to provide a comprehensive calculation of overhead. Instead, it shows the magnitude of difference and raises the concern that the wages of the people who work in the prison, the largest fixed cost, get squeezed to make up for high executive salaries and fees related to dealing with Wall Street. Top executives at private prisons make substantially more than their state counterparts, while those at the bottom are paid less than those working for the government, so inequality is one of the by-products of contracting out.

The second section takes a closer look at the efficiency of private prisons by reviewing attempts by CCA and GEO Group to do initial public offerings (IPOs) for prison real estate investment trusts (REITs). As explained briefly in chapter 3, these are entities that own real estate and pay no federal corporate income tax on the rent if they distribute most of their income to shareholders. CCA had an especially bad experience involving shareholder lawsuits, a stock price of $0.19 per share, and near bankruptcy. This extreme case, which involved multiple restructurings, sheds light on the larger legal and financial environment in which private prisons operate.

EXECUTIVE PAY

Many critics have noted that private prisons pay guards less and thus have high turnover, which creates problems in the facilities. This is why unions like the American Federation of State, County, and Municipal Employees oppose privatization. However, another angle to the problem also deserves exploration: executive pay. When private prisons pay executives substantially more than their government counterparts and pay guards less, contracting with a private prison directly contributes to income inequality. Further, examining the level of executive pay and the process by which it is set raises questions about the efficiency of private prisons. It might also provide useful context for reading the research findings that private prisons provide little or no cost savings.

The Securities and Exchange Commission (SEC) requires disclosure of executive pay each year, so part of the data necessary for a comparison is readily available on the agency's website. We used the annual report of private prison companies to see how many inmates or prison beds they had under management, then looked at Bureau of Justice Statistics (BJS) data to find states that housed approximately the same number of inmates. We then submitted Freedom of Information Act requests to those states to learn the annual salaries of the top department of corrections officials. As an additional point of comparison, we came up with a rough measure of the amount of money for which state correctional officials were responsible and the annual revenue of the private prison company.

Executive pay is broken down into many categories, and tables 5.1 and 5.2 provide a simplified version of what is reported to the SEC for CCA and GEO Group, respectively. The tables are simplified in that the "Stock Options and Awards" category includes several types of stock awards. The "All Other" category includes what both companies call a "nonqualified deferred compensation plan" through which the company matches a certain amount of pay that executives wish to defer for retirement. It also guarantees them a fixed rate of return on that money, with CCA paying 7.5 percent on contributions. GEO Group also includes tax gross-ups, which are payments companies make to executives to cover the income tax on other payments companies have made to executives. According to a tax law professor, the tax gross-ups are themselves taxable, so companies need to throw in additional tax gross-ups to cover the previous gross-ups. "The spiral ends when the ever-decreasing amount of new income reaches zero, or close to it. The bottom line: Grossing up an executive for taxes on $1 million can easily cost an additional $700,000 to $900,000" (Caron 2005). CCA does not specifically mention tax gross-ups in its filing on compensation, but another filing states that the Compensation Committee "may provide for additional cash payments to participants to defray any tax arising from the grant, vesting, exercise or payment of any award" (2007a). Additional items in the "All Other" category include life insurance, automobile allowances, and club dues.

Because we are interested in overhead costs, we will not include stock awards and options in our final comparisons. Debate rages over what the reported value of stock and option awards should be and what the actual "cost" to the company is. We note, however, that there are company costs related to stock registration and transfer and the administration of stock and option awards programs. Also, companies sell shares in secondary offerings to the public (see chapter 3) to raise money, and shares awarded to executives limit the number that can be sold to the public, indicating that awarding them to executives exacts an opportunity cost in forgone income.

Both tables include "Incentive Plan Compensation," which we will include in our calculations. To get more favorable treatment under IRS guidelines, this payment is not called a bonus and is mainly tied to the company's achieving certain performance targets (although it can also be related to certain individual accomplishments as well). Our review of previous SEC filings found that in each year from 2002 to 2007, the top executives of both CCA and GEO Group received incentive pay equaling between 72 and 222 percent of their base salary. Further, CCA states that "the *target* for bonuses was set at 75% of base salary" (2008, emphasis added). GEO Group (2008b) states that the target amount for the CEO is 150 percent of base salary. Finally, while the SEC requires companies to state at the beginning of the year the specific numbers the company finances must

Table 5.1. Corrections Corporation of America: Two Highest Executive Salaries, 2007

Principal Position	Salary	Stock Options and Awards	Incentive Plan Compensation	All Other	Total
John D. Ferguson: president, CEO, and vice chairman of the board	$712,249	$943,190	$1,068,374	$107,328	$2,831,141
Richard P. Seiter: executive vice president and chief corrections officer	$295,075	$632,826	$422,613	$40,138	$1,410,652

Source: CCA 2008b. Seiter was the second-highest paid because Irving Lingo stepped down as executive vice president, chief financial officer, and assistant secretary. He would have been paid more than Seiter if his resignation had not resulted in the forfeiture of his incentive plan compensation for that year.

Table 5.2. GEO Group: Two Highest Executive Salaries, 2007

Principal Position	Salary	Stock Options and Awards	Incentive Plan Compensation	All Other	Total
George C. Zoley: chairman of the board, CEO, and founder	$873,269	$933,388	$1,842,750	$210,794	$3,860,201
Wayne H. Calabrese: vice chairman, president, and COO	$613,654	$564,467	$1,036,152	$67,211	$2,381,484

Source: GEO Group 2008b.

meet in order for the bonus to be awarded, both companies note that they can disregard certain expenses when figuring whether the company met its goal: "Non-recurring and unusual items not included or planned for in our annual budget may also be excluded from net income after tax in the sole and absolute discretion of the Compensation Committee" (GEO Group 2008b). So, while in the strictest sense an incentive payment is not guaranteed, both expectations that some amount will be awarded and mechanisms to help insure that it is exist.

Future tables reporting on salary will thus include the total of salary plus incentive plan compensation plus all other pay. Payments in the form of stock and stock options will not be included so that the best comparisons can be made with what state officials make. This means that for 2007, the top wage earner at GEO Group made about $2.9 million, and the top wage earner at CCA made almost $1.9 million. For 2007, the second-highest wage earner at GEO Group made about $1.8 million, and the second-highest earner at CCA made almost $778,000. In calculating the second-highest earner's pay, we used only data for people who had a reported salary for the full year. Someone starting a certain executive position part way through the year may have a higher annual salary than is reported in the table, but this person would not receive that full amount, having only served in the position for part of the year. Thus, these tables may underrepresent the extent of difference between private prison executives and public officials. (The appendix discusses how the reader can access current filings for the most up-to-date executive pay of private prison officials.)

Making a fair comparison of government departments of corrections and private prisons requires matching them according to size. We use two measures. The first is based on the number of inmates in prison, which is generous to private prisons because states have probationers and parolees to deal with as well as prison inmates. CCA and GEO Group are not involved in these aspects of corrections (although the conclusion to this book notes that they certainly see them as important future markets). Because some states have contracts with private prisons, the number of inmates in private prison is subtracted from the reported number of inmates in state prison. Once again, this is a generous assumption for private prisons because the state department of corrections must still prepare the RFPs, review them, negotiate and monitor contracts, and deal with any problems that arise from placing state inmates in private prisons. Even if not involved in the day-to-day provision of services, the state is ultimately responsible for the inmates.

The second measure to help compare size looks at the amount of money top executives are responsible for managing—what we will call fiscal responsibility. For the states, the BJS reports direct current outlay for corrections, as well as capital outlays, which usually relate to prison construction, expansion, or renovation. Even though it would be appropriate to include this figure under fiscal responsibility, the direct current outlay allows for the best comparison with the total revenue of private prisons. (Private prisons both borrow money and have secondary stock offerings to raise money for activities that include prison construction, but financial data are not reported in a way that allows for a straightforward comparison with the states' direct and capital outlays.)

Table 5.3 presents the results of these comparisons for the highest wage earner in state departments of corrections and private prisons; table 5.4 presents findings for the second-highest wage earner. Even after making many assumptions favorable to private prisons, table 5.3 indicates that private prison executives are paid ten to twenty times as much as people running departments of correction for state governments. For example, putting aside the more than 200,000 people Michigan had on parole and probation, the state had 51,577 inmates under supervision—slightly less than the 54,000 the GEO Group had. Michigan paid its director of corrections $145,000, while GEO Group paid its top executive more than $2.9 million. Putting aside the nearly 280,000 people Florida had on probation and parole, the state had more than 86,000 inmates under supervision—more than the 72,000 CCA had. Florida paid its secretary of corrections $128,750, while CCA paid its top executive almost $1.9 million. Cornell Corrections only had 17,000 inmates under supervision, about one-quarter the number New York had, but the top earner at Cornell made about $1 million, while New York's public official made $157,000. Cornell has revenues of $360 million; New York has $2.3 billion in direct outlays for corrections. Putting aside the 120,000 inmates on probation and parole, Washington State has roughly the same number of inmates as Cornell, but the top wage earner at Cornell made about $1 million, while Washington's secretary was paid $141,552.

It is not surprising that executives in the private sector earn more than those in public service, but the degree of the difference in pay is noteworthy. Earlier filings, which reveal executive pay for years when the private prison companies were much smaller, also highlight this difference. For example, Wackenhut went public in 1994 and paid its president and CEO $190,000 when it had 11,414 inmates under supervision and total revenues of $105 million. This is more than the executive director of the Texas prison system made in 2007 ($165,000) for supervising more than 153,000 inmates, handling a parole and probation caseload of more than 532,000, and overseeing almost $3 billion in direct expenditures. Likewise, in 1993, the president and CEO of Esmor Correctional Services made $179,621 when the company had 829 inmates under supervision and annual revenue of $14.2 million.

The disparities for the second-highest wage earner reported in table 5.4, though not quite as extreme, are still significant. Using the same comparisons

Table 5.3. Top Wage Earner in Public Departments of Corrections and Private Prisons, 2007

State/Company	Position	Salary	Inmates under Supervision	Parole and Probation	Fiscal Responsibility: State Budget/Company Revenue (billions)
GEO	Chairman of the board, CEO	$2,926,813	54,000	—	$1
CCA	President, CEO, vice chairman of the board	$1,887,951	72,000	—	$1.5
Cornell Corrections	Chairman and CEO	$1,007,538	17,413	—	$0.4
California	Secretary	$225,000	172,365	520,299	$6.4
Texas	Executive director	$165,000	153,489	532,020	$3.0
New York	Deputy commissioner	$157,069	63,315	176,419	$2.3
Michigan	Director	$145,000	51,577	201,136	$1.7
Georgia	General counsel	$131,908	47,717	445,748	$1.3
Florida	Secretary	$128,750	86,619	277,767	$2.4
Ohio	Director	$118,205	47,086	261,559	$1.9
Washington	Secretary	$141,552	16,607	120,687	$0.9

Notes: Executive salary includes salary, plus incentive pay, plus "other"; it excludes stock and option awards—see text for discussion. For Georgia, the top wage earner was the director of medical services ($168,300), and Florida had a senior physician paid $154,266, so this table only includes the top wage earner engaged in corrections management. The salary for Florida's secretary of the Department of Corrections is for 2008. The top official in the Federal Bureau of Prisons made $205,312 in 2007. This BOP official was a regional director, who most likely made more than the director because of years in service. Because the region is unknown, statistics on prisoner, parole, probation, and fiscal responsibility were unavailable, and so the federal BOP is excluded from this table.

Sources: State salaries derive from Freedom of Information Act requests. Executive compensation for private prisons comes from GEO Group (2008b), CCA (2008b), and Cornell Corrections (2008b). Prison population numbers for states as of December 31, 2006 are from the Bureau of Justice Statistics (2007c, table 1 minus appendix table 4 [number of inmates in private facilities]). Private prison population numbers are for the year ending December 30, 2006, from GEO Group (2007), CCA (2007b), and Cornell (2007). State expenditures on corrections from 2006 are from Bureau of Justice Statistics (2008a, table 4, "Justice System Expenditure, by Character, State, and Type of Government, Fiscal Year 2006 [Direct Current Outlay—Excludes Capital Outlays]. Private prison revenue for the fiscal year ending December 30, 2007, comes from the 10-K filings for GEO Group (2008a), CCA (2008a), and Cornell (2008a). Parole and probation figures come from BJS (2007b, tables 1 and 3).

Table 5.4. Second-Highest Wage Earner in Public Departments of Corrections and Private Prisons, 2007

State/Company	Position	Salary	Inmates under Supervision	Parole and Probation	Fiscal Responsibility: State Budget/Company Revenue (billions)
GEO Group	Vice chairman, president, and chief operating officer	$1,817,017	54,000	—	$1
CCA	Executive president vice president and chief correctional officer	$777,826	72,000	—	$1.5
Cornell Corrections	Chief financial officer and treasurer	$366,607	17,413	—	$0.36
Federal BOP	Director	$197,200	193,046	113,929	$5.1
California	Undersecretary for programs	$158,760	172,365	520,299	$6.4
Washington	Deputy secretary for correctional operations	$138,500	16,607	120,687	$0.9
Georgia	Commissioner	$128,993	47,717	532,020	$1.3
Texas	Deputy executive director, director of financial services, and director of correctional institutions (three separate positions, same salary)	$128,124	153,489	176,419	$3.0
Michigan	Administrator for parole and probation, regional administrator (two separate positions, same salary)	$115,027	51,577	201,136	$1.7
Florida	Deputy secretary	$114,177	86,619	445,748	$2.4
New York	General counsel	$110,202	63,315	277,767	$2.3
Ohio	Assistant director	$96,692	47,086	261,559	$1.9

Notes: Executive salary includes salary, plus incentive pay, plus "other"; it excludes stock and option awards—see text for discussion. For Georgia, the top wage earner was the director of medical services ($168,300), and Florida had a senior physician paid ($154,266, so this table only includes the second-highest wage earner engaged in corrections management. Salary for Florida's deputy secretary of the Department of Corrections is for 2008. The Federal BOP director is the second highest paid; a regional director made $205,312 that year, probably because of a higher number of years in service.
Sources: See table 5.3. The figure from the Federal BOP is the 2007 estimate from the Department of Justice's Budget website at www.usdoj.gov/jmd/2008summary/html/024_2008_comparison.htm.

we made for table 5.3, the number two at GEO Group made $1.8 million compared with about $115,000 for the number two in Michigan's Department of Corrections; the second highest at CCA made almost $778,000, compared with about $114,000 for the second highest in Florida's Department of Corrections. In terms of historical comparisons, Esmor noted that it had a consulting agreement with William Banks for

> developing and implementing community relations projects on behalf of the Company and for acting as a liaison between the Company and local community and civic groups who may have concerns about the establishment of the Company's facilities in their communities, and government officials throughout the State of New York. As compensation for his services, Mr. Banks receives an amount equal to 3% of the gross revenue from all BOP, state or local correction agency contracts within the state of New York with a guaranteed minimum monthly income of $4,500. . . . [In] 1992 and 1993, Mr. Banks earned approximately $135,000 and $175,000, respectively. (1994)

So, back in the early 1990s, a consultant working in New York State for a small private prison company earned a salary about equal to that of New York's commissioner of corrections and higher than that of the state's second-highest-paid correctional official in 2007.

The pattern of public and private pay would hold for many positions beyond the top two reported here. Private prison companies report four to seven executive officers who receive more than $1 million in compensation or close to it. Further, in addition to executives, CCA and GEO Group have boards of directors whose members receive annual retainers plus pay for serving on committees and attending meetings. Directors who are not executives of CCA (so-called independent directors) receive $50,000 a year. With additional payments for committee work (discussed below), CCA had ten directors who made between $69,000 and $89,000 in 2007. Directors who are not executives of GEO Group receive $60,000 a year. With the additional payments for committee work, GEO Group had five directors who made between $68,800 and $97,100 in 2007. Being a director is not a full-time job. Most executives have other jobs, serve as directors of other companies, and/or do consulting work. As a point of comparison, median household income in 2007 was $50,233 (Census Bureau 2008, 5), so the pay for the part-time director position of a private prison was higher than that earned by half of all U.S. households from all their employment responsibilities.

While tables 5.3 and 5.4 present a great deal of information about annual executive pay, several other features are important to note for a full understanding. First, like most businesses, private prisons provide generous severance packages when contracts are not renewed. For example, in early 2009, GEO Group renewed contracts with several top executives, including

Chairman and CEO George Zoley. The agreement states that "the executive will be entitled to receive a termination payment equal to the following: (i) in the case of Mr. Zoley, 5 (five) times his annual base salary at the time of such termination together with any gross-up payments" (GEO Group 2009c). The prior agreement was for twice base salary. The new contract also increased his salary to $935,000 and stipulated that "under no circumstances shall the cost of living increase be less than 5% per annum" (GEO Group 2009b). Severance also includes "the continuation of the executive benefits (as defined in the employment agreement) for a period of ten years." Further, "the New Employment Agreements provide that upon such termination of the executive, GEO will transfer all of its interest in any automobile used by the executive pursuant to its employee automobile policy and pay the balance of any outstanding loans or leases on such automobile so that the executive owns the automobile outright." Finally, "if any payment to the executive there under would be subject to federal excise taxes imposed on certain employment payments, GEO will make an additional payment to the executive to cover any such tax payable by the executive together with the taxes on such gross-up payment" (GEO Group 2009c).

Such payments do not apply if the executive is fired "for cause," which includes acts like fraud or embezzlement against the company, "a felony or a crime involving moral turpitude," infringements of confidentiality or noncompetition agreements, or "gross negligence or willful misconduct that causes harm to the business and operations of the Company"(GEO Group 2009a). The final statement was in the contracts of the CEOs of many financial institutions that failed in 2008 and 2009. They were allowed to keep the severance payments because although they were fired for making bad decisions that drove the companies into ruin, their behavior did not rise to the level of "gross negligence or willful misconduct." Severance payments also do not apply for basic resignation, but executives do receive severance if they quit for "good reason," that is, if they quit because of a reduction in their executive power, a cut in their pay, or a move of the executive's office of more than fifty miles (GEO Group 2009a).

Second, unlike public officials, executives are eligible for "change-in-control" payments, such as after an acquisition or significant changes to the board of directors. The next section discusses how this applied to CCA, while here we note that this event happened in 2002 to what was then Wackenhut Corrections Corporation (WCC). A Danish multination security and correctional services company called Group 4 Falck acquired the Wackenhut Corporation, parent of WCC; thus, a majority interest, meaning control of WCC, transferred from Wackenhut Corporation to Group 4 Falck. (WCC then purchased all of their shares owned by Group 4 Falck and changed their name to GEO Group.) The change-in-control event meant that under their employment contracts, executives received "Change in

Control payments equal to three times the sum of the executive's annual salary as of the first day of the first month following a Change in Control and the annual bonus payment paid to the executive for fiscal year 2001, but payable in 24 equal consecutive monthly payments during an initial two-year employment term" (GEO Group 2003). For Zoley, this meant a payment of three times his 2002 salary of $632,500, plus his 2001 bonus of $373,500. That is a payment of $2.271 million over and above his regular salary.

Executives also received, as part of the change-in-control compensation, "all of WCC's interest in any automobile used by the executive and the payment of the balance of any outstanding loan or lease on such automobile." Finally, the executive was also entitled to "an acceleration of [his or her] retirement age from age 60 to age 55 and, upon reaching such accelerated retirement age, payment of the present value of all payments due under the Executive Retirement Agreements" (GEO Group 2003). So, for a change in control that did not affect the terms of their employment, all executives received a substantial lump sum on top of their regular salaries, a car, and accelerated retirement payments. Note that if any of the executives had been fired as a result of the change in control, the severance payments discussed above would have been paid out *in addition to* the change-in-control payments just discussed. (The term *golden parachute* refers specifically to this combination of generous severance and change-in-control payments for the ousted executive.)

The larger perspective on executive pay is best articulated in Lucian Bebchuk and Jesse Fried's Harvard University Press book *Pay without Performance: The Unfulfilled Promise of Executive Compensation* (2004). The "official view" of executive compensation is a "principal-agent" model in which shareholders delegate authority to the board of directors, which creates compensation packages that produce an "optimal" alignment of the interests of shareholders and executives. In contrast, Bebchuk and Fried argue for a managerial power model because frequently directors become "captured" by the CEO (directors want to keep their lucrative directorships and have the executives help them secure additional directorships, and so forth). The principal-agent model suggests that the executive "is paid just enough to keep him from going to another firm. In contrast, the level of pay in the managerial power approach is set as high as possible, with an upper bound on pay determined by public perceptions" (Weisbach 2007, 423). Put another way, in the managerial power model, executive pay is set as high as possible, subject to a public "outrage constraint."

Certain aspects of executive pay attempt to give executives incentives to manage well for the longer term, but other aspects of executive pay are hidden. "If managers are setting their own compensation subject to an outrage constraint, then compensation would be structured to minimize outrage" (Weisbach 2007, 425). One notable example of pay awarded to minimize outrage is deferred compensation plans, which are inefficient from a corporate tax perspective and "allow executives (but not other employees) to defer compensation until retirement, and typically guarantee a rate of return well in excess of market rates" (Weisbach 2007). In this respect, remember that both private prison firms had this system, and CCA guaranteed a 7.5 percent return. Tax gross-ups are another way to "camouflage" the amount of a payment, and GEO Group states, "The executive retirement agreements also require us to make tax gross-up payments with respect to the retirement payments in aggregate amounts that ensure that the executives receive the full amount of their retirement payments on an after tax basis" (2009b). Executives due, say, $2 million will receive enough that their after-tax payments will still be $2 million. (Remember that "grossing up an executive for taxes on $1 million can easily cost an additional $700,000 to $900,000" [Caron 2005].)

Before leaving the topic of executive pay, we must briefly examine the process for setting executive pay because it sheds light on both the "efficiency" and overhead costs (in addition to the pay itself) of the private sector. Executive pay comprises many parts and is far more complicated than the usual salary and benefits. Publicly traded firms, including private prisons, have a compensation committee that sets the company's "compensation philosophy." Based on this philosophy, every year the committee then sets the base salary; the measure of earnings for the performance targets for incentive pay; the specific amount of earnings tied to 50, 75, and 100 percent (and so forth) of base pay; systems for distributing and vesting stock awards and for distributing stock options; and levels for other payments. Incentive pay for executives can also be tied to nonfinancial criteria, like overseeing the successful implementation of a new system. As box 5.1 notes, however, incentive pay should not be tied to the absence of human rights abuses in company-run prisons, the achievement of fair labor standards, or other criteria related to social responsibility.

Members of the compensation committees of both CCA and Geo Group receive compensation in addition to their annual pay for serving on the board. For CCA, the chairman of the compensation, nominating and governance receives a fee of $5,000 annually and $2,500 per meeting. Other members of the committee each receive $2,000 per meeting. In addition, according to CCA's filings, the "Committee's compensation consultant and legal advisors" typically attend Compensation Committee meetings (CCA 2008b). And, "beginning in 2000 and continuing through 2008, the Committee has engaged PricewaterhouseCoopers LLP ('PwC') to assist it in reviewing the Company's compensation strategies and plans." For GEO Group, the Compensation Committee chair receives $5,000 annually, and each committee member receives $1,200 per meeting. In 2004, GEO Group hired Towers Perrin for consulting on executive pay, and "the Compensation Committee intends to periodically retain a nationally recognized independent compensation consulting firm in order to conduct updated reviews of our named executive officer compensation" (GEO Group 2009c).

BOX 5.1   GEO SAYS NO TO SOCIAL RESPONSIBILITY CRITERIA FOR EXECUTIVE COMPENSATION

Chapter 3 noted that the GEO Group and other private prisons argued against shareholder proposals for greater transparency for political contributions (box 3.2). The same group of shareholders, activist nuns, had previously introduced a proposal to make social responsibility—prisoners' human rights, health care standards, and fair labor, for example—criteria that should figure into executive pay. GEO Group argued against the proposal. The final count was 234,930 in favor and 7,294,538 against (GEO 2005b). The proposal mentions the American Legislative Exchange Council (ALEC), which is discussed in chapter 3 and the conclusion of this book. Here is the full proposal (GEO 2005b).

Proposal 4
Incorporate Social Criteria in Executive Compensation
Mercy Investment Program, 205 Avenue C, #10E, New York, New York 10009, beneficial owner of 200 shares of GEO stock, and The Province of St. Joseph of the Capuchin Order, 1015 North 9th Street, Milwaukee, Wisconsin 53233, beneficial owner of 272 shares of GEO stock, have co-filed the following shareholder proposal:

WHEREAS:

The size of executive compensation has become a major public as well as corporate issue. We believe that boards, in setting executive compensation, should consider a company's social as well as financial performance.

The relationship between a company's executive compensation and social responsibility is an important issue. For instance, should the pay of top officers be reduced if there is evidence that a company is associated with a pattern of unlawful discrimination or poor environmental performance, especially if the result may be damage to the company's reputation, costly fines, or protracted litigation?

The privatization of corrections services has raised concerns about the degree of public oversight over their operations, including:

• The quality of healthcare services in privately run facilities. See, "Hidden Hell: Women in Prison," *Amnesty Now* (Fall 2004), at 10.
• The role and propriety of the American Legislative Exchange Council (ALEC), funded in part by private prison companies, in advocating tougher sentencing laws in Wisconsin and other states. See, e.g., "Tough-on-Crime Measures Increase Prison Population," American Radio Works, http://americanradio works.publicradio.org/features/corrections/laws4html. See also, Karen Olson, "Ghostwriting the Law," *Mother Jones* (September/October 2002).

These and similar questions deserve the careful scrutiny of our Board and its Compensation Committee. Many companies are now using social responsibility criteria in setting executive compensation. For example, more than twenty-five percent of Fortune 100 companies report that they integrate workplace diversity or environmental criteria in setting their compensation packages; and several—including Chevron, Texaco, Coca Cola, and Proctor & Gamble—report that they use both of these criteria. At least seventy percent use at least one social responsibility criterion.

Tying social responsibility to executive compensation will provide a strong incentive for our Company's executives to improve its performance in the area of social responsibility. Social criteria, for example, may be added to the list of factors already noted in the Compensation Committee Charter (2004) that are used to determine the long-term incentive portion of CEO compensation. Further, such criteria are consistent with the objectives listed in our Company's Code of Business Conduct and Ethics (2004).

RESOLVED:

The shareholders request that the Board's Compensation Committee, when setting executive compensation, include social responsibility as well as corporate governance financial criteria in the evaluation.

SUPPORTING STATEMENT

We recommend that the criteria include:
1. Protection of the human rights of prisoners—civil, political, social, environmental, cultural and economic—based on internationally recognized standards.
2. Consistent standards for health care and safety with particular emphasis on inmates experiencing HIV/AIDS, mental health problems, pregnancy, and cancer.
3. Compliance with fair labor standards so that employees and their supervisors are trained appropriately and compensated justly for the management of immigration facilities, prisons and prisoners.
4. Services that are fairly priced for inmates and their families, e.g., telephone calls.

GEO's board of directors recommends a vote AGAINST the adoption of this proposal for the following reasons:

We believe that this proposal is unnecessary. Our executive compensation is already determined by the Compensation Committee of the board of directors which is comprised exclusively of independent directors, in accordance with the rules of The New York Stock Exchange. Our Compensation Committee considers all facts and circumstances which, in its business judgment, are appropriate in ensuring that our executive compensation is set at appropriate and competitive levels. This flexibility gives our Compensation Committee the latitude that it needs in order to ensure that our executive compensation policies are designed to maximize shareholder value over the long term and to attract, motivate and retain top executive talent. In undertaking its efforts, the Compensation Committee is separately advised by a nationally recognized, independent compensation consulting firm.

Based on our Compensation Committee's annual review of our executive compensation policies, we believe that our executive compensation programs adequately take into account all factors relevant to determining appropriate executive compensation. We also believe that our executive compensation policies are competitive and consistent with those at comparable companies, align executive compensation with our shareholders' interests, and link pay to the performance of the individual and the company. We believe that the shareholder proposal could have the effect of limiting the amount and type of compensation that could be offered to our senior executive officers, which would prevent us from aligning the interests of our senior executives with those of our shareholders, and put us at a competitive disadvantage for hiring and retaining top executive talent. The Compensation Committee's report explaining the criteria for executive officer compensation is included in this proxy statement beginning on page 22.

For these reasons, the board of directors unanimously recommends a vote AGAINST this proposal. The proxy holders will vote all proxies received AGAINST this proposal unless instructed otherwise.

EFFICIENCY

The ideology of government outsourcing rests on the belief that the private sector can do a better job and more cheaply than government because business is efficient, whereas government bureaucracy entails red tape. Though this belief is no doubt true at times, a critical examination of how it applies to private prisons must consider corporate restructuring, mergers, and acquisitions. While departments of correction do restructure, the process usually involves changes in the organizational chart, not extensive legal documents as is the case with the private sector. For example, chapter 3 noted that many corporations restructure in order to go public. Esmor Correctional Services notes in its IPO document that the company was incorporated in Delaware the month before the IPO, and before that it "operated as seven affiliated corporations all with identical shareholders" (Esmor 1993). Under the stock-transfer agreement drawn up to restructure for the IPO,

the stockholders of Esmor Management, Inc, Esmor (Brooklyn), Inc, Esmor Manhattan Inc, all of which are New York corporations, Esmor (Seattle), Inc, a Washington Corporation, Esmor New Jersey, Inc, a New Jersey Corporation, Esmor Texas, Inc and Esmor Houston, Inc, both of which are Texas corporations, (collectively referred to as the 'Affiliated Corporations') will transfer all of the outstanding shares of the Affiliated Corporations to the Company solely in exchange for 2,500,000 shares.

The IPO assumes the "effectiveness" of this process, and Esmor is waiting on "an opinion of tax counsel that there will be no tax consequences" from this restructuring (1993).

In addition to restructuring, private prisons engage in acquiring other companies, something the state departments of correction do not do. Acquisitions involve resources to locate suitable companies and perform "due diligence," which includes examining the company's finances and operating procedures. If the acquisition progresses, negotiations must be conducted regarding pricing and terms, with legal documents drawn up and filed with the SEC. One early Pricor acquisition involved buying "three California corporations which together conduct business as 'Advocate Schools.'" The cost was $4.7 million, and "the Company incurred $698,951 of costs related to the acquisition"; plus, "an additional $1,000,000 was paid for non-competition agreements" with former managers of those firms (Pricor 1987). The noncompetition agreement prevents these people from working for or consulting with any companies that could potentially compete with Pricor. Cornell was one company whose growth strategy mentioned acquisitions, and it listed as a risk factor that "no assurance can be given that the Company will be able to successfully integrate the operations and personnel of [recent acquisitions] with those of the Company on a profitable basis" (Cornell 1996). This final point highlights not just the risk from acquisitions but the expense incurred after the purchase to integrate the company, personnel, and finances.

Further, the rewards for growth in the private sector are far richer than they are in government service, which can lead to troublesome episodes. Chapter 3 briefly discussed the prison REITs in terms of the amounts of money they brought into the prison-industrial complex and the large number of Wall Street investment banks that involved. That chapter also briefly noted problems caused by these new corporate structures, and we return to that issue now to consider the multiple restructuring and shareholder lawsuits. This episode raises questions about the efficiency of private prisons in their quest to expand and the overhead costs of such endeavors. While it is not a typical period and does not reflect only usual business costs, we believe this extreme episode provides a revealing look at the legal and financial environment in which private prisons operate.

In April 1997, the CCA filed an IPO so that CCA Prison Realty Trust could go public "to capitalize on the opportunities created by the growing trend towards privatization in the corrections industry" (Prison Realty Trust 1997). Prison Realty Trust is an REIT, a vehicle created by federal tax law for owners of land and buildings. REITs pay no federal corporate income tax if they meet certain criteria like having a minimum number of shareholders and paying out 95 percent of their profits to shareholders. Because profits are not taxed and a substantial portion of them are paid out, REITs can be popular with shareholders. The Prison Realty Trust's IPO document notes an intention to pay shareholders $1.70 per share per year, which is 8.1 percent based on the $21 per-share IPO price. The share price can rise or drop, but this substantial dividend is attractive to investors because there should be an 8 percent return even if the share price does not change.

This move was helpful for CCA, which had conducted its IPO eleven years before, as a way to capture another significant infusion of cash. The

Prison Realty Trust prospectus states that CCA will receive $308 million from Prison Realty Trust for the purchase of nine facilities, with more cash if Prison Realty exercises options to buy more prisons in the future. Indeed, by the time CCA filed its quarterly report in August 1997, Prison Realty had bought ten facilities for $378 million, which allowed CCA to pay off $183 million in debt and earn some interest on part of the remaining amount (CCA 1997).

An REIT's income can only come from rent of land and buildings, so the idea is that Prison Realty will buy facilities from CCA, which it will lease back to CCA to manage. Note that at this point, the government contract with a private prison now also involves a contract that the private prison has with another entity essentially run by the same people. Although technically Prison Realty is a separate company, CCA is listed as a coregistrant on Prison Realty's SEC forms, and the prospectus notes, "As a result of these transactions, the Company and CCA will have several ongoing relationships after the Formation Transactions, some of which could give rise to possible conflicts of interest" (Prison Realty Trust 1997). Because Prison Realty has no operating history, the IPO document contains the required pro forma information, or results, as if it has been operating for the past year. This involves estimates of rental incomes from CCA, expenses for Prison Realty, and so forth. Based on the assumptions the company made, Prison Realty's pro forma financial statements suggest that for 1986 they would have had $41 million in revenue and turned a profit of $28.4 million.

While the prospectus contains some discussion of prisons and overcrowding, there is comparatively little discussion of criminal justice or privatization issues since this is largely a real estate–based venture. However, the extensive list of risk factors notes that Prison Realty Trust is dependent on CCA for revenues, which in turn means all the risk factors for CCA apply to Prison Realty Trust. For example, the short-term nature of contracts is a risk factor, as are the lack of assurance about renewal and the dependence "on government agencies supplying those facilities with a sufficient number of inmates to meet the facility's design capacities" (Prison Realty Trust 1997).

One of the major non-CCA risk factors was that Prison Realty will be taxed as a regular corporation if it fails to qualify as an REIT. If it fails to qualify, the company will be subject to federal tax, in which case it will be forced to reduce the distributions to shareholders and cannot qualify as an REIT for the next four years. Prison Realty's "lack of operating history and management's lack of experience in operating in accordance with the requirements for maintaining its qualification as a REIT" are part of the reason for the risk. Another facet is that Prison Realty must rely on tax counsel to negotiate "the application of highly technical and complex Code provisions" to qualify as an REIT. Indeed, the prospectus contains a seven-page "summary of material federal income tax considerations" relating to REIT requirements. It also lists four firms that have offered legal advice related to the proposed sale of shares (Prison Realty Trust 1997).

Since CCA successfully raised money by spinning off an REIT, Wackenhut decided to do the same. It formed Correctional Properties Trust in February 1998 "to capitalize on the growing trend toward privatization in the corrections industry by acquiring correctional and detention facilities from both private prison operators and governmental entities" (Correctional Properties Trust 1998). The company planned to use $113 million in proceeds to acquire eight prisons. Seven of these would be purchased from WCC and one from an entity called the Wackenhut Lease Facility for 122 percent of their initial cost. (Because of the requirements of certain government leases, a subsidiary called Wackenhut Corrections Corporation RE [Real Estate] Holdings handles certain leases.) Eighteen pages of the Correctional Properties Trust prospectus covers REIT qualification and tax status. For failure to qualify, "the Company might be required to borrow funds or liquidate certain of its assets to pay the applicable corporate income tax (and interest thereon plus the amount, if any, of penalties) arising from the Company's failure to maintain its status as a REIT" (1998).

For both CCA/Prison Realty and Wackenhut/Correctional Properties, doing business requires a large number of documents to specify the relation between companies that are supposed to be separate. The REIT can only make money from rent, and the IRS imposes a number of other restrictions to make sure companies do not restructure one part of themselves to avoid paying federal tax. Thus, the private prisons and their REIT counterparts establish operating companies, purchase agreements for the prisons, option agreements for future prison purchases, leases between the REIT and private prison company, and a right-to-purchase agreement so that the private prison can buy back the prisons if the REIT sells them in the future. Even though the private prison companies and their respective REITs share some executives and board members, the prospectuses suggest that rents from "related parties" undermine the qualification as an REIT, and "the applicable attribution rules, however, are highly complex and difficult to apply" (Correctional Properties Trust 1998).

In April 1998, CCA and Prison Realty Trust drafted a fifty-page merger agreement that would combine the two companies, even though Prison Realty Trust had been public by itself for a year (CCA 1998a). The accompanying press release quotes Doctor R. Crants, chairman of both companies, as saying, "The resulting company structure will combine the tax and dividend benefits of a REIT with the high growth prospects of a quality growth company to produce an exceptional investment opportunity." Specific benefits include a "stronger balance sheet" and "marketing synergies."

Because REITs can only receive rent, "after the merger, management of the REIT's facilities and contracts will be undertaken by three newly-formed private companies, all operating under the name of Corrections Corporation of America."

In September 1998, an amended and restated merger agreement was approved. Prison Realty Corporation was created from the mergers of CCA and Prison Realty Trust. Box 5.2 summarizes the details of the merger in the company's words. The box does not detail all the external transactions necessary to complete the merger—including the exchange of CCA stock for Prison Realty Corporation stock, the exchange of Prison Realty Trust common and preferred stock for Prison Realty Corporation stock, the conversion of bonds of many types and dates from both companies to Prison Realty Corporation bonds, and the conversion of all bank debt and credit facilities—in addition to the holding of shareholder meetings for both companies and the preparation of voting materials. Each of the companies hired a consultant to certify that the exchange ratios were fair. There were also legal expenses related to the transactions and whether the structure of the proposed merger could continue to qualify the company as an REIT. The annual report notes some $26 million in merger costs as a single line item on the financial statement (Prison Realty Corporation 1999b). That may or may not include $3.5 million to settle a lawsuit filed by a shareholder skeptical that the merger represented shareholders' best interests. The settlement required better disclosure of certain aspects of the merger and limits on payments from Prison Realty Corporation to the privately owned operating company that CCA would become. Because the privately held CCA would be run by the same executives as the publicly held Prison Realty Trust, shareholders were concerned that conflicts of interest (noted above) might lead executives to make deals benefiting the private company they owned rather than the shareholders of the public company they ran.

BOX 5.2   PRIVATE-SECTOR EFFICIENCY?

The text of this chapter reviews all the activity involved in corporate restructurings with an eye to highlighting their costs and providing some insight into the process. In simplifying this process for readers whose main interest is not corporate transactions, we run the risk of undermining our point about how involved these transactions are. So, here we present a summary of the 1998 merger as described by the company in its SEC filing (Prison Realty Corporation 1999b). This summary has itself been edited for brevity. This book's companion website has a link to the full filing; see PaulsJusticePage.com > Punishment for Sale.

The Merger-Related Transactions are summarized as follows:

On December 31, 1998, immediately prior to the Prison Realty Merger and in connection with the CCA Merger, CCA sold to a newly-formed management company, Correctional Management Services Corporation, a Tennessee corporation ("Operating Company"), all of the issued and outstanding capital stock of certain wholly owned corporate subsidiaries of CCA, certain management contracts and certain other non–real estate assets related thereto and entered into the Trade Name Use Agreement with Operating Company. In exchange, CCA received an installment note in the principal amount of $137.0 million (the "Operating Company Note"), 100% of the non-voting common stock of Operating Company and certain additional consideration under the Trade Name Use Agreement. The Operating Company Note is payable over 10 years and bears interest at a rate of 12% per annum. Interest only is generally payable for the first four years of the Operating Company Note, and the principal will be amortized over the following six years. Doctor R. Crants, Chairman of the Board of Directors and Chief Executive Officer of the Company and a member of the Board of Directors and Chief Executive Officer of Operating Company, has guaranteed payment of 10% of the outstanding principal amount due under the Operating Company Note.

On December 31, 1998, immediately prior to the Prison Realty Merger and in connection with the CCA Merger, CCA entered into a service mark and trade name use agreement with Operating Company (the "Trade Name Use Agreement"). Under the Trade Name Use Agreement, which has a term of 10 years, CCA granted Operating Company the right to use the name "Corrections Corporation of America" and derivatives thereof, subject to the terms and conditions therein, for a specified fee based, in general, on the gross revenues of Operating Company.

On December 31, 1998, immediately prior to the Prison Realty Merger and in connection with the CCA Merger, CCA transferred to Prison Management Services, LLC, a Delaware limited liability company, certain management contracts and all non–real estate assets relating to government-owned adult prison facilities managed by CCA. In exchange, CCA received 100% of the non-voting membership interest in Prison Management Services, LLC. This interest obligated Prison Management Services, LLC, to make distributions to CCA equal to 95% of its net income.

On December 31, 1998, immediately prior to the Prison Realty Merger and in connection with the CCA Merger, CCA transferred to Juvenile and Jail Facility Management Services, LLC, a Delaware limited liability company, certain management contracts and all non–real estate assets relating to government-owned jails and juvenile facilities managed by CCA, as well as all of the issued and outstanding capital stock of those corporate subsidiaries of CCA constituting its international operations. In exchange, CCA received 100% of the non-voting membership interest in Juvenile and Jail Facility Management Services, LLC. This interest obligated Juvenile and Jail Facility Management Services, LLC, to make distributions to CCA equal to 95% of its net income.

On January 1, 1999, immediately after the Prison Realty Merger, Prison Management Services, LLC, merged with and into Prison Management Services, Inc., a Tennessee corporation ("Service Company A"), with Service Company A as the surviving company. In connection with this merger, the Company received 100% of the non-voting common stock of Service Company A. The non-voting common stock obligates Service Company A to pay dividends to the Company equal to 95% of its net income.

On January 1, 1999, immediately after the Prison Realty Merger, Juvenile and Jail Facility Management Services, LLC, merged with and into Juvenile and Jail Facility Management Services, Inc., a Tennessee corporation ("Service Company B"), with Service Company B as the surviving company. In connection with this merger, the Company received 100% of the non-voting common stock of Service Company B. The non-voting common stock obligates Service Company B to pay dividends to the Company equal to 95% of its net income.

On January 1, 1999, immediately after the Prison Realty Merger, all leases between CCA and Prison Realty were cancelled, and the Company and Operating Company entered into a master lease agreement (the "Master Agreement to Lease") and leases with respect to each property owned by the Company and managed by Operating Company (collectively, the "Operating Company Leases"). The Operating Company Leases have terms of 12 years, which may be extended at fair market rates for three additional five-year periods upon the mutual agreement of the Company and Operating Company.

On January 1, 1999, immediately after the Prison Realty Merger, the Company and Operating Company entered into a right to purchase agreement (the "Right to Purchase Agreement") pursuant to which Operating Company granted to the Company a right to acquire, and lease back to Operating Company at fair market rental rates, any correctional or detention facility acquired or developed and owned by Operating Company in the future for a period of 10 years following the date inmates are first received at such facility. Additionally, Operating Company granted the Company a right of first refusal to acquire any Operating Company–owned correctional or detention facility should Operating Company receive an acceptable third-party offer to acquire any such facility.

On January 1, 1999, immediately after the Prison Realty Merger, the Company entered into a services agreement (the "Services Agreement") with Operating Company pursuant to which Operating Company is to serve as a facilitator of the construction and development of additional facilities on behalf of the Company for a term of five years from the date of the Services Agreement.

On January 1, 1999, immediately after the Prison Realty Merger, the Company entered into a tenant incentive agreement (the "Tenant Incentive Agreement") with Operating Company pursuant to which the Company will pay to Operating Company an incentive fee to induce Operating Company to enter into Operating Company Leases with respect to those facilities developed and facilitated by Operating Company.

On January 1, 1999, immediately after the Prison Realty Merger, each of Service Company A and Service Company B entered into an administrative services agreement with Operating Company (collectively, the "Administrative Services Agreements") pursuant to which employees of Operating Company's administrative departments perform extensive administrative services (including but not limited to legal, finance, management information systems and government relations services), as needed, for the Service Companies. As consideration for the foregoing, each Service Company pays Operating Company a management fee of $250,000 per month. This management fee will be increased annually at the rate of four percent per year. In addition, Operating Company entered into a trade name use agreement with each of the Service Companies under which Operating Company granted to each of the Service Companies the right to use the name "Corrections Corporation of America" and derivatives thereof, subject to specified terms and conditions therein.

Earlier in this section we noted that in addition to the government contract with a private prison, the private prison had a contract with another
entity essentially run by the same people. At this point, all those contracts
are cancelled and redrawn between Prison Realty Corporation and the various companies mentioned in box 5.2. Later filings clarify that the "Operating Company" mentioned in box 5.2 became "New CCA," so later filings
state that "Old CCA granted to New CCA the right to use the name 'Corrections Corporation of America'" (Prison Realty Corporation 1999c).

At the time of the first quarterly report, New CCA reported a net loss of
$25 million for the first three months of 1999 (Prison Realty Corporation
1999c), which created problems for Prison Realty Corporation because it
depended on New CCA's rent money as income. The loss happened even
though Prison Realty Corporation and New CCA had entered into an
amended and restated tenant incentive agreement providing more generous payments to New CCA that were retroactive back to January 1. Prison
Realty Corporation also disclosed that on January 1 it had entered into a
business-development agreement with New CCA to reward it for obtaining
new contracts, and the loss had happened in spite of payments from this
new agreement. Within days of the filing, a shareholder lawsuit was filed.
While inmates sue both public and private prisons, shareholder lawsuits
form a category of overhead costs specific to the private sector.

By May 26, 1999, fifteen similar complaints had been filed, alleging "violations of federal securities laws based on the allegation that the Company
and the individual defendants knew or should have known of the increased
payments to New CCA prior to the date on which they were disclosed to
the public and that, therefore, certain public filings and representations
made by the Company and certain individuals were false and misleading"
(Prison Realty Corporation 1999d). Shareholders felt that Crants and others had made misleading statements about the merged companies' strong
financial condition and the merger's benefits and that the agreements were
"material concerns" that should have been disclosed in a more timely manner. Shareholders of the earlier class action also filed in court saying that
"the increased payments to New CCA violate the terms of the Stipulation
of Settlement reached in that case and, therefore, also violate the order of
the court of February 26, 1999, approving the settlement" (Prison Realty
Corporation 1999d). They believed Prison Realty Corporation should be
held in contempt for violating the earlier court order.

New CCA's losses continued during the next two quarters in spite of the
new and revised agreements put in place. New CCA was borrowing money
and issuing shares as a private company to raise money to pay Prison Realty Corporation—an unsustainable practice. Further, the quarterly report
states, "New CCA expects to continue to use these sources of cash to offset
its anticipated losses from operations; however, amounts presently antici-

pated to be available to New CCA will not be sufficient to offset all of New CCA's expected future operating losses" (Prison Realty Corporation 1999e). Merrill Lynch was called in as a financial advisor to help the company evaluate options, and eventually another advisor was retained because the overlapping ownership of Prison Realty and CCA created conflicts of interest. Over the next four months, Merrill Lynch contacted forty-seven potential investors and merger partners and charged fees totaling $13.5 million; the other advisor received $2.4 million (Prison Realty 2000e).

In the last days of December 1999, Prison Realty Corporation announced another merger plan: the company, along with the three private operating companies, would be merged into one corporation that would no longer be an REIT. At the same time, the company announced that Fortress Investments, The Blackstone Group, and Bank of America ("the Investors") would invest up to $350 million in a new class of preferred stock, which would pay a guaranteed 12 percent per year in dividends (although the price of the stock could go up or down). The company could only buy back the stock "at a price which provides a total return of 18% per annum" (Prison Realty Corporation 1999a). This would have cost the company substantially more than what a government would pay on its bonds to finance activities. In addition, the company was liable to "pay to the Investors an aggregate transaction fee of $15.7 million" (Prison Realty Corporation 1999a). The deal would have allowed investors to appoint four members of the board and constitute a majority on a newly formed board of directors' Investment Committee, which would have had "exclusive power" over a number of important financial decisions.

The merger agreement comprised 86 pages plus a number of appendices to create a filing of more than 340 pages (Prison Realty 2000e). Privately held shares of the three operating companies (including New CCA) were converted into Prison Realty shares, although the company would use the name Corrections Corporation of America. If the merger went through, Credit Suisse First Boston would restructure the company's credit and provide a $1.2 billion line, dependent on the company's getting insurance to cover the shareholder lawsuits mentioned earlier. An entry on the sources and uses of funds for the credit line lists $9 million for the insurance policy and another $92.5 in merger fees and expenses (Prison Realty Corporation 1999a). Like many credit lines, CCA's had a variable rate linked to certain commonly used lending benchmarks, but the company also paid 0.5 percent interest on the unused balance. Governments do not pay when they do not borrow money, but CCA would pay $2.5 million if it did not use $500 million of its credit line (plus it would pay interest on the amount it did use).

In its filings, CCA admits that "the restructuring will also result in substantial transaction costs (a significant portion of which has already been incurred), including debt and equity financing fees and ongoing costs of capital to Prison Realty" (Prison Realty 2000e). In addition to the fees listed above, the company disclosed that "the equity investment and the changes in the composition of the Prison Realty board will constitute a change in control" because Crants had been forced to resign as chairman of the board and the board contained a majority of new members. So, Crants and Michael Devlin (the chief operating officer, who had also been forced to resign) "received severance benefits in connection with their resignation" (Prison Realty 2000e). CCA and Prison Realty also amended the terms of their leases, the annual base rent escalation features of the leases, the business development agreement, the amended services agreement, and the amended tenant incentive agreement. Whereas earlier the government had simply contracted with a private prison firm, the firm has not only contracted with itself but amended the amended agreements it has with itself. The company needed to obtain the consent of a number of banks and lenders to make these changes and deal with other provisions triggered by the change in control.

The situation had grown bad enough that the company disclosed that the auditors working on the 1999 financial statements "are currently evaluating whether their year-end report for each company will include a statement that there is doubt as to the ability of CCA to continue as a going concern, and, as a result of Prison Realty's financial dependence on CCA, the ability of Prison Realty to continue as a going concern" (Prison Realty 2000e). Certification as a "going concern" is crucial as it means the auditors believe the business is viable and will continue to operate for the foreseeable future. Banks do not lend to businesses that have not been certified as going concerns, and suppliers do not tend to work with them. The language triggers a number of provisions related to loans and credit that are not good for the company, including increased interest rates and the right to immediately demand loan repayment. And, what government would contract to house inmates with a business that might not be around for the foreseeable future?

The proposed equity investment from Fortress/Blackstone triggered another shareholder lawsuit alleging that "the directors breached their fiduciary duties to Prison Realty's shareholders by 'effectively selling Control' of Prison Realty for inadequate consideration and without having adequately considered or explored all other alternatives to this prospective sale or having taken steps to maximize shareholder value" (Prison Realty 2000e). The company also did not make a dividend payment because of cash flow concerns, which sparked another shareholder lawsuit that

alleges violations of federal securities laws based on the allegation that the defendants knew or should have known that Prison Realty would not make any further dividend payments on the shares of Prison Realty common stock, including the "special dividend" prior to the date on which it was disclosed to the public and therefore certain statements made by them prior to that time were false and misleading. (Prison Realty 2000e)

In the "Operations and Business Strategy" section immediately following the disclosure of these lawsuits, the company discussed the "efficient development and management of facilities" and "efficient application of financial resources" (Prison Realty 2000e).

Prison Realty finished 1999 with a loss of $53 million, and CCA incurred a loss of $202.9 million for the year (Prison Realty 2000b). The annual report disclosed that because of shareholder litigation, the company had incurred legal expenses of $6.3 million during 1999. The auditors stated that "there is substantial doubt about Corrections Corporation of America's ability to continue as a going concern."

Before the shareholders could vote on the merger and equity investment, Pacific Life Insurance, an existing shareholder, provided an alternative offer. Though similar in many respects to the earlier Fortress/Blackstone offer, it is marginally better for shareholders and the company. Prison Realty's board voted to accept the offer, which triggered a $7.5 million breakup fee to the Fortress/Blackstone investors. Prison Realty successfully secured waivers from lenders so as not to invoke some of the financially harsh conditions related to its default, although part of this waiver required the company to hire a management consultant acceptable to the lenders (Prison Realty 2000a). In this same filing, the company announced the contract with the Federal Bureau of Prisons to guarantee payments for 95 percent occupancy regardless of actual inmate population. This is the "bailout" noted in the previous chapter because of its timing and size. Revenues from these contracts for the three-year initial term and seven renewal options of one year would equal $760 million, "not including award fees" or "a bonus of up to 5 percent of annual revenues for superior performance" (Prison Realty 2000a).

On June 30, Prison Realty announced that the deal with Pacific Life had fallen through, but it planned to merge the various companies that comprise it into one that will not be taxed as an REIT. The federal contract seemed to have given the company confidence that it could sell shares in a secondary offering after the restructuring without the guarantees of Pacific Life, and an amended agreement with the banks gave Prison Realty time to make the stock offering (Prison Realty 2000d). The waiver had cost the company 0.75 percent of its $1 billion existing credit line ($7.5 million) and increased its interest rate. Waivers on other loans and preferred stocks also generated fees or worse terms for Prison Realty. CCA had paid its lender a $2 million waiver fee and needed to pay an extra $1 million to continue the waiver after the Pacific Life deal fell through. Although there were no breakup fees to Pacific

Life, the terms of agreement provided that Prison Realty had to reimburse Pacific Life for out-of-pocket expenses related to the offer.

Since the Pacific Life deal did not happen, Prison Realty refused to pay the breakup fee to Fortress Blackstone, which sued Prison Realty for the $7.5 million breakup fee and the $15.7 million transaction fee. Because the company failed to make required distributions in 1999 as required for its REIT status, it became liable for $5 to $7 million in taxes to the IRS. Prison Realty indicated "completion of the restructuring will require the companies to incur approximately $60.0 million of transaction costs (a substantial portion of which has either been incurred or contractually committed)" and "these resources could have otherwise been used by the companies to further their respective business objectives" (Prison Realty 2000d). Also, the company had a verdict against it for $753,000 for a construction dispute against U.S. Corrections Corporation, which it had acquired in April 1998. Further, a 428-page filing mentioned that the U.S. Corrections Corporation employee stock ownership plan (ESOP) filed suit against Prison Realty

> alleging numerous violations of the Employees Retirement Income Security Act ("ERISA"), including but not limited to failure to manage the assets of the ESOP in the sole interest of the participants, purchasing assets without undertaking adequate investigation of the investment, overpayment for employer securities, failure to resolve conflicts of interest, lending money between the ESOP and employer, allowing the ESOP to borrow money other than for the acquisition of employer securities, failure to make adequate, independent, and reasoned investigation into the prudence and advisability of certain transaction, and otherwise. (Prison Realty 2000c)

Prison Realty originally indicated that insurance would likely cover whatever liability it had, but a later filing indicated that "the Company's insurance carrier has indicated that it did not receive timely notice of these claims and, as a result, is currently contesting its coverage obligations in this suit" (CCA 2001).

Following the merger and restructuring, the company, now doing business as Corrections Corporation of America, faced removal from the New York Stock Exchange because its share price dropped below $1 for a period of time. Because the company was on its way to losing more than $700 million in 2000, during the last three months of the year the share price hit a low of $0.19 (down from more than $24 during the early part of 1999). This process, known as delisting, is potentially serious because it would mean the company's shares would be traded in ways reserved for so-called penny stocks. These stocks do not have much credibility when it comes to raising additional money through secondary offerings; they are expensive to trade, so fewer people deal with them; and many mutual funds are prohibited from holding them. CCA prepared to do a reverse stock split, whereby ten shares of the company's stock become one share, which elevated the share price by ten times (ten shares worth $0.86 each become one share worth $8.60). Also, following the merger, Merrill Lynch submitted an additional bill for $8.1 million because it saw the merger as a "restructuring transaction" under the terms of its agreement with CCA, which provided for additional payments if the company's consulting resulted in such an outcome. Finally, in analyzing its situation, CCA decided to abandon a series of facilities they had started developing and on which they had already spent $2.1 million (CCA 2001).

A few of the items mentioned above were ultimately settled on more reasonable terms for the company: the shareholder litigation involved $75 million in stock and cash from insurance, Blackstone settled for $15 million rather than the full $23.2 million, Merrill Lynch settled for $3 million rather than the full $8.1 million, and the insurance paid for the claims of U.S. Corrections Corporation's retirement plan. However, the issue involved not only the final cost entailed but the amount of time, energy, and resources spent dealing with these matters. (Indeed, in 2002, the company paid the IRS $54 million to settle problems arising from an audit of the company's tax returns from 1997 [CCA 2002a].) Further, these items were a small part of a much larger constellation of fees and charges paid by the company over these years.

CONCLUSION

While private business can be more efficient and effective than government at times, the question is whether this assumption holds for private prisons, a debate that has frequently focused on research into the cost savings of private prisons. As an alternative to rehashing the debate over how best to do cost comparisons and as a way of moving beyond the platitudes about government red tape, this chapter has examined some issues related to how private prisons actually function. The first finding, beyond the convoluted process of setting executive pay, is that the pay of private prison executives generates enormous overhead costs that must be recovered elsewhere if the business is to turn a profit and provide the service more cheaply than government.

Remember that in 1994 Wackenhut paid its top executive $190,000 when it had 11,414 inmates under supervision, and Esmor paid $179,621 to its top executive when it had 829 inmates under supervision in 1993. By way of comparison, the executive director of the Texas prison system made $165,000 in 2007 for supervising more than 153,000 inmates, plus a parole and probation caseload of more than 280,000. This inflated pay scale for private prison executives is inefficient and generates more overhead costs than the state prison system's. These additional overhead costs must be recouped, for instance, by lowering the salary and benefits of prison workers. So, in exchange for whatever benefits private prisons allegedly provide, one cost is increased inequality in society as private prisons make up for paying those at the top more than states do by paying those at the bottom less. (Another other cost is having an industry that lobbies against sentencing reform.)

This concern about inequality is compounded by the fact that the overhead costs of participating in the corporate world and relying on Wall Street include the many fees that go to those who are already well-off. Taxpayer money goes to government, which then pays a private prison firm, which then pays fees to an array of large banks, law firms, consultants, lobbyists, and marketing firms. In our concluding chapter, we review the other concerns about private prisons that this book has detailed based on their operating histories and raise questions about future expansion plans.

Conclusion

Back to the Future

One important premise of this book has been that private prisons were born of an incarceration binge that was wasteful of taxpayer money, produced only a small effect on crime, and contributed greatly to injustice—especially racial injustice. Private prisons and the shareholders and lending institutions that have billions of dollars invested in them now depend on the continuation of those trends for revenue and growth. Further, these prisons' ongoing operation contributes to economic inequality because, in order to make up for high overhead in the form of executive pay, lobbying, and fees to Wall Street firms, they pay lower-level staff less than the government would.

These critiques are not always visible in the debate over criminal justice policy or prison privatization. For example, within the narrowly framed discussion of corporate responsibility, *Corporate Responsibility Officer* magazine has named the Corrections Corporation of America (CCA) among the nation's "100 Best Corporate Citizens," even though on multiple occasions the company urged shareholders to vote against greater transparency for political contributions and other socially responsible proposals initiated by shareholders. Governments that debate whether to contract with private prisons focus extensively on cost savings, usually based on the daily charge rather than the full array of costs imposed by a variety of contractual clauses. The iron triangle of interests in the prison-industrial complex—government bureaucracy, key members of legislative bodies, and private business interests—each side protects itself as well as the other sides from external influence, regulation, and public accountability. As we noted in chapter 3, this subgovernment has the potential to determine public policy free from scrutiny with far-reaching economic, political, and social consequences.

Criminal justice textbooks, likewise, generally include a short section or box on prison privatization. They usually strive to appear "balanced," so they review some points on which there is debate. But they do not include the deeper concerns that arise from "following the money" and leave discussions of ideas like the prison- or criminal justice–industrial complex to a small number of theoretically critical texts. This is especially unfortunate in that it leaves many students and the public without an understanding of what is really driving policy—and thus gives an incomplete picture of today's criminal justice system. Indeed, just as "tough on crime" started off as a code for controlling blacks, it soon also became code for economic development: build a prison to take care of areas with high unemployment due to lost manufacturing jobs, declining natural resources, or other economic dislocations. The contradiction between political promises to expand the prison system and cut taxes always threatened to slow down the incarceration binge but never really did, partly because private prisons raised billions in private capital to build prisons and relieved governments of those construction costs.

The extreme financial crisis of 2008 has the potential to impact expenditures on prison and privatization, although, as we write the conclusion to this book, it is still too early to tell what the effect will be. Because many states' corrections budgets have grown so large, they are prime targets for cost cutting. The financial crisis gives some leeway for politicians to "get smart" and not just "get tough." This will entail realizing that many offenders in prison, costing an average of $25,000 a year, would pose no threat to public safety if released or put on some form of community corrections. The transition from President George W. Bush's administration to that of President Barack Obama also holds out hope for increased questioning of our reliance on incarceration and a directional change in the pendulum of punishment policy.

However, rather than overhauling the problematic sentencing policy at the root of many problems, some governments are simply considering the option of switching to private prisons in the belief they will save money. In fact, some local governments are considering using taxpayer money for private police as well—a notable departure from private businesses using their own money for private security. But caution is warranted on both fronts. John Macdonald, a criminology professor and lead researcher of a Rand study on private police, notes, "If an unfortunate event were to happen it could cost the public more in the long term than what the city believes it could save" (White 2009). The same applies to private prisons, although we believe they cost the public more in the long run, even in the absence of unfortunate events.

First, a government must hire or (retrain) people to write a request for proposals (RFP) to solicit bids from private prison companies. This step is critical in specifying the level of services and becomes the basis for a subsequent contract. Responses to the RFP must be evaluated and a contract negotiated. Governments are at a disadvantage generally because the company deals with contracts more often and has a better understanding of the implications of certain clauses and language than governments might, especially when negotiating early contracts. This contract language, in turn, means that the daily fee per inmate does not really capture all the costs for the government. But debates tend to focus on the daily fee as a point of comparison with the costs of the public system.

Second, paying a private prison company means that the state will be using some taxpayers money to pay high executive compensation and Wall Street consulting fees. Even if a state is not concerned with contributing to inequality, the issue partially entails the fact that money previously spent on corrections, which stayed in the state, will now leave the state economy. If prisoners are housed out of state, then the state or local economy will lose even more money. And, even if the private prison is located in state, its jobs will pay less than the state jobs being replaced. Having fewer jobs or jobs that pay less undercuts any marginal gain in savings or cash flow to the state, hurting the state's economy and recovery. Of course, interest in privatization will bring in money in the form of campaign contributions that may help certain politicians, but it is doubtful that having corporate policies influence crime policy will benefit taxpayers.

Further, the claim that private prisons' treatment programs are more effective rests on a single problematic study that appeared in the journal *Crime and Delinquency*. It showed that inmates from private prisons had lower recidivism rates than those released from public prisons based on ninety-nine pairs of inmates (Lanza-Kaduce, Parker, and Thomas 1999). All authors were identified as affiliated with the Center for Studies in Criminology and Law, University of Florida. A follow-up article raised concerns that the third author, Charles Thomas, was director of the Private Corrections Project, housed within the Center for Studies in Criminology, which was primarily funded (to the tune of $400,000) by private prison companies and received a $25,000 summer stipend. Thomas had also been board member for CCA's Prison Realty Trust (see chapter 5), for which he received $12,000 a year, plus $1,000 for each board meeting and $500 for each subcommittee meeting (Geis, Mobley, and Shichor 1999, 374). A 1998 Securities and Exchange Commission filing listed a $3 million fee to Thomas for consulting (Geis, Mobley, and Shichor 1999, 380), and he owned shares of Prison Realty Trust, which at the time were worth $600,000 (Geis, Mobley, and Shichor 1999, 377). The company's stock option plan has, as its avowed, purpose "to increase their proprietary interest in the company" (quoted in Geis, Mobley, and Shichor 1999, 375).

This raises concerns about a conflict of interest; specifically, Thomas's financial interest in private prisons could have conflicted with his charge as a social scientist to report data fully, regardless of whether findings support or contradict desired outcomes (Leighton and Killingbeck 2001). Disclosure is one minimal tactic for dealing with real and perceived conflict of interest—and it was clearly not employed here. An additional concern is the short follow-up period—one year—for the study's assessment of recidivism: "When a man associated with the private prison industry in a money-making position uses such a short follow-up period in his study it inevitably arouses the suspicion that there was a desire, perhaps over-riding, to get the favorable news legitimated by its appearance in a scholarly publication" (Geis, Mobley, and Shichor 1999, 374). (Thomas had other conflicts as well and was fined $20,000 by the Florida Ethics Commission for sitting on the Florida Correctional Privatization Commission, formed to advise the state on privatization, at the same time that he was a paid consultant for the private prison industry [Stern 2006, 114].)

Even if states and localities reduce their prison populations and dependence on private prisons, private firms will persist because of expanding federal contracts for detaining immigrants. In November 2008, GEO Group chairman George Zoley assured investors, "These federal initiatives to target, detain, and deport criminal aliens throughout the country will continue to drive the need for immigration detention beds over the next several years and these initiatives have been fully funded by Congress on a bipartisan basis" (quoted in Barry 2008). The shift of power to Democrats seems to be of little relevance to private prisons. Zoley pointed out that "the president only asked for a program funding of $800 million. It was the Democratic chairman [of the Homeland Security subcommittee] . . . that added another $200 million to this program" (Barry 2008). James Hyman, president of Cornell Companies, adds, "We do not believe we will see a decline in the need for detention beds particularly in an economy with rising unemployment among American workers" whose jobs politicians will promise to protect by detaining and deporting immigrants (Barry 2008).

The expansion of private prisons due to the detention of immigrants is not a new development; rather, it is an extension of policies put in place after the terrorist attacks of September 11. However, the new groups of marginalized "raw materials" for industry profit include women and children, despite the outcry of human rights and community groups. Currently, though, the Immigration and Customs Enforcement Division (ICE) pays CCA, GEO Group, and Cornell Corrections from $200 to $272 per night per detainee—including for women and children who have committed no criminal violations. While reasons are given for detaining families, an approach based on following the money would highlight that "in 2004, when Congress passed legislation authorizing ICE to triple the number of immigration beds, CCA's lobbying expenditures reached $3 million; since then it has spent an additional $7 million on lobbyists" (Martin 2009, 1). (These figures do not include the lobbying expenses of other private prison firms; nor do they include campaign contributions made by any firm to further this initiative.) As of early 2009, ICE plans to double its capacity, which includes opening three new family-detention facilities in 2010 (Martin 2009, 1).

Even if the number of prison beds is reduced and government relies less on privatization, the industry is now accustomed to the flow of government money. Companies are ready to follow the money and push for more privatization by identifying social problems that will enable them to rely on the same set of claims used to promote operational prison privatization: high quality and cost savings, increasing public safety, innovation, experience, and historical success, combined with the appeal of public-private partnerships. The industry has broadened its market to include what it refers to as "specialized" populations: the mentally ill, drug addicts, youth offenders, probationers, and those recently or soon to be released from prison. They require more specialized services, which have a higher price and, more important, a greater profit margin.

Two specific "specialized" areas of market expansion—mental health and community corrections—are noteworthy and deserve attention. Developments in policy and practice in each of these areas have the potential to impact millions of people. In addition, the people (raw materials) that make up these populations are among the most vulnerable, yet the easiest to construct as dangerous and thus in need of the specialized services offered by private businesses. Below we examine private companies' entry into these markets and the policies that opened the doors to them, current problems in each, and the potential expansion of markets like privatized parole.

MENTAL HEALTH

After sharp reductions in funding to mental health facilities, prisons became warehouses for those suffering from mental health issues. However, only recently has this emerged as a "crisis" of importance to the private prison industry. In 2002, President Bush's New Freedom Commission on Mental Health described the system as "broken and in shambles." According to Human Rights Watch (2003), at least one in six prisoners in the United States is mentally ill, equaling well over three hundred thousand men and women. Prison guards in Wisconsin chillingly describe the conditions within the prison walls: "We are equipped to handle 317 mentally ill patients, but we have 4,610. These seriously mental ill inmates have been recklessly integrated into the general population and their presence presents a very dangerous dichotomy to the corrections setting" (Milam 2004, B1). The Michigan Bar Association describes the number of severely mentally ill who end up in prison in Michigan as "an out of control crisis" (Weeks 2004, A7).

Just as the corrections officers, prison officials, prisoners' rights activists, judges, and politicians found themselves on the same page in their response to overcrowding, which played a crucial role in the buildup of prisons and their eventual privatization, they now find themselves in agreement that something else is terribly wrong with the criminal justice system. The nation's prisons and jails have become mental health facilities, a role for which they are ill equipped. Governors across the country have established mental health commissions to fix the broken mental health system. For example, Michigan governor Jennifer Granholm stated, "There is one goal for this commission, that no one enters the juvenile or criminal justice system because of inadequate mental health care" (quoted in Weeks 2004, A7).

The industry is less interested in how mentally ill offenders get into prison than with the profit margin they generate. Since specialized services command premium payments and high margins, the industry in 2001 formed the Association of Private Correctional and Treatment Organizations (APCTO). This nonprofit trade association comprises private prison firms—CCA, Wackenhut (now GEO Group), Cornell, Management Training Corporation—and prison-service groups, including Community Education Centers, Correct Rx Pharmacy Services, MHM (a mental health provider), Corrections Services Corporation (a rehabilitation provider), and Physicians Network Association (a healthcare provider). Andrew LeFevre—a former private prison industry executive and director of the American Legislative Exchange Council's (ALEC) Criminal Justice Task Force, which shapes criminal justice policy—heads APCTO. The group's self-description and mission statement follow a script remarkably similar to that of prison privatization: linking humanitarianism, public duty, cost savings, professionalism, and innovation to promote the further privatization of rehabilitation and treatment. The group states that members are

> committed to new correctional solutions that rehabilitate inmates and reduce recidivism and offer a variety of adult programs designed to help inmates become productive members of society. APCTO member companies provide high quality service and generate cost savings as part of public agencies' comprehensive correctional efforts at the federal, state and local level. Member companies also specialize in the provision of residential and outpatient programs to help offenders transition from the institutional setting into society. Because many inmates enter the corrections system with substance abuse and behavioral problems, our programs include comprehensive counseling and specialized behavioral health services that focus on helping clients overcome substance abuse and/or behavioral health issues. All these programs have been

developed from years of experience interacting with and treating individuals entrusted to our care. (APCTO 2005)

At the same time, private prison executives were commenting on expectations for services such as mental health: "We expect our government clients will seek more specialized services for more targeted populations. We have begun to see it less and less as a monolithic population. It is a diverse population with various needs," said Wackenhut executive Wayne Calabrese, citing the "evolution" of the industry. "I think the best is ahead of us" (Slevin 2001, A03). In 1998, Wackenhut had taken over management of a state mental health hospital in southern Florida, "a historic milestone for public sector mental health services and a significant diversification of the Company's service offerings" according to its annual report (Wackenhut 2002).

Several years later, the Mentally Ill Offender Treatment and Crime Reduction Act of 2003 became law, supported by ALEC and sponsored by CCA supporters Senator Mike DeWine and Representative Ted Strickland, both of Ohio. The law aims to ensure access to mental health and other treatment services for mentally ill adults or juveniles. It requires these programs to target nonviolent adults or juveniles who (1) have been diagnosed with a mental illness or with co-occurring mental illness and substance-abuse disorders or manifest obvious signs of such an illness or disorder during arrest or confinement or before any court, and (2) face criminal charges and are deemed eligible on the grounds that the person's mental illness produced the commission of the offense. The law directs that $50 million in grants should be used to create or expand—among other efforts—programs that offer specialized training to officers and employees of criminal or juvenile justice agencies in identifying symptoms in order to respond appropriately to individuals with mental illnesses (Bossolo 2004).

Of course, in this new market, problems quickly surfaced (Carter 2002; *Business Week* 2004). And while it is better for the mentally ill to get treatment than not, the APCTO humanitarian rhetoric obscures the point made by President Bush's New Freedom Commission on Mental Health:

> The mental health delivery system is fragmented and in disarray . . . lead[ing] to unnecessary and costly disability, homelessness, school failure, and incarceration. . . . In many communities, access to quality care is poor, resulting in wasted resources and lost opportunities for recovery. More individuals could recover from even the most serious mental illnesses if they had access in their communities to treatment and supports that are tailored to their needs. (Quoted in Human Rights Watch 2003)

The "crisis" of mentally ill prisoners is rooted in the lack of community mental health treatment, which causes much of the incarceration in the first place. But the private prison industry wants to profit from the incarcerated mentally ill rather than fix the bigger problem. Just as private prisons have no interest in crime prevention and as private hospitals are in the business of "sick care" with minimal interest in public health, the "service" and "innovation" here are very narrowly defined. In the introduction, we noted that focusing on incarceration to control crime is like mopping the floor while the tub is overflowing. Once again, private interests claim to be serving the public with better and cheaper mops than government can make while obscuring the root problems.

COMMUNITY CORRECTIONS

Privatization started with community corrections in the form of halfway houses and residential treatment centers. This history, touched on in chapter 2, became the basis for the push into managing prisons. But private prison firms are interested in expanding back into community corrections because the parole and probation populations dwarf that of inmates. As of year end 2007, over five million adults were under some type of community supervision, or about 70 percent of the total number of people under the control of the criminal justice system.. This number includes almost 4.3 million on probation and 824,000 on parole (BJS 2008b).

Further, this issue has received attention due to growing awareness of the challenges people leaving prison and attempting to reenter society face. In his 2004 State of the Union address, President Bush put prisoner reentry in the national spotlight:

> Tonight I ask you to consider another group of Americans in need of help. This year, some 600,000 inmates will be released from prison back into society. We know from long experience that if they can't find work or a home or help, they are much more likely to commit crime and return to prison. So tonight, I propose a four-year, $300 million Prisoner Re-Entry Initiative to expand job training and placement services, to provide transitional housing and to help newly released prisoners get mentoring, including from faith-based groups. (Bush 2004)

The Second Chance Act sat in the Republican-controlled Congress for several years before being passed into law in 2008. The final bill authorized expenditures of $400 million over four years to fulfill the president's goal that America become "the land of the second chance. . . . When the gates of the prison open, the path ahead should lead to a better life" (Bush 2004; Congressional Budget Office 2008).

The private prison industry started by capitalizing on President Bill Clinton's initiatives to allow states to contract more easily with faith-based organizations—policies accelerated by Bush. GEO Group, for example, recruits large numbers of religious volunteers, which provides the company with free labor and qualifies it for certain faith-based grants. CCA partnered in 2003 with Bill Glass Champions for Life, the operator of the nation's largest evangelical prison ministries program. In the same year, CCA hired Donna Alvarado, who, in addition to having held several senior management positions in government such as deputy assistant secretary of defense and counsel for the judiciary on immigration and refugee policy, is the former director of ACTION, the federal domestic volunteer agency. CCA quickly recognized the value of her "access to and knowledge of organizing and funding regarding faith-based and community-based programs" (CCA Source 2003). The following year CCA entered into an agreement with the Institute in Basic Life Principles. While some raise concern about the worldview and theology of the faith-based organizations (Berkowicz 2004), a larger point is that the line between "for-profit" and "not-for-profit" organizations has been blurred. For-profit organizations have established nonprofit arms, and for-profit companies have created partnerships with nonprofit organizations, so it is increasingly difficult to distinguish business interests masquerading as public service from genuine humanitarian interests. Some of the not-for-profit organizations have been incorporated into the prison-industrial complex and provide cover for the iron triangle of interests that dictate policy.

The expansion of for-profit community corrections has led to inevitable problems as businesses try to reduce their labor costs to maximize profits. For example, an investigative report revealed that escapes were commonplace at two private detention centers near Horizon City, Texas. Avalon, Inc., a member of APCTO, operates the minimum-security halfway houses for parole violators. During their incarceration, inmates said escaping was easy. Residents took advantage of guard-staffing shortages and the center's reliance on security cameras to slip away undetected. Cutting back on staff pay rates and replacing positions with surveillance equipment enabled Avalon's private prisons to cut the costs of housing residents (*El Paso Times*, August 29, 2001). Halfway houses run by Cornell Corrections have experienced such problems as poor living conditions, sexual harassment, and an incident in which an inmate walked away from a halfway house and raped a former girlfriend (resulting in a suit not just against the company but the state as well) (*Anchorage Daily News* 2001; Clark 2001). Also, the Promontory Community Correctional Center in Utah managed by APCTO member Management and Training had parolees who disappeared completely. In less than nine months, 102 parolees enrolled in the program walked away, compared with only 41 parolees from halfway houses operated by the Utah Department of Corrections outside of prison (Burton 1999).

Obviously public programs also have problems, but the larger point is the lack of evidence to support private prisons' main contention: that they do a better job. While most people's ideological belief that private business does do better lends credence to the industry's claim, the bar should be higher. If they are generally going to pay staff less and give them fewer retirement benefits and holidays, private prisons will have higher staff turnover, which inherently creates problems with quality. Likewise, aggressively replacing people with technology has its limits, and private firms are more likely to push technology to reduce labor costs. While governments also have an interest in keeping costs low to appease taxpayers, they are more directly accountable to citizens for mistakes that endanger public safety. Prison businesses are accountable to the governments they contract with, but there is little accountability if contracts are poorly written and/or have minor penalties for noncompliance.

In addition, as with operational prison privatization, conflicts of interest and ethical concerns have characterized private industry's foray into community corrections. For example, in 2001 Georgia's attorney general began looking into consulting contracts between two members of the state board of pardons and parole and private security companies. Parole board chairman Walter Ray and board member Bobby Whitworth acknowledged that they had been paid consultants for the probation company Detention Management Services, a firm with state contracts. Ray was paid $11,000 over two years, and Whitworth was paid $75,000 over three years, plus over $120,000 in consulting fees from the Bobby Ross Group, another firm with state contracts (*Atlanta Journal-Constitution* 2002). In 2003, "a jury found Whitworth guilty of public corruption for accepting $75,000 from the company to draft and lobby for legislation that dramatically expanded the role of private probation companies" (Perry 2008). Whitworth served six months, but two powerful Republican lobbyists kept the privatization law on the books and have pushed to give private firms felony parole and probabtion cases as well.

As private firms seek to influence legislation and expand markets, further conflicts of interest and ethically dubious payments to public officials are inevitable. The point, made by the prosecutor in Whitworth's case, is not whether the law on privatization is a good one; the point is that the law prohibits certain payments to public officials in exchange for influence. As to whether the privatization of probation is a good idea, law enforcement in Georgia opposed the law and its expansion: "One sheriff told lawmakers last year that among his peers, private probation was seen mostly 'as a moneymaking fee-collection service.' Another said there is generally 'not a lot of emphasis on supervision as much as there is on collection'" (Perry 2008, online). The Southern Center for Human Rights supports this concern:

> Privatization of misdemeanor probation has placed unprecedented law enforcement authority in the hands of for-profit companies that act essentially

as collection agencies. These companies, focused on profit rather than public safety or rehabilitation, are not designed to supervise people or connect them to services and jobs. Rather, they charge exorbitant monthly fees and use the threat of imprisonment and a variety of bullying tactics to squeeze money out of the men and women under their supervision. (2008, 4)

Any money paid by probationers goes first to defraying the private company's fees, then to paying their criminal fine, with a risk of jail even for technical violations if payments are not high enough to make progress on the actual fine. Some case officers receive bonuses for meeting collection goals and may be fired for insufficient collections from people in their caseload. Since an arrest warrant removes a person from the caseload, private probation officers have a personal financial incentive to seek an arrest warrant for clients who are too poor to pay (Southern Center for Human Rights 2008).

While private prison firms seek to profit from the poor by using coercive collection tactics against parolees, they also have a plan to profit from the rich by letting them buy their freedom. Private prisons profit from everyone equally, but in a way that reinforces inequality and ensures "the poor get prison" (Reiman and Leighton 2010). The proposal is based on the idea that states can reduce prison costs through early release. But the cost of release, proposed by the Conditional Post-Conviction Bond Release Act, is similar to a bail bond issued by a private company. This proposed model legislation, developed by the ALEC (see chapter 3), claims to reduce prison crowding and violent crime by allowing for early release of prisoners who can provide a surety bond issued by private companies. ALEC argues that this plan would not burden taxpayers as it would be funded primarily by the convicts and their families, and it would free up the much needed prison space for violent offenders. In the same fashion that proponents of private prisons argued the need for private prisons, ALEC argues that the current early release program, parole, is a failure, citing Department of Justice statistics such as "67% of criminals released from prison were rearrested for felonies or serious misdemeanors within 3 years" and "15 murders a day are committed by people under government supervision" (Reynolds 2008). The proponents of privatized parole draw on the same techniques of creating fear of a particular group while at the same time stressing government's inability to keep us safe.

Members of the task force that created this model legislation are members of the corrections-commercial complex, including officers of CCA. Thus, it comes as no surprise that the "solution" to this new "crisis" is fundamentally more of the same: shift profits to private companies while ignoring the larger issue of the overuse of our taken-for-granted ways of punishing. This type of thinking allowed the debate on private versus public prisons to go on without any questioning of the fundamental problem of imprisonment itself, ensuring that other solutions—even painfully obvious ones, like crime-prevention programs—were ignored or dismissed. This contributes to the production and reproduction of an "underclass" population by consistently funneling the poor through the system and stigmatizing them so they end up excluded from many aspects of society. The Conditional Post-Conviction Bond Release Act makes the problem worse by allowing those with means to buy their freedom—and allowing private interests to profit from an increasing number of inmates in an increasing number of ways.

The construction of the newest undeserving populations—criminal and not-so-criminal aliens, the mentally ill, parolees, and probationers—as political, economic, and moral threats continues the melding and strengthening of moral, business, and government interests. In this situation, the debate over privatization is no longer about public versus private prisons but the "optimal" mix of the two. Moreover, there is no room in this debate, nor has there been for quite some time, to question the fundamentally flawed implementation of punishment.

BIG BROTHER, INC.

The private corrections companies have acknowledged that any change in drug or immigration laws or an overall shift from incarceration as the preferred method of control will devastate their financial status, so they have plans to expand into community corrections as previously discussed. An especially ominous part of this strategy involves private services that use Global Positioning Systems (GPS) to track parolees and probationers. The idea started with sex offenders and has snowballed. Sex offenders must be monitored for longer periods; for instance, California's Proposition 83 requires lifetime monitoring (Simerman 2008). Other jurisdictions are interested in expanding monitoring to people who have served a sentence for a violent felony—or for any felony and for nonfelony domestic violence; some hope to monitor potential juvenile gang members or any juvenile subject to curfew (Simerman 2008; Malan and Sussman 2008). Information can easily be shared, and other interested agencies can also log into the computer system to track suspects or receive notifications.

Delaware's Division of Youth and Rehabilitative Services contracted with Big Brother, Inc., to monitor the state's youth offenders with GPS devices (Sanginiti 2004). Tennessee embarked on a $2.5 million pilot project to use GPS to keep track of violent sex offenders on parole. The chairman of the state's Corrections Oversight Committee explained the future: "Taken statewide the program could include other types of offenders, those behind in child support and those convicted of domestic violence. This could reduce our demand for prison beds and allow us to stiffen penalties for felons that pose a risk to society" (Associated Press 2004).

The promise is not just public safety but cost savings. The cost usually highlighted for monitoring services is about $3,000 to $5,000 a year, as opposed to $30,000 to $40,000 a year for incarceration. But "active" monitoring requires people to review the alerts twenty-four hours a day and respond when subjects enter a "zone of exclusion," any area they are prohibited from entering, like school zones or high-drug-traffic areas. This is a way to try to "confine" people to certain sections of a city, to allow them to travel only between home and work, or to impose a curfew. Tracking people throughout the day, however, also requires a great many personnel resources. These personnel cannot simply be moved from other probation and parole tasks to monitoring, because agents must still meet with clients to help them with the enormous issues they face either reentering society or creating an environment less conducive to reoffending.

Further, false alerts are common because of faulty equipment, low batteries, or interference in tunnels, subways, parking garages, and other "urban canyons." Officials complain that at times false alerts are so overwhelming, they must shift resources from other public-safety activities (Malan and Sussman 2008). "Passive" monitoring is cheaper and easier but only provides a listing of violations at the end of the day or week. A *Seattle Post-Intelligencer* article on Washington State's experience with GPS noted, "As more states use GPS, some have found it to be a devil's bargain. Corrections officers praise the tool's helpfulness, but curse the immense amount of work it creates" (Ho 2007).

The problems and cost have not prevented states from requiring more monitoring, so Cornell Corrections and the GEO Group have already established electronic-monitoring services. A vice president of Pro Tech Monitoring said in 2007, "We have so much business that we can hardly keep up with manufacturing. We're exploding" (Ho 2007). Doctor R. Crants (cofounder of CCA), Steven W. Logan (cofounder of Cornell Corrections and founding president of APCTO), Joseph F. Johnson (former director of CCA and member of the Board of Directors National Democratic Governors' Association), Brian Moran (former director of General Dynamics Corporation), and Greg Utterback (former director of business development at Cornell Companies) came together to form Satellite Tracking of People, LLC (STOP). Their system, Veritracks, adds crime-mapping technology to the monitoring of offenders so it can plot an individual's movements against crime incidents (PR Newswire 2005).

Within limits, GPS tracking of people convicted of crimes can be a helpful tool for criminal justice. But, like prison, it can easily be overused because of political and media responses to serious, but unusual, cases in which GPS could make a difference. An article in the newsletter of the Association for the Treatment of Sexual Abusers noted,

> Politicians who want to appear "hard on crime" are clamoring to have all registered sexual offenders fitted with GPS tracking devices for life and a public, frightened by media exploitation of admittedly horrifying but nonetheless rare events, seems largely supportive of such measures. When used in concert with other management tools, GPS does hold promise for supervising predatory sex offenders. But a more careful examination of salient facts indicate that universal GPS monitoring of all registered sex offenders would be ill advised. First, most sex offenders, rather than being predatory, victimize in places where we expect them to be (i.e. their own homes and the homes of people they know well.) Second, GPS uses relatively new and expensive technology with known flaws and limitations. There is as yet, little scientific research regarding its effectiveness for management of even predatory sexual offenders. And finally, there are unresolved civil liberties issues that will most likely make their way through the court system during the coming few years. These facts seem to lead to the conclusion that carefully documented trials of varying approaches should continue, but that universal GPS monitoring of all predatory registered sex offenders is premature, and GPS monitoring of non-predatory sex offenders will likely never make much sense. (Delson 2006, 7)

In case the media and politicians do not take GPS tracking to excess on their own, the industry has already hired lobbyists and is building the next iron triangle of the prison-industrial complex. Former Texas House Corrections Committee chair Ray Allen became a lobbyist for STOP (as well as GEO Group) (Texans for Public Justice 2007). STOP is also a corporate sponsor for the National Juvenile Court Services Association, among other organizations.

STOP has also figured out a new angle for preventing bad publicity. Its agreement with Santa Barbara County contains a clause in the intellectual property section stating that "neither party shall use the other party's Trademarks in a manner that disparages the other party or its products or services, or portrays the other party or its products or services in a false, competitively adverse or poor light." STOP is a trademarked name, as is its product, BluTag. Santa Barbara County Department of Corrections is not a formal trademark and the county is not in a competitive environment when it comes to criminal justice, so these provisions protect STOP not just from false statements but also from true statements by county officials about the problems with BluTag and STOP. (The full text of this contract is available on the companion website for this book, PaulsJusticePage.com > Punishment for Sale.)

The entanglements of the many private and government participants, the expansion of the areas of potential profit, and the increased number of populations affected by privatization call for a rethinking of the phrase "prison-industrial complex," which fails to capture the emerging trends. Just as the industry has broadened its markets to follow the money, so too must criminologists broaden their understanding of the complexities of privatized criminal justice—especially as it interfaces with the politics of criminal justice. Frankly, embracing such a larger understanding of criminal justice runs counter to current disciplinary practices, which view criminal law as the outcome of consensus rather than lobbying and political contributions and which discuss criminal justice practices in terms of retribution, deterrence, and rehabilitation rather than high-profit-margin markets for companies seeking perpetual growth.

More pointedly, philosopher Michel Foucault provided a powerful caution about government's desire for a powerful social-control apparatus:

> Historians of ideas usually attribute the dream of a perfect society to the philosophers and jurists of the eighteenth century; but there was also a military dream of society; its fundamental reference was not to the state of nature, but to the meticulously subordinated cogs of a machine, not to the primal social contract, but to permanent coercions, not to fundamental rights, but to indefinitely progressive forms of training, not to general will, but to automatic docility. (1979, 169)

The incarceration binge has illustrated exactly how difficult it can be to control the excessive buildup of social control, especially when combined with for-profit corporate interests. The emerging issue is to ensure that the United States does not repeat the mistake of the incarceration binge with the latest incarnation of punishment. Any government desire for docility on the part of marginalized citizens should not become too closely wed to the profits of companies with billions of dollars in publicly traded shares, billions more on loan from Wall Street bankers who become vested interests, no concerns for transparency about campaign contributions or lobbying, and disregard for social responsibility.

The identification of strategies for profiting from additional marginalized populations means that the seeds for future growth in the private prison industry have already been planted and begun to sprout. The political, economic, and cultural conditions are ripe for even more growth in privatization, and the claims and strategies used to promote prison privatization are surfacing to turn even more marginalized people (raw materials) into profitable commodities. The nation has hit extreme economic troubles, with high levels of unemployment. Local, state, and federal governments are struggling with funding priorities, including decisions about the growing correctional system, both private and public. The question is, how will the United States respond? Will the nation merely use privatized "solutions" as a Band-Aid for the failed experiment in excessive incarceration? Or will it seize the opportunity to question our fundamentally flawed punishment policies and pursue socially just remedies to problems like racism, crime, and economic disparities? Our goal with this book has been to provide a thoughtful examination of the political, cultural, historical, and economic entanglements of privatization because they are essential to understanding how the nation will respond. Our hope is that this knowledge can help support a posture of resistance to this existing form of domination and that the future expansion of formal control mechanisms—especially for the sake of private profit—can be redirected to confront social inequality.

Appendix

Using the Securities and Exchange Commission Website to Research Private Prisons

Starting in the mid-1990s, the Securities and Exchange Commission (SEC) started to post on its website the filings of companies traded on the stock exchange. So, many documents about private prisons are freely available on the Web for further exploration, investigation, or updating. Because private companies are not subject to the Freedom of Information Act and try to lock down as much information (other than that related to public relations) as possible, this is one of the few sources of detailed information about developments in the private prison industry. And the information presented here can be used to research any company traded on the stock exchange.

The process is not complicated, but a little information can help people zero in on what they would like to find. So, this appendix briefly describes where to go on the Web, how to find the company whose filings interest you, and what specific forms contain which information.

Where: www.sec.gov. Some sites want to charge for filings that are freely available, so make sure to go to this site. As it is organized in early 2009, the next step is to select "Filings & Forms," followed by "Search for Company Filings." (The name of the system is EDGAR.) Finally, select the option for "Company or fund name, ticker symbol, CIK (Central Index Key) . . . "

Finding private prison companies: Searching by the company name normally works well, but the spin-offs and reacquisitions discussed in chapter 5 have rendered the commonsense search options dead ends for current filings. A search for the Corrections Corporation of America ends in 2006, for example. Table A.1 provides a list of CIK numbers, which are assigned to companies and carried through name changes.

Table A.1.   SEC Identifiers for Private Prisons

Company	*CIK*
Corrections Corporation of America/Prison Realty Trust	0001070985. Use 0000739404 to access documents from 1994–1998.
GEO Group/Wackenhut	0000923796 (a search for GEO Group will bring up all the company filings)
Esmor Correctional Services (now Correctional Services Company)	0000914670
Cornell Corrections	0001016152
Children's Comprehensive Services	0000816247
Avalon Correctional Services	0000872202

Identifying important forms: A search will bring up numerous forms for each year, so knowing where key information is can save a great deal of time. Table A.2 presents this information.

Table A.2.   Most Relevant SEC Forms for Private Prison Research

Form	*Information Contained*
10-K	Annual report. Review of business, financials, management discussion, risk factors, listing of directors and executive officers, summary of executive-compensation information, and significant events of the past year.
10-Q	Quarterly report. Financial information, management discussions, legal proceedings, and risk factors. Results of shareholder votes from 14A are frequently reported here.
DEF 14A	Definitive 14A or proxy. Detailed executive-compensation information, proposals for shareholders to vote on, and corporate-governance information.
8-K	Current report. Any "material information." These contain everything from press releases to announcements of contracts awarded or terminated, significant legal events, changes in executives, executive employment agreements, and so forth.

Note that the EDGAR search defaults to exclude "Ownership Forms." Ownership forms allow someone to see who—person, company, or investment fund—owns a substantial number of shares in a company. There tend to be many of these forms, which is why the default setting excludes them.

References

Adams, Gordon. 1984. The Department of Defense and the military-industrial establishment: The politics of the iron triangle. In *Critical Studies in Organization and Bureaucracy*, ed. F. Fischer and C. Siranni, 320–34. Philadelphia, PA: Temple University Press.

AFSCME Resolution # 69. 1982. Available at www.afscme.org/resolutions/

Alcorn, Stanley, and Ben Solarz. 2006. The autistic economist: How and why the dismal science embraces theory over reality. *Yale Economic Review* (summer) www.yaleeconomicreview.com/issues/2006_summer/autistic_economist.html

Anchorage Daily News. 2001. Halfway house faces suit. *Anchorage Daily News*, May 1.

Anrig, Greg, Jr., and Gregory Crouch. 1986. Getting a lock on the private-prison business. *Money* 15 (May): 32.

Associated Press. 2004. State to shadow parolees with GPS. *Wired*, July 13. Available at www.wired.com/politics/law/news/2004/07/64202

———. 2008. Private prison company is subject to Tenn. open-records law. First Amendment Center, July 30. Available at www.firstamendmentcenter.org/news.aspx?id=20355

Association of Private Correctional and Treatment Organizations (APCTO). 2005. Learn about members. APCTO. Available at www.apcto.org

Atlanta Journal-Constitution. 2002. Paper trails, fees, bills among issues in probe of parole board. *Atlanta Journal-Constitution*, June 14.

Austin, James, and Garry Coventry. 2001. Emerging issues on privatized prisons. Washington, DC: Bureau of Justice Assistance. Available at www.ncjrs.org/pdf-files1/bja/181249.pdf

Avalon Enterprises. 1991. Form S-18. Filed with the Securities and Exchange Commission, January 31.

———. 1992. Form 10-K. Filed with the Securities and Exchange Commission May 5.

Bakan, Joel. 2004. *The corporation: The pathological pursuit of profit and power.* New York: Free Press.

Barak, Gregg, Paul Leighton, and Jeanne Flavin. 2007. *Class, race, gender, and crime,* 2nd ed. Lanham, MD: Rowman & Littlefield.

Barry, Tom. 2008. Immigrants drive prison profits. Immigrant Solidarity Network, December 3. Available at www.immigrantsolidarity.org/cgi- bin/datacgi/database .cgi?file=Issues&report=SingleArticle&ArticleID=1039

———. 2009. Immigrant prison burns in Pecos. Americas Program, February 6. Available at http://americas.irc-online.org/am/5849

Bates, Eric. 1998. Private prisons. *The Nation,* January 5, 266 (1).

Bebchuk, Lucian A., and Jesse M. Fried. 2004. *Pay without performance: The unfulfilled promise of executive compensation.* Cambridge, MA: Harvard University Press.

Beckett, Katherine, and Theodore Sasson. 2000. *The politics of injustice: Crime and punishment in America.* Thousand Oaks, CA: Pine Forge Press.

Bender, Edwin. 2000. Private prisons, politics and profits. National Institute on Money in State Politics, July 1. Available at www.followthemoney.org/press/ ZZ/20000701.phtml

Berens, Michael. 2000. Nursing mistakes kill, injure thousands: Cost-cutting exacts toll on patients, hospital staffs. *Chicago Tribune,* September 20, A1.

Berkowicz, Bill. 2004. Prisons, profits and prophets. The November Coalition, September 2. Available at www.november.org/stayinfo/breaking2/Prophets.html

Beutler, Brian. 1999. Oklahoma House Bill No. 1053, First session of the Forty-seventh Legislature. Available at www.afscme.org/workers/10203.cfm

BI Incorporated. 1983. Form S-18. Filed with Securities and Exchange Commission March 16.

———. 2000. Form 10-K. Filed with Securities and Exchange Commission June 30.

Biewen, John. 2002. Corrections Inc. American Radio Works, April. Available at http://americanradioworks.publicradio.org/features/corrections

Bivens, T. 1986. Can prisons for profit work? *Philadelphia Inquirer Magazine,* August 3, 14–15.

Blumstein, Alfred. 2001. Why is crime falling—or is it? In *Perspectives on Crime and Justice: 2000–2001 Lecture Series.* Washington, DC: National Institute of Justice.

Blumstein, Alfred, and Joel Wallman. 2000. *The crime drop in America.* New York: Cambridge University Press.

Bossolo, Laura. 2004. Mentally Ill Offender Treatment and Crime Reduction Act becomes law. American Psychological Association Press Release, November 4. www.apa.org/releases/S1194_law.html

Boston, J. 1991. Reorganizing the machinery of government. In *Reshaping the State,* ed. J. Boston, J. Martin, J. Pallot, and P. Walsh, 233–67. Auckland, NZ: Oxford University Press.

Brakel, S. J. 1988. Prison management, private enterprise style: The inmates evaluation. *New England Journal of Criminal and Civil Confinement* 14: 175–244.

Bureau of Justice Statistics. 1992. *Drugs, crime and the justice system* (NCJ 133652). Washington, DC: U.S. Department of Justice.

———. 2001a. *Justice expenditure and employment extract series* (NCJ 194802). Washington, DC: U.S. Department of Justice.

———. 2001b. *Prisoners in 2000* (NCJ 288207). Washington, DC: U.S. Department of Justice.

———. 2002a. *Immigration offenders in the federal criminal justice system, 2000* (NCJ 191745). Washington DC: U.S. Department of Justice.

———. 2002b. *Prisoners in 2001* (NCJ 195189). Washington, DC: U.S. Department of Justice.

———. 2003. *Prevalence of imprisonment in the U.S. population, 1974–2001* (NCJ 197976). Washington, DC: U.S. Department of Justice.

———. 2006. *Justice expenditure and employment in the United States, 2003* (NCJ 212260). Washington, DC: U.S. Department of Justice.

———. 2007a. *Prison and jail inmates at midyear 2006* (NCJ 217675). Washington, DC: U.S. Department of Justice.

———. 2007b. *Probation and parole in the United States, 2006* (NCJ 220218). Washington, DC: U.S. Department of Justice.

———. 2007c. *Prisoners in 2006* NCJ (219416). Washington, DC: U.S. Department of Justice.

———. 2008a. *Justice expenditure and employment extracts 2006* (NCJ 224394). Washington, DC: U.S. Department of Justice.

———. 2008b. *Probation and parole in the United States, 2007 statistical tables* (NCJ 224707). Washington, DC: U.S. Department of Justice.

———. 2009. *Prison inmates at midyear 2008—statistical tables* (NCJ 225619). Washington, DC: U.S. Department of Justice.

Burton, Greg. 1999. Hefty cost endangers prison plan. *Salt Lake Tribune,* October 3, A1.

Burton-Rose, Daniel, ed. 1998. *The celling of America: An inside look at the U.S. prison industry.* Monroe, ME: Common Courage Press.

Bush, George W. 2004. State of the Union address. American Rhetoric, January 20. Available at www.americanrhetoric.com/speeches/stateoftheunion2004.htm

Business Week. 2004. Psychiatric solutions: You might be shocked. *Business Week,* August 2. Available at www.businessweek.com/print/magazine/content/04_31/b3894152_mz026.htm

Butterfield, Fox. 1996. Intervening early costs less than '3 strikes' law, study says. *New York Times,* June 23, A24.

Callanan, Valerie. 2005. *Feeding the fear of crime: Crime-related media and support for three strikes.* El Paso, TX: LFB Scholarly Publishing.

Carceral, K. C. 2005. *Prison, Inc: A convict exposes life in a private prison.* New York: New York University Press.

Carey, Bill. 2005. *Master of the big board: The life, times and businesses of Jack C. Massey.* Nashville, TN: Cumberland House Publishing.

Caron, Paul. 2005. WSJ on tax-free gross-ups for corporate execs. Tax Prof Blog, December 22. Available at http://taxprof.typepad.com/taxprof_blog/2005/12/wsj_on_taxfree_.html

Carrillo, Karen. 2002. Locking away profits: Capitalizing on immigrant detentions has turned into a booming business for Lehman Brothers. *ColorLines* (September). Available at www.thefreelibrary.com/Locking+away+profits:+capitalizing+on+immigrant+detentions+has+turned...-a090794907

Carter, Kate. 2002. State tells juvenile facility to shape up. *Online Athens,* February 26. Available at onlineathens.com/archive

Cavender, Gray. 2004. Media and crime policy: A reconsideration of David Garland's *The Culture of Control. Punishment and Society* 6: 335.

CCA Source. 2003. Q&A: CCA past, present & future: Co-founders Don Hutto and Tom Beasley. *Correct Perspectives,* January 1. Available at www.fundinguniverse .com/company- histories/Corrections-Corporation-of-America-Company-History.html

Census Bureau. 2008. *Income, poverty and health insurance coverage in the United States, 2007.*

Center for Public Integrity. 1999. Hidden agendas: How state legislators keep conflicts of interest under wraps. Minnesota Public Radio, February 15. Available at http://news.minnesota.publicradio.org/features/199902/15_smiths_hiddenagendas/cpi_report.shtml

Charry, Rebecca. 1999. Locked out on the prison decision. *Washington Post,* June 13, B8.

Cheves, John. 2004a. Battle brews over privatizing prison; GOP touts savings in Elliott County plan. *Lexington Herald-Leader,* February 3, A1.

———. 2004b. DeLay took charitable gift in Lexington. *Lexington Herald-Leader,* December 1, A1.

Choudry, Aziz. 2003. The paydirt of paranoia. *Z-Net Commentary,* February 20. Available at http://au.geocities.com/mdcwatcharchive/reading/paydirt.txt

Christie, Nils. 1993. *Crime control as industry.* New York: Routledge.

Clark, Maureen. 2001. Women win suit over halfway house guard's sexual misdeeds. *Anchorage Daily News,* January 23, A1.

Clear, Todd. 2002. The problem with addition by subtraction. In *Invisible Punishment,* ed. Marc Mauer and Meda Chesney-Lind, 181–93. New York: The New Press.

Clendinen, Dudley. 1985. Officials of counties debate private jail operation. *New York Times,* November 14, A27.

Cody, W., and A. Bennett. 1987. The privatization of correctional institutions: The Tennessee experience. *Vanderbilt Law Journal* 40: 829–49.

Collins, Michael. 2001. Patriots don't use heroin. *Cincinnati Post,* September 28, www.mapinc.org/drugnews/v01.n1718.a06.html

Collins, William. 2000. *Contracting for correctional services provided by private firms.* Middletown, CT: Association of State Correctional Administrators.

Colvin, M. 1997. *Penitentiaries, reformatories and chain gangs: Social theory and the history of punishment in nineteenth-century America.* New York: St. Martin's Press.

Congressional Budget Office. 2008. Second Chance Act of 2007, H.R. 1593, 110th Congress.

———. 2007. GovTrack.us. Available at www.govtrack.us/congress/bill.xpd?bill=h110-1593

Conklin, John. 2003. *Why crime rates fell.* Boston: Allyn & Bacon.

Cornell Corrections. 1996. Form 424B1. Filed with Securities and Exchange Commission October 4.

———. 1997. Form 10-K. Filed with Securities and Exchange Commission March 31.

———. 2007. Form 10-K. Filed with the Securities and Exchange Commission March 16.

———. 2008a. Form 10-K. Filed with the Securities and Exchange Commission March 14.

———. 2008b. Form DEF 14A. Filed with Securities and Exchange Commission April 25.

———. 2009. Form 10-K. Filed with Securities and Exchange Commission March 6.

Correctional Properties Trust. 1998. Form 424B1. Filed with the Securities and Exchange Commission April 24.

———. 1999. Form 10-K. Filed with the Securities and Exchange Commission March 31.

Corrections Corporation of America. 1986. Form S-1. Filed with Securities and Exchange Commission August 15 and revised prospectus filed October 1.

———. 1987. Form 10-K. Filed with Securities and Exchange Commission March 31.

———. 1994. Annual report. Nashville, TN: Corrections Corporation of America.

———. 1995. Form DEF 14A. Filed with the Securities and Exchange Commission April 14.

———. 1997. Form 10-Q. Filed with the Securities and Exchange Commission August 14.

———. 1998a. Form 8-K. Filed with the Securities and Exchange Commission April 22.

———. 1998b. Form 10-K. Filed with the Securities and Exchange Commission March 30.

———. 1998c. Form 10-Q. Filed with the Securities and Exchange Commission August 28.

———. 1998d. Form S-3. Filed with the Securities and Exchange Commission November 13.

———. 2001. Form 10-K. Filed with the Securities and Exchange Commission April 17.

———. 2002a. Form 8-K. Filed with the Securities and Exchange Commission October 28.

———. 2002b. Form 10-K. Filed with the Securities and Exchange Commission.

———. 2007a. Form 8-K filed with the Securities and Exchange Commission May 11.

———. 2007b. Form 10-K. Filed with Securities and Exchange Commission February 27.

———. 2008a. Form 10-K. Filed with Securities and Exchange Commission February 27.

———. 2008b. Form DEF 14A. Filed with the Securities and Exchange Commission April 14.

———. 2009. Form 10-K. Filed with Securities and Exchange Commission February 25.

Coyle, Andrew, Allison Campbell, and Rodney Neufeld, eds. 2003. *Capitalist punishment: Prison privatization and human rights.* Atlanta, GA: Clarity Press.

Crane, Richard. 2000. Monitoring correctional services provided by private firms. Association of State Correctional Administrators. Available at www.asca.net/documents/monitor.pdf

Cullen, Francis, and Paul Gendreau. 1989. The effectiveness of correctional rehabilitation. In *The American prison,* eds. Lynne Goodstein and Doris Layton MacKenzie, 23–44. New York: Plenum Press.

Cullen, Francis, and Karen Gilbert. 1982. *Reaffirming rehabilitation.* Cincinnati, OH: Anderson Publishing.

Current Population Reports, P60-235. Washington, DC: U.S. Government Printing Office.

Currie, Elliott. 1985. *Confronting crime: An American challenge.* New York: Pantheon.

———. 1998. *Crime and punishment in America.* New York: Metropolitan Books.

Davey, Joseph Dillon. 1998. *The politics of prison expansion: Winning elections by waging war on crime.* Westport, CT: Praeger Publishers.

Davis, Angela. 1999. Globalism and the prison industrial complex. *Race and Class* 40: 2–3.

Delson, Niki. 2006. Using global positioning systems (GPS) for sex offender management. *The Forum: Newsletter for the Association for the Treatment of Sexual Abusers* (summer), 1–9.

Dickinson, Laura. 2007. Public participation/private contract. *Social Justice* 34, nos. 3–4: 149.

DiIulio, John J., Jr. 1988. What's wrong with private prisons. *The Public Interest* 92 (summer): 66–83.

Donziger, Steven R., ed. 1996. *The real war on crime.* New York: Harper Perennial.

Douglas, William O. 1954. *An almanac of liberty.* Garden City, NY: Doubleday.

Driscoll, Amy. 1999. UF prof who touted privatized prisons admits firm paid him. *Miami Herald,* April 27, B3.

Dyer, Joel. 2000. *The perpetual prisoner machine.* Boulder, CO: Westview Press.

Eisenhower, Dwight. 1961. Farewell address. Wikisource, January 17. Available at http://en.wikisource.org/wiki/Eisenhower%27s_farewell_address

El Paso Times. 2001. Escapes common place at Horizon City halfway house. *El Paso Times.* August 29. Available at www.privateci.org/rap_avalon.html

Esmor Correctional Services. 1993. Form SB-2. Filed with Securities and Exchange Commission November 4.

———. 1994. Form 10-KSB. Filed with Securities and Exchange Commission April 1.

Federal Register 68, no. 19 (January 29): 4580–679. Available at www.ftc.gov/os/2003/01/tsrfrn.pdf

Federal Trade Commission. 2003. 16 CFR Part 310: Telemarketing Sales Rule; Final Rule.

Fitzgerald, Lehn. 2000. Office of Wisconsin Senator Gwendolynne Moore; August 3. Special Report on Wisconsin's Prisoners. 2000. Wisconsin State Legislature, 1–13.

Foucault, Michel. 1979. *Discipline and punish: The birth of prison.* New York: Random House.

Fox, Susan Byorth. 1998. Cost comparisons between state and private correctional facilities: Apples to Apples? Report prepared for the Correctional Standards and Oversight Committee. Montana Legislature, February. Available at http://leg.mt.gov/css/publications/research/past_interim/cor_rpt4.asp

Frank, Nancy, and Michael Lynch. 1992. *Corporate crime, corporate violence.* New York: Harrow and Heston.

Friedman, Alex. 1997. Strange bedfellows. CorpWatch, June 1. Available at www.corpwatch.org/article.php?id=869

Gehrke, Robert. 2000. Private prison plans scrapped. *Desert News* (Associated Press), August 16, B1.

Geis, Gilbert, Alan Mobley, and David Shichor. 1999. Private prisons, criminological research, and conflict of interest: A case study. *Crime & Delinquency* 45: 372–88.

General Accounting Office. 1991. *Private prisons: Cost savings and BOP's statutory authority need to be resolved.* Washington, DC: General Accounting Office.

———. 1999. *Prison work programs: Inmates' access to personal information* (GAO/GGD-99-146). Washington, DC: General Accounting Office.

———. 2007. *Cost of prisons: Bureau of Prisons needs better data to assess alternatives for acquiring low and minimum security facilities.* Washington, DC: General Accounting Office.

GEO Group. 2003. Form DEF 14A. Filed with the Securities and Exchange Commission April 7.

———. 2005a. Form 10-Q. Filed with the Securities and Exchange Commission August 16.

———. 2005b. Form DEF 14A. Filed with the Securities and Exchange Commission April 11.

———. 2007. Form 10-K. Filed with Securities and Exchange Commission March 2.

———. 2008a. Form 10-K. Filed with Securities and Exchange Commission February 15.

———. 2008b. Form DEF 14A. Filed with Securities and Exchange Commission April 3.

———. 2009a. Form 8-K (exhibit 10.1). Filed with the Securities and Exchange Commission January 7.

———. 2009b. Form 10-K. Filed with Securities and Exchange Commission February 18.

———. 2009c. Form DEF 14A. Filed with Securities and Exchange Commission March 30.

Gildemeister, G. A. 1987. *Prison labor convict competition with free workers in industrializing America, 1840–1890.* New York: Garland.

Goodsell, Charles T. 1984. The Grace Commission: Seeking efficiency for the whole people? *Public Administration Review* 44: 196–204.

Gragg, Randy. 1996. A high security, low risk investment: Private prisons make crime pay. *Harper's* (August): 50.

Gran, Brian, and William Henry. 2007 Holding private prisons accountable: A socio-legal analysis of "contracting out" prisons. *Social Justice* 34, nos. 3–4: 175.

Greenberg, David, and Drew Humphries. 1980. The cooption of fixed sentencing reform. *Crime and Delinquency* (April): 206–25.

Greene, Judith. 2001. Federal government bails out failing private prisons. *The American Prospect* (September 10). Available at www.projectcensored.org/top-stories/articles/25-federal-government-bails-out-failing-private-prisons/

———. 2003. Entrepreneurial corrections: Incarceration as a business opportunity. In *Invisible punishment: The collateral consequences of mass incarceration*, ed. Marc Mauer and Meda Chesney-Lind, 200–20. New York: New York Press.

Hallett, Michael. 2004. Commerce with criminals: The new colonialism in criminal justice. *Review of Policy Research* 21, no. 1: 49–62.

———. 2007. *Private prisons in America: A critical race perspective.* Champaign: University of Illinois Press.

Hallett, Michael, and Sue Hanauer. 2001. Selective celling: Inmate population in Ohio's private prisons. *Policy Matters Ohio.* Available at www.policymattersohio. org/pris.html

Hallett, Michael, and Frank Lee. 2001. Public money, private interests: The grass-roots battle against CCA in Tennessee. In *Privatization in criminal justice: Past, present, and future,* ed. David Shichor and Michael J. Gilbert, 227–43. Cincinnati, OH: Anderson Publishing.

Hallinan, Joseph T. 2001. Federal government saves private prisons as state convict population levels off. *Wall Street Journal,* November 6. Available at www.common dreams.org/headlines01/1106-05.htm

Harding, Richard. 1997. *Private prisons and public accountability.* Buckingham UK: Open University Press.

Hatry, H. P., P. J. Brounstein, R. B. Levinson, K. Chi, and P. Rosenberg. 1989. *Comparison of privately and publicly operated corrections facilities in Kentucky and Massachusetts.* Washington, DC: The Urban Institute.

Herbers, John. 1987. The new federalism: Unplanned, innovative and here to stay. *Governing* (October): 30.

Herivel, Tara, and Paul Wright, eds. 2003. *Prison nation: The warehousing of America's poor.* New York: Routledge.

Herron, Matt. 2004. Private prisons: The debate rages on. *The Snitch,* August 4, A1.

Hightower, Jim. 1998. *There's nothing in the middle of the road but yellow stripes and dead armadillos.* New York: HarperPerennial.

Hill-Collins, Patricia. 1990. *Black feminist thought: Knowledge, consciousness and the politics of empowerment.* New York: Routledge.

Ho, Vanessa. 2007. GPS for state sex offender gets split verdict. *Seattle Post-Intelligencer,* December 12. Available at www.seattlepi.com/local/343247_sexoffenders12.html

Huling, Tracy. 2002. Building a prison economy in rural America. In *Invisible punishment: The collateral consequences of mass imprisonment,* ed. Meda Chesney-Lind and Marc Mauer, 194–213. New York: The New Press.

Human Rights Watch. 2003. *Ill equipped: U.S. prisons and offenders with mental illness.* New York: Human Rights Watch. Available at www.hrw.org/reports/2003/usa1003

Humphrey, Tom. 1985. Prison overcrowding in Tennessee forces emergency legislative session. *Christian Science Monitor,* November 6, 3.

Internal Audit Report, Office of the Inspector General. 2005. Contract management of private correctional facilities: Evaluation report. State of Florida, Office of Inspector General, Number 2005-61. June 30.

International Centre for Prison Studies. 2009. Entire world—prison population rates per 100,000 of the national population. King's College London World Prison Brief. Available at www.kcl.ac.uk/depsta/law/research/icps/worldbrief/wpb_stats.php?area=all&category=wb_poprate

Irwin, John. 2005. *The warehouse prison.* Los Angeles, CA: Roxbury.

Irwin, John, and James Austin. 2001. *It's about time: America's imprisonment binge.* 3rd ed. Belmont, CA: Wadsworth Publishing.

James, Joni. 2005. Audit: 2 prison vendors overpaid. *St. Petersburg Times,* July 27. Available at www.sptimes.com/2005/07/27/State/Audit__2_prison_vendo.shtml

Jefferies & Company. 2002. *Report on CCA,* July 19, 3.

Johnson, Robert. 1987. *Hard time: Understanding and reforming the prison.* Monterey: Brooks/Cole.

Kamen, Al. 1983. Hill hearing of DC jail: Implications of overcrowding "tragic." *Washington Post,* July 13. Available at www.prisoncommission.org/public_hearing_2.asp

Katz, Michael. 1989. *The undeserving poor.* New York: Pantheon Books.

Kennedy, William, and Robert Lee. 1984. *A taxpayer survey of the Grace Commission report.* Ottawa, IL: Greenhill Publishers.

Kennickell, Arthur. 2006. *Currents and undercurrents: Changes in the distribution of wealth, 1989–2004.* Washington, DC: Federal Reserve Board. Available at http://federalreserve.gov/pubs/oss/oss2/papers/concentration.2004.5.pdf

Kesey, Ken. 1963. *One flew over the cuckoo's nest.* New York: Signet.

Kihss, Peter. 1981. New York group opposing bond issue for prisons. *New York Times,* June 28, Section 1, A43.

King, Colbert I. 1998. Correct the corrections mess. *Washington Post,* December 5, A23.

King, Ryan. 2006. *A decade of reform: Felony disenfranchisement policy in the United States.* Washington, DC: The Sentencing Project. Available at www.sentencingproject.org/Admin/Documents/publications/fd_decade_reform.pdf

Kolbert, Elizabeth. 1989. Who wants new prisons? In New York, all of upstate. *New York Times,* June 9, B1.

Kramer, Ronald. 1984. The ideological construction of crime: An analysis of the L.E.A.A. Career Criminal Program. *Deviant Behavior* 5: 217–37.

Kuttner, Robert. 1996a. Columbia/HCA and the resurgence of the for-profit hospital business, part I. *New England Journal of Medicine* 335, no. 5 (August 1): 362–68.

———. 1996b. Columbia/HCA and the resurgence of the for-profit hospital business, part II. *New England Journal of Medicine* 335, no. 6 (August 8): 446–51.

LaFranchi, Howard. 1986. Texas prisons crowd way into hot contest for governorship. *Christian Science Monitor,* June 24, National, 5.

Land, Greg. 2000. Private prisons: Specter of slavery? *Atlanta Journal Constitution,* December 16, 14A.

Lanza-Kaduce, Lonn, Karen Parker, and Charles Thomas. 1999. A comparative recidivism analysis of releases from private and public prisons. *Crime & Delinquency* 45: 28–47.

Leighton, Paul, and Donna Killinbeck. 2001. Professional codes of ethics. In *Criminal Justice Ethics,* ed. Paul Leighton and Jeffrey Reiman. Upper Saddle River, NJ: Prentice Hall. Available at http://paulsjusticepage.com/cjethics/ethics_appendix.htm

Leighton, Paul, and Jeffrey Reiman. 2004. *A tale of two criminals: We're tougher on corporate criminals, but they still don't get what they deserve.* Boston: Allyn and Bacon. Available at www.paulsjusticepage.com/RichGetRicher/fraud2004.htm

Lilly, R., and P. Knepper. 1993. The corrections-commercial complex. *Crime & Delinquency* 39, no. 2: 150–66.

Linowes, David F. 1988. Privatization: Toward more effective government—report of the President's Commission on Privatization. Washington, DC: U.S. Government Printing Office.

Lockyer 2003. Petition for Certiorari. Available at http://caselaw.lp.findlaw.com/scripts/getcase.pl?court=US&vol=000&invol=01-1127

Logan, C. H. 1987. The propriety of proprietary prisons. *Federal Probation* 51, no. 3: 35–40.

———. 1990. *Private prisons: Cons and pros.* New York: Oxford University Press.

Logan, C. H., and B. W. McGriff. 1989. *Comparing costs of public and private prisons: A case study.* Washington, DC: National Institute of Justice.

Loury, Glenn. 2007. Why are so many Americans in prison? Race and the transformation of criminal justice. *Boston Review* (July/August). Available at bostonreview .net/BR32.4/article_loury.php.

Lynch, James. 1993. A cross-national comparison of the length of custodial sentences for serious crimes. *Justice Quarterly* 10, no. 4: 801–23.

Lynch, Michael J., Raymond Michalowski, and W. Byron Groves. 2000. *The new radical primer in radical criminology: Critical perspectives on crime, power, and identity.* Monsey, NY: Criminal Justice Press.

Maggi, Laura. 2004. Blanco transition draws $1 million; political, business donors open wallets. *Times-Picayune*, March 18.

Malan, Douglas, and Paul Sussman. 2008. Rapist's case reveals flaws in using technology to track offenders. Sex Offender Issues, September 22. Available at http:// sexoffenderissues.blogspot.com/2008/09/ct-false-alarms-common-with-gps.html

Mancini, Matthew J. 1996. *One dies, get another: Convict leasing in the American South, 1866–1928.* Columbia: University of South Carolina Press.

Martin, Brian. 2000. Columbia/HCA. Corporate Health Care, October 2007. Available at www.uow.edu.au/arts/sts/bmartin/dissent/documents/health/access_ columbia_hca.html

Martin, Courtney. 2009. The big business of family detention. *The American Prospect,* February 2 (Web only). Available at www.prospect.org/cs/articles?article=the_ big_business_of_family_detention

Martin, S. J., and Sheldon Ekland-Olson. 1989. Texas prisons: The walls came tumbling down. *Social Forces* 68, no. 2: 667–68.

Martinson, Robert. 1974. What works?—Questions and answers about prison reform. *Public Interest* (spring): 22–54.

Mattera, Philip, and Mafruza Khan. 2001. *Jail breaks: Economic development subsidies given to private prisons.* Washington, DC: Institute on Taxation and Economic Policy. Available at www.soros.org/initiatives/justice/articles_publications/publi- cations/jailbreaks_20011001

Mattera, Phillip, Mafruza Khan, and Stephen Nathan. 2004. *Corrections corporation of America: A critical look at its first twenty years.* Charlotte, NC: Grassroots Leadership.

Matthews, Roger. 1989. *Privatizing criminal justice.* Newbury Park, CA: Sage Publications.

Mauer, Marc, and Meda Chesney-Lind, eds. 2002. *Invisible punishment: The collateral consequences of mass imprisonment.* New York: The New Press.

McDonald, Douglas. 1994. Public imprisonment by private means: The emergence of private prisons and jails in the United States, the United Kingdom and Australia. *British Journal of Criminology* 34: 29–48.

———. ed. 1990. *Private prisons and the public interest.* New Brunswick, NJ: Rutgers University Press.

McDonald, Douglas, Elizabeth Fournier, M. Russell-Einhourn, and S. Crawford. 1998. Private prisons in the United States: An assessment of current practice. Cambridge, MA: Abt Associates Inc., July 16.

McGonigle, Steve. 2007. Fired TYC monitors had worked for facility's operator. *Dallas Morning News*, October 12. Available at www.dallasnews.com/sharedcontent/ dws/news/texassouthwest/stories/101207dntextyc.3515586.html

Milam, Stan. 2004. Four guards highlight state prison problems. *Wisconsin State Journal*, July 26, Business, C8.

Miller, Jerome G. 1996. *Search and destroy: African-American males in the criminal justice system.* Cambridge: Cambridge University Press.

Mobley, Alan, and Gilbert Geiss. 2001. The corrections corporation of America aka the Prison Realty Trust, Inc. In *Privatization in criminal justice: Past, present and future*, ed. David Shichor and Michael Gilbert, 207–23. Cincinnati, OH: Anderson Publishing.

Mokhiber, Russell, and Robert Weissman. 1997. The ten worst corporations of 1997. *The Multinational Monitor* 18, no. 12. Available at http://multinational-monitor.org/hyper/mm1297.05.html#columbia

Montgomery, Cliff. 2000. The new cold war: Making crime pay. *3:AM Magazine*, November. Available at www.3ammagazine.com/politicsarchive/nov2000_prison_politics_1.html

Montgomery, Lori. 2000. Rural jails profiting from INS detainees. *Washington Post*, November 24, A1.

Morain, Dan. 2003. Private prison company donates $53,000 to governor. *Los Angeles Times*, November 28. Available at http://archives.lists.indymedia.org/ imc-houston/2003-November/008127.html

Morrison, Courtney. 2009. The big business of family detention. *The American Prospect*, February 2. Available at www.prospect.org//cs/articles?article=the_big_business_of_family_detention

Morse, Janice. 1998. Guards faulted in escapes. *Cincinnati Enquirer*, August 5. Available at www.enquirer.com/editions/1998/08/05/loc_escapes05.html

Mullen, Joan K. 1985. *The privatization of corrections.* Washington, DC: National Institute of Justice.

Myers, M. A. 1998. *Race, labor and punishment in the New South.* Columbus, OH: Ohio State University Press.

National Institute of Justice. 1995. *NIJ research plan, 1995–1996.* National Criminal Justice Reference Service, March. Available at www.ncjrs.gov/txtfiles/nijrespl.txt

New York Times. 1984. Overcrowded state prisons burden counties. *New York Times*, September 16, Section 1, A46.

Nixon, Richard. 1970. State of the Union address. The American Presidency Project, January 22. Available at www.presidency.ucsb.edu/ws/index.php?pid=2921

Office of Management and Budget. 1983. OMB circular A-76. Executive Office of the President. Washington, DC, August 4 (revised 1999).

Ollson, Karen. 2002. Ghostwriting the law. *Mother Jones* (October). Available at www.motherjones.com/news/outfront/2002/09/ma_95_01.html

Oshinsky, David. 1996. *Worse than slavery: Parchman Farm and the ordeal of Jim Crow justice.* New York: Free Press.

Palast, Gregory. 1999. Wackenhut's free market in human misery. *Observer* (London), September 26. Available at www.gregpalast.com/free-market-in-human-misery/

Palmer, Heather. 2001. Private prisons can't ignore public access laws. *The News Media and the Law* 25, no. 4, 20. Available atwww.rcfp.org/newsitems/index.php?i=5846

Parenti, Christian. 1999. *Lockdown America: Police and prisons in the age of crisis.* New York: Verso.

PBS *NewsHour.* 1997. Doctoring the books. PBS, July 31. Transcript available at www.pbs.org/newshour/bb/medicare/july-dec97/medicare_fraud_7–31.html

Perrone, Dina, and Travis C. Pratt. 2003. Comparing the quality of confinement and cost-effectiveness of public versus private prisons: What we know, why we do not know more, and where to go from here. *The Prison Journal* 83: 301–22.

Perry, Celia. 2008. Probation for profit: In Georgia's outsourced justice system, a traffic ticket can land you deep in the hole. *Mother Jones* (July/August). Available at http://findarticles.com/p/articles/mi_m1329/is_4_33/ai_n28048749

Pew Center on the States. 2008. *One in 100: Behind bars in America 2008.* Washington, DC: Pew Charitable Trusts. Available at www.pewcenteronthestates.org/uploadedFiles/8015PCTS_Prison08_FINAL_2-1-1_FORWEB.pdf

Pew Public Safety Performance. 2007. *Public safety, public spending: Forecasting America's Prison Population, 2007–2011.* Washington, DC: Pew Charitable Trusts. Available at www.pewcenteronthestates.org/uploadedFiles/Public%20Safety%20Public%20Spending.pdf

Pollack, Jessica M., and Charis E. Kubrin. 2007. Crime in the news: How crimes, offenders and victims are portrayed in the media. *Journal of Criminal Justice and Popular Culture* 14, no. 1: 59–83.

PR Newswire. 2005. STOP acquires two leading offender monitor technologies. PR Newswire, January 6. Available at www.stopllc.com/en/art/19/

Pratt, T. C., and J. Maahs. 1999. Are private prisons more cost effective than public prisons? A meta-analysis of evaluation research studies. *Crime and Delinquency* 45, no. 3: 358–71.

Pricor, Inc. 1987. Form S-1. Filed with Securities and Exchange Commission June 12.

———. 1988. Form 10-K. Filed with Securities and Exchange Commission June 29.

Prison Realty Corporation. 1999a. Form 8-K. Filed with the Securities and Exchange Commission December 28.

———. 1999b. Form 10-K. Filed with the Securities and Exchange Commission March 30.

———. 1999c. Form 10-Q. Filed with the Securities and Exchange Commission May 14.

———. 1999d. Form 10-Q. Filed with the Securities and Exchange Commission August 16.

———. 1999e. Form 10-Q. Filed with the Securities and Exchange Commission November 10.

———. 2000a. Form 8-K. Filed with the Securities and Exchange Commission June 13.

———. 2000b. Form 10-K. Filed with the Securities and Exchange Commission March 30.

———. 2000c. Form 424B4. Filed with the Securities and Exchange Commission July 31.

———. 2000d. Form PRER14A. Filed with the Securities and Exchange Commission June 30.

———. 2000e. Form PRES14A. Filed with the Securities and Exchange Commission February 17.

Prison Realty Trust. 1997. Form 424B1. Filed with the Securities and Exchange Commission. July 15.

———. 1998b. Form 10k. Filed with the Securities and Exchange Commission March 30.

Prisoners of the Census. 2007. The Prison Policy Initiative. Available at www .prisonersofthecensus.org/

Ray, O. S. 1972. *Drugs, society and human behavior.* St. Louis, MO: C. V. Mosby.

Reagan, Ronald. 1981. Inaugural address, January 20. The Ronald Reagan Presidential Foundation and Library. Available at www.reaganlibrary.com/reagan/ speeches/first.asp. www.bartleby.com/124/pres61.html

Reiman, Jeffrey, and Paul Leighton. 2010. *The rich get richer and the poor get prison.* 9th ed. Boston: Allyn and Bacon.

Reynolds, Morgan. 2008. Privatizing Probation and Parole. NCPA Policy Report No. 233.

Robbins, Ira. 1988. *The legal dimensions of private incarceration.* American Bar Association. Washington, D.C.

Robert, Reginald. 2001. U.S. senator tells Irvington that cartels are decimating the town. *NJ Star-Ledger,* October 2. Available at www.mapinc.org/drugnews/v01/ n1735/a09.html

Rosa, Erin. 2009. GEO Group, Inc: Despite a crashing economy, private prison firm turns a handsome profit. CorpWatch, March 1. Available at www.corpwatch. org/article.php?id=15308

Russell, Katheryn K. 1998. *The color of crime: Racial hoaxes, white fear, black protectionism, police harassment, and other macroaggressions.* New York: New York University Press.

Ryan, Mark, and Tony Ward. 1989. *Privatization and the penal system: The American experience and the debate in Britain.* New York: St. Martin's Press.

Sanginiti, Terri. 2004. GPS tracks state's youth offenders. *Delaware News Journal,* March 26. Available at www.nlada.org/DMS/Documents/1080329801.11/ 26gpstracksstates.html

Savas, E. S. 2000. *Privatization and public-private partnerships.* New York: Seven Bridges Press.

Schiller, Bradley. 2003. *The economy today.* 9th ed. New York: McGraw-Hill Irwin.

Schlosser, Eric. 1998. The prison-industrial complex. *The Atlantic* 282, no. 6 (December). Available at www.theatlantic.com/doc/199812/prisons

Schmalleger, Frank. 2003. *Criminal justice today.* 7th ed. Newark, NJ: Prentice Hall.

Schroeder, Jana. 2001. American friends service committee memorandum. Ohio Public Safety and Justice Campaign, May 8. Available at www.geocities.com/ opsjc/Schroeder.html

Sclar, Elliott D. 2000. *You don't always get what you pay for: The economics of privatization.* Ithaca, NY: Cornell University Press.

Segal, Geoffrey. 2004. States tap private prisons. Heartland Institute, July 1. Available at www.heartland.org/Article.cfm?artId=15289

Sellers, Martin P. 1993. *The history and politics of private prisons.* Cranbury, NJ: Associated University Presses.

Serial 40: Privatization of Corrections. 1986. *Hearings before the Subcommittee on Courts, Civil Liberties and the Administration of Justice of the Committee on the Judiciary, House of Representatives.* Ninety-ninth Congress, first and second sessions. November 13, 1985, and March 18, 1986. Washington, D.C.: U.S. Government Printing Office.

Sharpe, John. 1992. *Texas crime, Texas justice: A report from the Texas Performance Review.* Austin, TX: Office of the Comptroller of Public Accounts.

Sherrill, Robert. 2001. Death trip: The American way of execution. *The Nation,* January 8. Available at www.thenation.com/doc/20010108/sherrill

Shichor, David. 1995. *Punishment for profit.* Thousand Oaks, CA: Sage Publications.

Shichor, David, and Michael J. Gilbert, eds. 2001. *Privatization in criminal justice: Past, present, and future.* Cincinnati, OH: Anderson Publishing.

Simerman, John. 2008. Panel hears concerns about sex offender law. *Oakland Tribune,* January 9. Available at http://findarticles.com/p/articles/mi_qn4176/is_20080109/ai_n21191155

Simon, David. 2005. *Elite deviance.* 8th ed. Boston: Allyn and Bacon.

Sinden, Jeff. 2003. The problem of prison privatization: The U.S. experience. In *Capitalist Punishment: Prison Privatization and Human Rights,* ed. Andrew Coyle, Allison Campbell, and Rodney Neufeld, 245–79. Atlanta, GA: Clarity Press.

Slevin, Peter. 2001. Prison firms seek inmates and profits; management woes, loss of business noted. *Washington Post,* February 18, A3.

Smalley, Suzanne. 1999a. A stir over private pens. *National Journal* 3, no. 18 (May 1): 1168.

———. 1999b. For-profit prisons offer privatization lessons. GovernmentExecutive.com, May 3. Available at www.governmentexecutive.com/dailyfed/0599/050399b2.htm

Solomon, Alisa. 2002. Detainees equal dollars: The rise of immigrant incarcerations drives a prison boom. *Village Voice,* August 14–20. Available at www.villagevoice.com/issues/0233/solomon.php

Sourcebook Online. *Sourcebook of Criminal Justice Statistics,* Available at www.albany.edu/sourcebook/

Southern Center for Human Rights. 2008. *Profiting from the poor: A report on predatory probation companies in Georgia.* Atlanta, GA: Southern Center for Human Rights. Available at www.schr.org/files/profit_from_poor.pdf

Stein, Herbert. 1996. Corporate America, mind your own business. *Wall Street Journal,* July 15.

Stern, Vivien. 2006. *Creating criminals: Prisons and people in a market society.* London: Zed Books.

Sutton, Charlotte. 1987. Hernando to put new jail in private hands. *St. Petersburg Times,* December 18 section 16B.

Tatge, Mark. 1998a. Judge to rule on Youngstown prison security issue. *Plain Dealer,* July 17, 5B.

———. 1998b. More CCA prison assaults revealed. *Plain Dealer,* August 18, 5B.

———. 1998c. Officials apologize for escape, but lawmakers get few answers. *Plain Dealer*, August 5, 5B.

———.1998d. Warden at beleaguered private prison replaced. *Plain Dealer*, March, 21, 4B.

———. 1998e. Youngstown says prison is no longer welcome; officials wanted facility's jobs, sold site to CCA for $1. *Plain Dealer*, August 3, 1A.

Terry, Charles. 2003. *The fellas: Overcoming prison and addiction.* Belmont, CA: Wadsworth Publishing.

Texans for Public Justice. 2007. Eight more lawmakers morph into lobbyists. *Lobby Watch*, April 11. Available at http://info.tpj.org/Lobby_Watch/2007Revolvers.pdf

Tharp, Paul. 2001. Prison companies get hot; terror threat fueling firms' stocks. *New York Post*, October 4, 35.

Thomas, Paulette. 1994. Triangle of interests creates infrastructure to fight lawlessness. *Wall Street Journal*, May 12, A1.

Thompson, Charles C., and Tony Hays. 2000. Gore brings back $640 toilet seat. *WorldNetDaily*, October 27. Available at www.wnd.com/index.php?pageId=4314

Thompson, Cheryl W. 1998a. DC must stop sending inmates to Ohio prison; court says city failed to cull violent ones. *Washington Post*, February 26, A8.

———. 1998b. DC sues private prison firm in contract dispute; CCA failed to protect and defend the city in two lawsuits, complaint contends. *Washington Post*, December 19, B7.

———. 1998c. Prison company assailed; report slams firm hoping to build DC facility. *Washington Post*, October 8, B1.

———. 1998d. Report galvanizes DC prison critics. *Washington Post*, December 10, J1.

Thompson, Joan. 1996. Laws lag behind booming private prison industry. Associated Press, November 5. Available at http://articles.latimes.com/1996-12-01/news/mn-4574_1_private-prison-industry

Thompson, Tracy. 1989. Drug purchase for Bush speech like "Keystone Cops." *Washington Post*, December 15, C1.

———. 1990a. DC student is given 10 years in drug case. *Washington Post*, November 1, B11.

———. 1990b. Subject of Lafayette Square crack sale guilty in other cases. *Washington Post*, January 1, C5.

Thompson, Tracy, and Michael Isikoff. 1990. Getting too tough on drugs. *Washington Post*, November 4, C1.

Tocqueville, Alexis de. 1904. Democracy in America. Vol. 1. New York: D. Appleton and Company.

Tolchin, Martin. 1985a. Company offers to run Tennessee's prisons. *New York Times*, September 13, A12.

———. 1985b. Experts foresee adverse effects from private control of prisons. *New York Times*, September 17, A17.

———. 1985c. Governors caution in endorsing the private operation of prisons. *New York Times*, March 3, A26.

———. 1985d. New momentum in the selling of government. *New York Times*, December 18, B12.

———. 1985e. New studies are planned on trend toward privately operated jails. *New York Times*, February 25, A18.

———. 1985f. Privately operated prison in Tennessee reports $200,000 in cost overruns. *New York Times*, May 21, A14.

———. 1985g. Prospect of privately run prisons divides Pennsylvania legislators. *New York Times*, December 15, 78.

Tonry, M. 1987. Sentencing guidelines and sentencing commissions: The second generation. In *Sentencing Reform: Guidance or Guidelines?* ed. Ken Pease and Martin Wasik. Manchester, NY: Manchester University Press.

Trevison, Catherine. 1998. CCA fires back at critics of private prisons. *Tennessean*, September 9, 1A.

U.S. Department of Justice. 1998. U.S. joins lawsuit against Columbia and Quorum hospital chains. Department of Justice, October 5. Available at www.usdoj.gov/opa/pr/1998/October/462civ.htm

———. 2003. Largest health care fraud case in U.S. history settled: HCA investigation nets record total of $1.7 billion. Department of Justice, June 26. Available at www.usdoj.gov/opa/pr/2003/June/03_civ_386.htm

Vieraitis, Lynne, Tomislav Kovandzic, and Thomas Marvell. 2007. The criminogenic effects of imprisonment. *Criminology and Public Policy* 6, no. 3: 589–622.

Vindy.com. 2004. Private prison poised to grow 1,200 federal inmates to arrive in '05. December 24. Available at www.vindy.com/print/299134106115372.php

Vise, David A. 1985. Private company asks for control of Tenn. prisons; 99-year contract bid gets mixed reception. *Washington Post*, September 22, F01.

Vogel, Richard D. 2004. Silencing the cells: Mass incarceration and legal repression in U.S. prisons. *Monthly Review* (May). Available at www.monthlyreview.org/0504vogel.htm

Vogel, Todd. 1987. Jails could be Texas' next ten-gallon business. *Business Week*, April 20, 33.

Wackenhut Corrections Corporation. 1994. Form S-1. Filed with Securities and Exchange Commission May 24.

———. 1995. Form 10-K. Filed with Securities and Exchange Commission March 24.

———. 2002. Form 10-K405. Filed with Securities and Exchange Commission March 1.

Wagner, Peter. 2007. *Prisoners of the census*. The Prison Policy Initiative. Available at www.prisonersofthecensus.org

Walker, D. R. 1988. *Penology for Profit: A history of the Texas prison system*. College Station: Texas A&M Press.

Wallace, George. 1963. Inaugural address as governor of Alabama. University of Tennessee, Knoxville, January 14. Available at http://web.utk.edu/~mfitzge1/docs/374/wallace_seg63.pdf

Washington Post. 1997. Sentenced to private prison; DC inmates say they face abuse at Ohio facility. *Washington Post*, September 21, A21.

———. 1998. In Ohio, but still the District's. *Washington Post*, July 31, A24.

Weeks, George. 2004. Michigan renews focus on mentally ill. *Detroit News*, December 26, B8.

Weisbach, Michael S. 2007. Optimal executive compensation versus managerial power. *Journal of Economic Literature* 45 (June): 419–28.

Welch, Michael. 1999. *Punishment in America: Social control and the ironies of imprisonment.* Thousand Oaks, CA: Sage Publications.

White, Bobby. 2009. Cash-strapped cities try private guards over police. *Wall Street Journal,* April 21. Available at http://online.wsj.com/article/SB124027127337237011.html

Wilson, William Julius. 1987. *The truly disadvantaged.* Chicago: University of Chicago Press.

Woolley, John, and Gerhard Peters. 2007. Political party platforms. The American Presidency Project 2007. Available at www.presidency.ucsb.edu/platforms.php

Wray, Harmon. 1986. Cells for sale. *Southern Changes* 8, no. 3: 3–6. Available at http://realcostofprisons.org/blog/archives/2007/07/1986_article_by.html

Zahn, Mary, and Richard P. Jones. 2000. Bill would keep federal cash, inmates out of private prisons. *Milwaukee Journal Sentinel,* January 24, B9.

Ziedenberg, Jason, and Vincent Schiraldi. 2001. JPI analysis of Bureau of Justice Statistics' "Prisoners in 2000" release: Nations' incarcerated population went up, not down, in 1999–2000. The Justice Policy Institute, August 10. Available at www.prisonpolicy.org/scans/jpi/prisoners2000.html

Zimring, Franklin. 2007. *The great American crime decline.* New York: Oxford University Press.

CASES CITED

Costello v. Wainwright, 397 F. Supp. 20 (M.D. Fla. 1975)

Costello v. Wainwright, 489 F. Supp. 1100, 1102 (M.D. Fla. 1980)

Finney v. Arkansas Board of Correction, 505 F.2d 194 (1974)

Finney v. Hutto, 410 F. Supp. 251 (1976)

Gideon v. Wainwright, 372 U.S. 335 (1963)

Holt v. Hutto, 363 F. Supp. 194 (1973) [*Holt III*]

Holt v. Sarver, 300 F. Supp. 825 (1969) [*Holt I*]

Holt v. Sarver, 309 F. Supp. 362 (1970) [*Holt II*]

Hutto v. Finney, 437 U.S. 678 (1978)

Hutto v. Finney, 548 F.2d 740 (1977)

Lockyer v. Andrade, 538 U.S. 63 (2003)

Mapp v. Ohio, 367 U.S. 643 (1961)

Miranda v. Arizona, 384 U.S. 436 (1966)

Pugh v. Locke, 406 F.Supp. 318 (1976)

Ruiz v. Estelle, 503 F. Supp. 1295 (1980)

Rummel v. Estelle, 445 U.S. 263 (1980)

Index

conditions, 64. *See also* Prison Realty
  Trust
Corrections Oversight Committee, 170
cost savings, xii, 11–12, 60, 63, 70,
  111, 114, 116–17, 131, 157, 159,
  163–64, 171
Costello v. Wainwright, 41
Crane, Richard, 63–65, 68, 118–19
Crants, Doctor R., 91, 97–98, 111, 148,
  150, 152, 154, 171; founding of
  CCA and, 55–56, 58, 62, 65, 96
Credit Suisse First Boston, 86, 153
crime: deterrence of, 4, 78, 173;
  domestic problem, 35, 51; fear of,
  35, 39–40, 79–80, 103
crime prevention, ii, xi, 2, 26, 79, 166
crime prevention programs, 170
crime rates, 4, 6, 11, 21–22, 24, 27, 31,
  34–35, 37–39, 44, 51, 61, 79, 90,
  92–93, 121
Criminal Alien Contracts (CAR), 122
criminalblackman, 40
criminal justice system, xii, 4, 8, 11, 25,
  28–29, 32, 34, 39, 43, 44, 51, 81,
  93, 160, 164, 166
criminal justice–industrial complex
  104. *See also* prison–industrial
  complex and military–industrial
  complex
criminal laws, 38, 92
culture of poverty thesis, 32
Cuomo, Mario, 54

D.C. Prisoners' Legal Services Project,
  108
Declaration of Independence, 47
Deconcini, Dennis, 96
decriminalization, 37, 45
deindustrialization, 37, 45
DeLay, Tom, 98
Dell, 102
democracy, 18, 79, 95
Department of Corrections, 56–57, 97,
  110, 129–31, 135–36, 145, 167,
  172
Department of Defense, 51, 80
Department of Homeland Security, 125

Department of Justice, 59, 80, 111, 169
De Tocqueville, Alexis: *Democracy in
  America*, 18
Detention Management Services
  (DMS), 168
deterrence, 4, 78, 173
DeWine, Mike, 123–24, 165
Dirty Harry, 40
discrimination, 33–34, 143
Division of Youth and Rehabilitative
  Services, Delaware, 170
domestic violence, 170
domicile, 91
domination of politics, 35
Donahue, J. David, 97
Douglas, William, Supreme Court
  Justice, 49
drug abuse: as a public enemy, 33
Drug Enforcement Administration
  (DEA), 37

Easley, Michael, 98
economy, 3, 5–6, 10, 24, 26, 31, 37,
  45, 47, 51, 115, 121, 123, 161–62
education, 2, 4, 25–26, 31, 36, 50, 65
Eighth Amendment, 3, 25, 41–42
Eisenhower, Dwight D., 4, 78–79, 103
Employee stock ownership plan
  (ESOP), 156
Esmor Correctional Services, 91, 93,
  130, 136, 139, 145, 157
ethnicity, 28
executions, 1, 37, 40, 48, 55
executive pay, xii, 2, 6, 12, 127, 130–
  32, 135–36, 139, 141–43, 157, 159
Executive Retirement Agreements,
  141–42

facility maintenance, 116–17
faith-based organizations, 166–67
false alerts, 171
Federal Bureau of Prisons, 65–66, 70,
  77, 96, 106, 113, 155
Federal Trade Commission (FTC), 77
fees: lawyers, xii, 2, 57, 58; lobbyists, 2;
  Wall Street investment banks, xii, 2
felony disenfranchisement, 28

About the Authors

Donna Selman is an assistant professor in the Department of Sociology, Anthropology and Criminology at Eastern Michigan University. She earned her Ph.D. from Western Michigan University in sociology. Her research interests include prisoner reentry, community justice, law enforcement training, and labor issues. She is coauthor with Kasey Tucker-Gail on several articles related to law enforcement training and deaths. She has contributed to *Battleground Criminal Justice* (2007), edited by Gregg Barak, and *Constructing Crime: Perspectives on Making News and Social Problems* (2006), edited by Gary W. Potter and Victor E. Kappeler. She has served on the executive board of the Division on Critical Criminology and is an executive committee member of the local chapter of the American Association of University Professors in addition to serving as the grievance officer.

Paul Leighton is a professor in the Department of Sociology, Anthropology and Criminology at Eastern Michigan University. He received his Ph.D. from American University in sociology/justice. His research interests include violence, white collar crime, criminal justice policy, and punishment. He is a coauthor with Jeffrey Reiman on the ninth edition of the *Rich Get Richer and the Poor Get Prison* (2010); they also coedited *The Rich Get Richer: A Reader* (2010) and *Criminal Justice Ethics* (2001). He has coauthored—with Gregg Barak and Jeanne Flavin—*Class, Race, Gender and Crime*, 2nd ed (2007). He was North American Editor of *Critical Criminology: An International Journal*, and named Critical Criminologist of the Year by the American Society of Criminology's Division on Critical

Criminology. In addition, Leighton is webmaster for StopViolence.com, PaulsJusticePage.com, and PaulsJusticeBlog.com. He is vice president of the local chapter of the American Association on University Professors and is vice president of the Board of SafeHouse, the local shelter and advocacy center for victims of domestic violence and sexual assault.